PUBLIC
ADMINISTRATION

PUBLIC ADMINISTRATION

Archana Chaturvedi

Commonwealth

Public Administration

Edition : 2026

ISBN 81-7169-977-4

Published by :

COMMONWEALTH PUBLISHERS
4831/24, Prahlad Street,
Ansari Road, Darya Ganj,
New Delhi - 110002
Ph. : 23272541, 23257835
e-mail : campusbooks@hotmail.com

Typesetting by :

Arnav Computers
Delhi - 110051

Printed at :
S.P. Printech
Delhi

PREFACE

Public administration is administration by state. It covers the entire gamut of state activity which in turn is influenced by the nature of state itself. It is a continuous search by the state for a value based management. It is the oldest human activity which involves every step from planning to action and final appraisal.

Aim of this book is to make available to our readers some important material, useful both, to the subject of political science as well as to the public administration. A critique of Administrative reforms and reforms of the civil service along with a detailed bibliography has been included to facilitate further research on the subject.

We take this opportunity to acknowledge the authorities on the subject.

Librarians and their staff members have been kind and helpful. They deserve our thanks.

My publisher and staff members at different levels have worked really hard. They deserve my readers love and patronage.

Dr. Archna Chaturvedi

Contents

1

Introduction

Administrative reform has become a significant phenomena all over the world. International Round Table on Public Administration in 1983 in Tokyo was attended by representatives of liberal democracies carrying out sweeping reforms in their administrative systems. The United Nations publication, *Enhancing Capabilities for Administrative Reform in Developing Countries*[1] highlighted the measures needed for shaping the administrative systems in developing countries.

The study of Indian administration assumes importance, since it is enjoined to serve as a "change-agent" to bring about equal opportunity for all and to secure the maximum development of human and material resources of a vast country.[2] As a consequence, none of the segments of Indian administration has remained untouched by committees and commissions that have "investigated politico-administrative problems and suggested ways and means for the administrative structure."[3] The state have also set up administrative reforms committees for examining their administrative systems from a holistic angle and several other bodies that have investigated specific aspects of the State administration.[4] All these committees, however, in their recommendations have sought to achieve the objective of welfare society in India through peaceful and democratic means without making a sharp break with the past. Tentatively, the reform activities in India since 1947 to the present may be divided into three periods for the purpose of analysis:

(a) the period of consolidation (1947-66);

(b) the period of reconstruction (1966-80); and

(c) the period of modernization 1980.

Period of Consolidation

A number of problems emanating from the partition of India surfaced in this period. Even before Independence, the Secretariat Reorganization Committee was constituted and it submitted its report on August 10, 1947.[5] In 1949, the Ayyangar Committee suggested the regrouping of ministries and the creation of organization and methods division for surveillance upon the ministries to effect economy and efficiency. Paul Appleby, an American expert, studied the Indian Administrative system between 1953 and 1956 and called it "archaic, feudalistic and unimaginative."[6] His suggestions consisted of "improving work procedure and the capabilities of administrative organization."[7] Preceded by it was the A.D. Gorwala Report in 1951 emphasizing the need for introduction of organization and method procedures in various organizations of the government.[8]

With the promulgation of the Constitution, the entire perspective of administrative reform in India underwent a sea-change.

> The Constitution by itself is a fundamental and mandatory instrument of administrative reform. It, in fact, laid the ground rules of the relationship between the citizens and the state on the one hand and the state and the civil servants on the other. It also enunciated the parameters within which all the future endeavours of reforms of the administrative system would have to remain confined.[9]

In reality, the Gorwala Report (1951), the Appleby Report (1953) and the Report of the States Reorganisation Commission (1956) took into account the changed context of the administration in India. The Second Pay Commission (1957-59) produced a valuable report in the field of personnel administration. Its strong advocacy for the establishment of Whitely Councils on the British lines for resolving the problems in employer-employee relations may be regarded as an important milestone in administrative reform, Corruption had extended its tentacles throughout the country and was responsible for malfunctioning of the system. To probe into this problem, the Government appointed the Santhanam Committee in 1962 which, *inter alia*, recommended for strengthening of vigilance organization and a code of conduct for civil servants. In 1963, the Central Vigilance Commission was created.

The setting up of the Administrative Reforms Department under the Government of India in 1964 might be regarded as a landmark signifying the Government's firmness to achieve efficiency, integrity and economy in the administration.

These attempts were piecemeal and a cross-section of the population, particularly the intelligentsia, was not satisfied with the then state of affairs in the administration. There was a spate of articles and reviews published in various journals and leading dailies examining the findings of the reform committees in the light of the Government's constitutional commitment to planned change through democratic means. *The Indian Journal of Public Administration* published a special issue on Administrative Reforms since Independence in 1963 in two volumes.[10] By and large, there was unanimity among its contributors against transplanting of foreign concepts and models.

Critical writings of the intellectuals in the U.K. since 1964, according to Caiden and Siedentopf:

> [L]aunched ideas that became embodied in the thinking of leaders, probably because of economic failure to which they had no answer, led those in authority to seek salvation in governmental reform rather than intrinsic force of the ideas themselves. In much the same way, managerialism found its way through the Fulton Report, into Civil Service reform.[11]

In August, 1965, Prime Minister Lal Bahadur Shastri came out with an announcement that the Government contemplated the establishment, of a high-powered Commission for making a comprehensive examination of the administrative system. The issue of formal notification, though delayed till January, 1966, for the constitution of Administrative Reforms Commission marked the inauguration of the period of restructuring the administrative system in India.

PERIOD OF RESTRUCTURING (1966-80)

The period 1960-80 witnessed the setting up of the Administrative Reforms Commission with the widest possible terms of reference to deal with the problems of organization and management, programme administration and functional areas like personnel administration and financial administration. Indeed the Commission could not have wished for more. While preparing the terms of reference, the Administrative Reforms Department had before it the model of the Hoover Commission in the USA. The setting up of the Commission with such a wide sweep of tasks raised a doubt whether it was possible for any agency, even though manned by highly competent persons, to accomplish the task efficiently and in a reasonably short time.[12] It may be mentioned that the Hoover Commission on Organization of the Executive branch of the Government (1953-55) carried with ranging terms of reference but wilfully did not go beyond the scope of the federal executive. Likewise, the Royal Commission on Government Organization (1960-63) appointed in Canada took case of the reform of the federal government alone. The Fulton Committee (1966-68) in the U.K., however, did not like to confine itself to the Home Civil Service only and therefore, brought the machinery of government and its personnel within the scope of its examination.[13] Going by the experiences in other federations, in India also the scope of the Administrative Reforms Commission should have been restricted to the federal sphere alone. The Hoover Commission was established after more than 170 years of independent existence of the USA during which period consensus on national goals and objectives had been built up assiduously and the machinery of the administration got stabilized.

The setting up of the Administrative Reforms Commission, it was contended by some, with a vast sweep of duties barely within two decades of India's independence was a premature act.

But such an argument seemed untenable. A number of important considerations weighed in favour of constituting the Administrative Reforms Commission in India: Firstly, if the reforms were delayed the administrative machinery would have developed without conscious direction inflicting more hardship on the people and insurmountable obstacles in the achievement of national goals and objectives. Secondly. India had been passing through the most difficult period because of two consecutive years of crop failure and consequently, spiraling of prices, devastating results of the Third Five Year Plan hastened the setting up of the Commission to recommend measures needed for overhauling the administrative machinery of the country.[14]

Another important issue, *i.e.;* membership of the Commission, may be highlighted here. To make a comprehensive study the Commission should have drawn members from contrasting background ensuring reconciliation and synthesis of different experiences and outlooks in the conclusions reached.[15] It would have been realistic too, But members nominated to the Commission were drawn from the Rajya Sabha and the Lok Sabha. To associate parliamentarians in the process of administrative reforms was pragmatically sound to enlist political support for implementation of the Commission's recommendations. But burgeouning dominance of the executive over the legislature remains an incontrovertible fact. Faced with a complex web of problems, a developing country requires a strong government. The Executive, being at the center of political power, initiates and monitors the reforms in the administration. For instance, the Reforms Commission in the Philippines was converted into the Presidential Commission in 1978. An independent agency, the Reforms Commission in South Korea was located in the office of the President. The Administrative and Services Reorganization Committee (ASRC) in Bangladesh was appointed under the supervision and control of the Executive. Yet, the track record of the Administrative Reforms Commissions in these countries does not seem to be promising at all.[16]

However, the Administrative Reforms Commission in India generated an awareness of administrative restructure in the country. By and large, consensus of opinion was built around the following: (a) the extant administration, its structure and procedure, was entirely out of tune with development tempo released through Five Year Plans; (b) behavioral aspect of administrators was equally important for ensuring social justice and equity in a developing society like India.

According to Caiden,[17] from academic standpoint, administrative reform was deeply interwoven with other reforms in society and other influences that interact and it was not merely an application of radical proposals for grappling with problems of stagnation. Following the ARC's report on Personnel Administration, the Third Pay Commission (1970-73) was appointed. Examining the importance of pay structure in a developing country like India the Third Pay Commission noted: "We attach importance to the pay structure in a society not merely as a provision for the needs of the employees or stimulus to efficiency but also as an instrument of social change."[18] Besides providing policy direction in regard to employees' emoluments, the Third Pay Commission introduced the concept of classification of posts contingent upon assumed equivalence of the work content of various occupational groups at different levels.

Recruitment and selection of the personnel is inextricably linked with personnel administration. The Committee on Recruitment Policy and Selection Methods was appointed in February 1974 for the purpose of reforming recruitment method in the civil service. The Committee's main recommendation for holding single examination for All India services was accepted by the Government in November, 1978, Such an examination would consist of two parts; a qualifying preliminary examination (objective test) and the main examination (written and interview test).[19]

The question of reforming the police system in India has also been to the fore since the advent of independence. Admittedly, the role of police in this country has to undergo a profound and all-pervasive change for achieving the goals of welfare state. In order to study the problems relating to the entire police systems the National Police Commission was appointed in 1977, which was asked to look into the question of modernization of law enforcement machinery and institutional arrangements for preventing the misuse of powers by the police. Its eight reports embodying five hundred recommendations extended over a wide area of interest regarding police administration. The Government had not made known its decision on many aspects; its desire, however, for gradually restructuring the police administration was clearly discernible.[20]

To a large extent these parameters of the administrative system cannot be insulated from the nature and character of the education system and in particular, the products it makes available for different occupational categories. The appointment of the Radha Krishnan Commission (1949) and the Kothari Commission (1963-64) manifested clear intention of the Government for molding human resources in tune with administrative development of the country. Critics, however, argued, that a parade of reform commissions reflects mere intent, not action.[21] Within the broad framework of the reforms as posited down here restructuring of governmental reorganization had been in progress.

PERIOD OF MODERNIZATION (1980—)

The country ushered in an era of modernization as it was implementing the recommendations of various reform commissions. As the entire world was increasingly exposed to technological innovations, India could hardly shut it up. Indeed, there existed a strong logic of applying scientific and technological methods in administration. The recommendations of the National Police Commission (1977-81), *inter alia*, meant to modernize the logistics of the police for the control of crime and maintenance of public order. The National Education Policy (1986) constituted an integral part of modernizing programme of the country. In brief, the NEP emphasized universalization of primary education vocationalization of secondary education and consolidation of higher education in India. Although objective were laudable, implementation remained tardy. In a developing country, if the implementation of these reform proposals is not fast enough, tissues of resistance in the system develop leading to distortion of objectives and dilution of purposes.

Administrative reforms can ignore economic reforms at its own peril. Economy is the core of the better government. The establishment of the Economic Reforms Commission in March 1981 had two purposes: (a) initially, to suggest measures for rationalization and improvement of the tax administration; and (b) in the long run, to develop well coordinated rational approach to the proposals for the establishment of a new economic order.[22]

Thus, critical areas of reform as identified in the reports of different commissions and committees appointed by the Government of India may be summed up; general administration, plan administration, fiscal and financial administration, police and education. The key areas of administrative reform, however, vary from one country to another. Administrative reform programmes in South America concentrated on the areas like law, criminal justice, tax, financial administration, police, public administration, control and accountability of state enterprises, government contract and management of public works.[23] To any careful observer the key areas on which the reform has been concentrated in India are analogous with those in Southern America. In reform initiatives, the Government has to depend on the quantum of expendable national resources.

Reports of the Administrative Reforms Commission and the National Police Commission, for illustration, were multi-dimensional touching upon various aspects of the administrative system. Again, the report of the Santhanam Committee on Corruption was unidimensional as it dwelt on corruption alone. By focussing the important areas of reform these commissions called for intensive action both at the Central and the State levels. In fact, a number of states of India wanted to travel along the path of reforms and they did not lag behind in the appointment of reform commissions and committees. It would suffice here to name some of them: Kerala Administrative Reforms Commission (1958), Andhra Pradesh Reforms Enquiry Committee (1960), Rajasthan Administrative Reforms Committee (1963) and the Administrative Reforms Committee of West Bengal (1983). One is likely to be amazed by the variety of administrative standards prevailing in the Centre and the States and even among the States in our federal polity. Noting this identical feature in South America, Caiden wrote:

> There are islands of excellence, comparable to the best anywhere but there are also islands of shame in a sea of indifference, ineptitude and apathy. The fact that good and bad co-exist often close to one another suggests that there are few overwhelming cultural or environmental or contextual obstacles to making improvements. . . .[24]

STRATEGY OF REFORMS

The most important and controversial area where there is no agreement is the strategy of administrative reform, Strategy is concerned with thinking and action designed to ensure that the balance of advantage rests with the initiator of the plan, strategy may be comprehensive, incremental or limited. The former is an interdepartmental or government-wide reform while the latter refers to reforms focussed on a particular agency or on a particular process, *e.g.*, budgetary process, or position classification. The advantage of comprehensive reform lies chiefly in the fact that it is "better suited to catch the imagination of top political leadership,"[25] but "much time and resources could be wasted with very limited results, often breeding widespread cynicism among the clientele and lost morale and momentum among the change-agents."[26] The Administrative Reforms Commission is a case in point. Indeed, guided by lofty ideas the ARC started functioning and set up a number of study teams on various aspects of administration. In all, the Commission could submit twenty reports, but it failed to submit seven more reports that were stipulated. Its plan to submit a final report embodying the recommendations of all its reports remained unfulfilled owing to its sudden termination. The final report, as was envisaged, would have summed up all its reports and laid down the lines on which its reform proposals should have been scrutinized. The last days of the Commission presented a pathetic picture. Without consulting other members the chairman had written to the Central government suggesting the abolition of the Commission on 30 June. 1970.[27] In regard to its unfinished task, the Government held that the Department of Administrative Reforms would take care of it.

The reports of the ARC were received with mixed reactions. Scholars sharply differed in regard to the contribution of the ARC. According to some, the total impact of ARC reports on India's administrative system was minimal and that it did not usher in a major transformation of traditional administrative system. Others, however, contested this view and commented that nearly five hundred recommendations given by the Commission had their own merit.[28] It is true that the Commission which started functioning with fanfare and publicity could not live up to the expectation in the long run. The Government's decision to abolish the Commission was received with relief all over the country. Many newspapers brought out editorials dwelling on utter futility of this venture and welcoming the step.[29] In fact, this had been the story of many comprehensive reform efforts in Asia during the last decade.[30]

Grandiose schemes for wholesale transformation have been generally replaced by incremental, quickly attainable substantive improvements.[31] According to incremental and intra-departmental strategy, the reform or restructuring of responsibilities and authority is done in a given ministry or department. Being gradualist in character, incremental strategy has the advantage of experimentation and confidence building among the reform agents. As the strategy seeks to fulfil limited objective, the resistance to the reform proposal may not be stiff and insurmountable. But the danger of having inconsistent and, at times, contradictory reform proposals, not supplemental to each other, cannot be ruled out. In order to monitor the proposal, the need for a permanent agency can hardly be ignored. In fact, keeping in view the importance of administrative reforms, an independent Ministry of Personnel and Training, Administrative Reforms and Public Grievances and Pensions was brought into being in 1985. It was rightly put under the charge of the Prime Minister. Placing the reform agency under a nodal ministry, the Home or the Finance, has not been found as an effective strategy in the Asian context.

Comprehensive or incremental strategy for the purpose of translating reform proposals may be resorted to depending on the situation and time. This is known as optimum strategy. Such a strategy presupposes prior determination as to whether the existing situation is congenial for administering the reform proposal or not. Thus, this approach is reactive rather than 'proactive' Timing for reforms is a crucial factor and it determines to a great extent the success or failure of a given reform experiment. Administrative reform may be introduced in normal period or crisis situation. Reform in the normal period is primarily oriented toward system-maintenance. Such reform may be structural and limited in scope. But radical changes are introduced for meeting crisis situation and the people and urged to conform to the values of the emergent situation. In crisis situation, power rolls back in the hands of the executive facilitating the formulation and implementation of reform programmes. People are generally found receptive to changes designed to terminate the crisis. From the experiences during the emergency period in India, it had been found that the reforms introduced in various sectors of the administrative system could not be sustained owing to people's apathy.[32] Normally, the trend in India has been to introduce reforms and adopt strategies only to enhance the capabilities of the development administration.

LESSONS FROM REFORMS

Public administration in India is dominated by the view that it is an instrument of public action and its success depends on the effective implementation of decisions made by representative institutions. Administrative reform has stemmed out of the concern of making such administrative action more effective. Academically speaking, the most important paradigm guiding research has been that of Max Weber. Despite exhortation from academics and professionals no significant attempt has been made so far to develop alternative conceptual framework for the purpose. The Gorwala reports on public administration and on public enterprises (1951) and Appleby reports on public administration (1953) and public sector undertaking (1956) are regarded as "classics in Indian administration."[33] Gorwala believed that efficiency and discipline in the civil service was deteriorating, but Appleby still rated the Indian government as among the dozen or so most advanced governments of the world.[34] Pursuing the British model, Gorwala stressed on efficiency and discipline in the civil service and on the development of understanding between politics and administration. Appleby identified structural and procedural deficiencies and emphasized the need for training considering the requirements of development administration.[35]

In an effort to reform Indian administration, technical measures and adjustments have been offered by most of the reform committees and commissions, but the premises and assumptions that supported the form and operation of public administration were hardly questioned and considered,

One of the arguments advanced in favour of establishing Administrative Reforms Commission in sixties was to restore Indianness of Indian administration. To what extent the hope had come to be realized was a matter of opinion. According to one view, the ARC had a comprehensive probe into public administration at all levels and in all segments of administration during 1966-70 and its recommendations were relevant to Indian context. By 1979, action on over five hundred recommendations had been initiated.[36] Contrary to this view, it was observed that the Administrative Reforms Commission did not address itself to this basic task of evolving a philosophy of administration and its numerous reports cannot be threaded into an integrated whole. While noting the existence of tension between the generalist and the specialist it was argued that the Commission helped to accelerating the polarization of the generalist and the specialist in Indian administration. Moreover, the reform proposals of the ARC had limited effectiveness and applicability for "the reforms model adopted in disregard to its ecology was bound to be dysfunctional."[37] The controversy reinforced the argument in favour of embedding public administration in the realities of Indian situation. An old and archaic society was slowly to be transformed into a more just and human society. This calls for new agenda for public administration in India. "If the American scholars could give a call for a new public administration in their social crisis, why can't scholars in India raise a similar debated?"[38]

CONCLUSION

Not much serious studies have been undertaken to fathom into the factors and forces responsible for non-implementation of the reform proposals in India.[39] A few observations from the studies already undertaken in other countries in this regard may be ventured only to help in better understanding of Indian reforms activities. In Africa, administrative reform initiatives collapsed due to bureaucratic inertia and social disharmony.[40] Indian subcontinent bureaucratic resistance defeated reform campaigns.[41] Political corruption has been responsible for the failure of the administrative reforms in the Philippines, Indonesia, South Africa and Taiwan.[42] It can reasonably be argued that in an atmosphere of political corruption as it exists in India it is difficult to push through reform proposals. Pressure groups and vested interests stand in the way of implementing reforms in India. Reform initiatives also fail in India due to dilution to goals and objectives and misplaced emphasis on priorities.[43] These are some of the factors and forces at work against reform initiatives in this country. But they are all tentatively focussed. More critical and in-depth studies are urgently needed in this sphere.

Success of the reform proposals rests on political support, administrative capacity and public participation for implementing the reforms.[44] The value for money approach in administrative reform has been greatly assisted by the upsurge over the past decade of policy analysis and public productivity research,[45] dispelling the doubt that much of the government performance cannot be measured and evaluated. It is acknowledged that reforms in administration have to be implemented by and within the same bureaucracy. In other words, it has to be consulted and involved with the reform process. Bureaucracy has to be seen not as the inevitable enemy but as a willing partner having talent and experienced professionals who know where the problems lie and what should be done with minimum of dislocation. Not only do the bureaucrats bow to the inevitable but their professional obligations impel them to deflect public criticism by improving public services and by demonstrating that bureaucratic inertia can be overcome.[46] This line of argument postulates that panacea for government ills cannot be "found in political abstractions or business practices or purely managerial prescriptions or constant harassment of public officials."[47] Indian bureaucracy has grown with the colonial tradition. Since Independence, its functional contours and ethos have vastly changed in keeping with the changed political environment. To lay the entire blame for inefficiency in administration on bureaucracy is to sideline other issues. Administratively, success of a reform plan demands from the hundreds of thousands of permanent officials who handle public business daily to devise for themselves better ways of doing their jobs.[48]

Indian experience can make a definite contribution to the theory of administrative reform. By resorting to both incremental and comprehensive approaches for reforms, India has been able to identify their respective functional and dysfunctional aspects. Like other administration, Indian administration is culture-bound and it has to be reformed considering Indian genius and culture.

REFERENCES

1. United Nations, *Enhancing Capabilities of Administrative Reform in Developing Countries* (New York: Department of Technical Cooperation, 1983).
2. Paul Appleby, *Public Administration in India: Report of a Survey* (New Delhi: Cabinet Secretariat, 1953).
3. M.A. Muttalib, "Trends in Administrative Reforms", in *A Survey of Research in Public Administration (1970-79)* (New Delhi .

Concept Publishing Co. for ICSSR, 1986), 112.

4. Ibid.
5. The Secretariat Reorganisation Committee in its report (1947) suggested: (a) optimum use of the available manpower, (b) induction of provincial civil service into Central Secretariat; and (c) reorganization of work in the Central secretariat.
6. P.K. Mattoo, "Administrative Reforms at the Central Level," *Indian Journal of Public Administration*, XXXI (1985), 535.
7. Ibid.
8. A.D. Gorwala, *Report on Public Administration* (New Delhi, 1951), 34.
9. Mattoo, "Administrative Reforms at the Central Level," 54 1.
10. *Indian Journal of Public Administration*, Special number on Administrative Reforms since Independence, 1963, surveyed the trends of administrative reforms in various articles.
11. Gerald Caiden and Siedentopf, eds. *Strategies of Administrative Reforms* (Lexington: Mass, 1982), 5-6.
12. See discussion on the terms of reference of A.R.C, in S.R. Maheshwari, *The Administrative Reforms Commission* (Agra: Laxmi Narayan Agarwal, 1972), 29.
13. H.M.S.O., *Committee on the Civil Service, Report*, Vol. I (London, 1968), 107.
14. See discussion on the genesis of the Commission of ARC, Maheshwari, *The Administrative Reforms Commission*, 24.
15. See discussion on membership of A.R.C. *Ibid.*, 37.
16. Raul P. De Guzman, Arturo Pacho and Ric Tan Legada, "Reforms in Asia and Pacific Region Nations," *IJPA*. XXXI (1985), 972.
17. Gerald E. Caiden, *Administrative Reforms* (London: The Penguin Press, 1970), 65.
18. Government of India, *Report of 'Third Pay Commission* Vol. IV. See dissenting note by A.K. Das Gupta and N.K. Roy, p. 100, para 2.
19. UPSC, Committee on Recruitment Policy and Selection Methods, *Report* (New Delhi, 1976), 14.
20. G.C. Singhvi, "Some Aspects of Reforms in Police Administration," *IJPA*, XXXI (1985), 797.
21. Caiden, "The Vitality of Administrative Reform," *International Review of Administrative Sciences*, Vol. 54, p. 331.
22. Mattoo, "Administrative Reforms at the Central Level," 538.
23. Caiden, *Public Administration in South America; Some Reflections*

(Los Angeles: University of Southern California, 1984), 2.

24. *Ibid.*, 4.
25. Hahn-Been Lee and Abelardo G. Samonte, eds. *Administrative Reform in Asia* (Manila: Eropa, 1970).
26. *Ibid.*, 17.
27. Maheshwari, *The Administrative Reforms Commission*, 72.
28. See P.R. Dubhashi, "Administrative Reforms: Lessons form the Experiences Abroad," *IJPA*, XXIV (1983), 276-77; and Muttalib, "Trends in Administrative Reforms," 119.
29. Maheshwari, *The Administrative Reforms Commission*, 72..
30. Lee and Samonte, eds., *Administrative Reforms in Asia*, 28.
31. Caiden, "*Vitality of Administrative Reforms*, " 350.
32. See *Shah Commission Report*, Vol. I (New Delhi), 77.
33. Muttalib, "Trends in Administrative Reforms," 117.
34. *Ibid*
35. *Ibid*.
36. *Ibid.*, 119.
37. Maheshwari, *The Administrative Reforms Commission*, 154-157.
38. Mohit Bhattacharya, "Public Administration in India: A Discipline in Bondage, *IJPA*, XXXII (1986), 225.
39. Sec *IJPA* special issue on "Administrative Reforms Revisited" (1985).
40. See B.C. Chikolu, "The Zambian Administrative Reforms: An Alternative View *Public Administration and Development* (1981), 55-56; and Williams Robert; *Political Corruption in Africa* (Aldershot: Gower, 1987).
41. M.M. Khan, "Administrative Reform," *IJPA*, XXIV (1979), 170-80; "Ruling Elites and Major Administrative Reforms: The Case of the Pakistan Civil Service," *Indian Journal of Political Science*, XL 729-60; and Krishna K. Tummala, *The Ambiguity of Ideology and Administrative Reform* (Bombay: Allied Publisher, 1979).
42. Caiden. "The Vitality of Administrative Reforms," 349.
43. *The Statesman* (Calcutta), 23 Nov., 1988.
44. See Al-Saigh M. Nassir, ed., *Administrative Reform in the Arab World: Readings* (Amman, AQAS, 1986); and I. Mayo-Smith and N.L. Rutter, *Achieving Improved Performance in Public Organizations: A Guide for Managers* (West Hartfold, CT: Kumarian Press, 1986).
45. David, L. Dillman, "Personnel Management and Productivity Reform: Taming the Civil Service in Great Britain and the United

States," *International Journal of Public Administration*, VIII (1986), 347-67; Trudi C. Miller, ed., *Public Sector Performance: A Conceptual Turning Point* (Baltimore: Johns Hopkins University Press, 1984); Willian Plowden, *et ai*, "New Directions in Administrative Reforms," *International Review of Administrative Sciences*, 49 (1983), 96-109.

46. Caiden "The Vitality of Administrative Reforms," 351.
47. *Ibid.*
48. *Ibid.*

2

Mughul Administration

I. Nature of the Mughul Government

The establishment of the Mughul administration, on ideas and principles different from those of the Sultans of Delhi, was mainly the work of Akbar. Of his two predecessors, Babur and Humayun, the former had neither time nor opportunity, and the latter neither inclination nor ability, to elaborate a system of civil government. While gifted with political genius of a high order, Akbar was indebted in certain respects to the Sur example of administrative organisation. The Mughul government was a "combination of Indian and extra-Indian elements". It was, more correctly speaking, "the Perso-Arabic system in an Indian setting". It was also essentially military in nature and every officer of the Mughul State had to be enrolled in the army list. It was necessarily a centralised autarchy, and the king's power was unlimited. His word was law, and his will none could dispute. He was the supreme authority in the State, the head of the government, the commander of the State forces, the fountain of justice, and the chief legislator. He was the Khalifah of God, required to obey the scriptures and Islamic traditions, but in practice a strong king could act in defiance of sacred law if he so liked. There was nothing like a cabinet of ministers in the modern sense of the term. The ministers could not claim to be consulted as a matter of right; it was entirely a matter of the Emperor's pleasure to accept their advice or not. Much depended, indeed, on the personality of the Emperor and his ministers. A wise ruler like Shah Jahan wanted invariably to consult a Sadullah Khan, while a minister like Husain Ali Khan would have littie regard, even open contempt, for his crowned puppets. The first six Mughul rulers of India possessed, however, a strong commonsense, and their autocracy did not, therefore, degenerate into an unbearable tyranny trampling on the rights and customs of the people. Endowed with the spirit of "benevolent despots", these rulers worked hard for the good of their subjects, in one way or another, especially in the regions round the central capital and the seats of viceregal governments in the provinces. But the State in those days "did not undertake any socialistic work, nor interfered with the lives of the villagers so long as there was not violent crime or defiance of royal authority in the locality". From one point of view, the enormous power of the Mughul emperors was strictly limited. Their orders could not always be easily enforced in the distant corners of the Empire, not to speak of certain hilly parts of Chota Nagpur and the Santal Parganas, which most probably never acknowledged their sway. When we find almost each and every Emperor issuing orders for the abolition of the same kind of taxes and cesses in the very first year of his reign, we are led to conclude that previous attempts to abolish these had proved ineffectual and inoperative. There are copious references in the records of the English factories in India to show that even in the days of Shah Jahan and Aurangzeb, not to speak of the reigns of their weak successors, the *subahdars,* the provincial *diwans,* and the customs-officers, occasionally acted contrary to the orders of the central government, mostly out of selfish motives,

2. The Nobility

Owing to several factors, the Mughul nobility was a heterogeneous body, composed of diverse elements like Turk, Tartar, Persian and Indian, Muslim and Hindu, and could not, therefore, organise itself as a powerful baronial class. Some Europeans also received titles of nobility. In theory, the nobility was not hereditary but purely official in character. A noble had only a life interest in his *jagir,* which escheated to the crown on his death; and the titles or emoluments could not usually be transmitted from father to son. The effect of the system of escheat was, as Sir J. N. Sarkar has observed, "most harmful". The nobles led extravagant lives and squandered away all their money in unproductive luxury during their life-time. It also "prevented India from having one of the strongest safeguards of public liberty and checks on royal autocracy, namely, an independent hereditary peerage, whose position and wealth did not depend on the king's favour in every generation, and who could, therefore, afford to be bold in their criticism of the royal caprice and their opposition to the royal tyranny".

3. Public Service and Bureaucracy

To maintain the military strength of the Empire, it was necessary for the Mughuls to employ a large number of foreign adventurers. Though Akbar inaugurated the policy of "India for Indians" and threw open official careers to the Hindus, yet the foreign elements predominated in the Mughul public service. The general character of the public services remained unaltered during the reigns of Jahangir and Shah Jahah. But deterioration in their efficiency began during the reign of the former, and became striking during the reign of his son and more so in the reign of Aurangzeb. Thus Prince Akbar wrote to Aurangzeb plainly in 1681: "The clerks and officers of state have taken to the practice of traders, and are buying posts with gold and selling them for shameful considerations. Every one who eats salt destroys the salt-cellar."

Every officer of the State held a *mansab* or official appointment of rank and profit, and, as such, was bound theoretically to supply a number of troops for the military service of the State. Thus the *mansabdars* formed the official nobility of the country, and this system was the "army, the peerage, and the civil administration, all rolled into one". Akbar classified the office-holders into thirty-three grades, ranging from "commanders of 10" to "commanders of 10,000". Till the middle of Akbar's reign, the highest rank an ordinary officer could hold was that of a commander of 5,000; the more exalted grades between commanders of 7,000 and 10,000 were reserved for members of the royal family. But towards the end of his reign this restriction was relaxed, and, under his successors, the officers rose to much higher positions. The *mansabdars* were directly recruited, promoted, suspended or dismissed by the Emperors. Each grade carried a definite rate of pay, out of which its holder was expected to maintain a quota of horses, elephants, beasts of burden and carts. But the *mansabdars* rarely fulfilled this condition. Irvine writes that "in spite of musterings and brandings we may safely assume that very few *mansabdars* kept up at full strength even the quota of horsemen for which they received pay". A *mansabdari* dignity was not hereditary. The State Service was not specialised, and an officer might be entrusted at any moment with an entirely new duty. Akbar's wonderful capacity for "picking the right man for the right job" checked the evils of this system, but a deterioration set in later on with the change in the personality of the rulers.

The officers of the Mughul government received their salaries in two ways. Either they received them in cash from the State, or occasionally they were granted *jagirs* for a temporary period. They were not, however, given any ownership over the lands in their *jagirs*, but were only allowed to collect and enjoy the land revenue, equivalent to the amount of their salaries, from the assigned tracts. "Any excess collected not only involved injustice towards the cultivators; it was a fraud against the State as well." *Jagirs* were frequently transferred from one *mansabdar* to another. The *jagir* system, however, gave some undue power and independence to the holders of *jagirs*; and Akbar, like Sher Shah, was justified in trying to remunerate his officers by cash payments, and in converting *jagir* into *khalsa* lands, whenever possible. Whether paid in cash or in *jagirs*, the Mughul public servants enjoyed, as we know from the *Ain-i-Akbari*, inordinately high salaries,[1] which attracted most enterprising adventurers from Western and Central Asia. Various evils crept into the Mughul public services after the reign of Aurangzeb, if not earlier.

4. Departments of Government and Chief Officers

Though the Mughul Emperors had absolute powers, they appointed a number of officers in the different departments of the Government for the transaction of its multitudinous affairs. The chief departments of the State were: *(a)* the Imperial Household under the *Khan-i-Saman*, *(b)* the Exchequer under the *Diwan*, *(c)* the Military Pay and Accounts Office under the *Mir Bakhshi*, *(d)* the Judiciary under the *Chief Qazi*, *(e)* Religious Endowments and Charities under the Chief *Sadr* or *Sadr-us-Sudur*, and (f) the Censorship of Public Morals under the *Muhtasib*. The *Diwan* or *Wazir* was usually the highest officer in the State, being a sole charge of revenues and finance. The *Bakhshi* discharged a variety of functions. While he was the Paymaster-General of all the officers of the State, who "theoretically belonged to the military department", he was also responsible for the recruiting of the army, and for maintaining lists of *mansabdars* and other high officials; and when preparing for a battle he presented a complete muster-roll of the army before the Emperor. The *Khan-i-Saman* or the Lord High Steward had charge of the whole imperial house-hold "in reference to both great and small things". The *Muhtasibs* or Censors of Public Morals looked after the enforcement of the Prophet's commands and the laws of morality. The other officers, somewhat inferior in status to those mentioned above, were the *Mir Atish* or *Daroga-i-Topkhana* (head of the artillery), the *Daroga of Dak chowki* (head of the correspondence department), the *Daroga* of the Mint, the *Mir Mal* or the Lord Privy Seal, the *Mustaufi* or the Auditor-General, the *Nazir-i-Buyutat* or the Superintendent of the Imperial Workshop, the *Mushriff* or the Revenue Secretary, the *Mir Bahri* or the Lord of the Admiralty, the *Mir Barr* or the Superintendent of Forests, the *Waqa-i-navis* or News-Reporters, the *Mir Arz* or the officer in charge of petitions presented to the Emperor, the *Mir Manzil* or the Quartermaster-General, and the *Mir Tozak* or the Master of Ceremonies.

5. The Police

So far as the rural areas were concerned, the Mughuls introduced no new arrangements for the prevention and detection of crimes. These remained, as from time immemorial, under the headman of the village and his subordinate watchmen. This system, which afforded a fair degree of security in the local areas with only occasional disturbances in times of disorder, survived till the beginning of the nineteenth century. In the cities and towns, all police duties, including the task of maintaining public order and decency, were entrusted to the *Kotwals*, whose duties, as enumerated in the *Ain-i-Akbari*, were multifarious: (i) to detect thieves, (ii) to regulate prices and check weights and measures, (iii) to keep watch at night and patrol the city, (iv) to keep up registers of houses, frequented roads, and of citizens, and watch the movements of strangers, (v) to employ spies from among the vagabonds, gather information about the affairs of the neighbouring villages, and the income and expenditure of the various classes of people, (vi) to prepare an inventory of, and take charge of, the property of deceased or missing persons who left no heirs, (vii) to prevent the slaughter of oxen, buffaloes horses or camels, and (viii) to prevent the burning of women against their will, and circumcision below the age of twelve. Sir J. N. Sarkar believes that this long list of the *Kotwals* duties in the *Ain* represents "only the ideal for the *Kotwal*" and not "the actual state of things". But Manucci also gives from personal observation an exhaustive account of the *Kotwal's* duties. It is, however, certain that the *Kotwals* main business was to preserve peace and public security in the urban areas. In the districts or *sarkars*, law and order were maintained usually by officers like the *Faujdars*. "The *faujdar*, as his name suggests, was only the commander of a military force stationed in the country. He had to put down smaller rebellions, disperse or arrest robber gangs, take cognizance of all violent crimes, and make demonstrations of force to overawe opposition to the revenue authorities, or the criminal judge, or the censor." The police arrangements were in some respects effective, though "the state of public security varied greatly from place to place and from time to time".

6. Law and Justice

Nothing like modern legislation, or a written code of laws, existed in the Mughul period. The only notable exceptions to this were the twelve ordinances of Jahangir and the *Fatdwa-i-'Alamgiri*, a digest of Muslim law prepared under Aurangzeb's supervision. The judges chiefly followed the Quranic injunctions or precepts, the *Fatawas* or previous interpretations of the Holy Law by eminent jurists, and the *qanuns* or ordinances of the Emperors. They did not ordinarily disregard customary laws and sometimes followed principles of equity. Above all, the Emperor's interpretations prevailed, provided they did not run counter to the sacred laws.

The Mughul Emperors regarded speedy administration of justice as one of their important duties, and their officers did not enjoy any special protection in this respect under anything like Administrative Law. "If I were guilty of an unjust act," said Akbar, "I would rise in judgment against myself." Peruschi writes on the authority of Monserrate that "as to the administration of justice he is most zealous and watchful". The love of justice of the other Emperors, like Jahangir, Shah Jahan and Aurangzeb, has been testified to by some contemporary European travellers. Though approach to the Emperor through all kinds of official obstructions was not very easy, at least two Mughul Emperors, Akbar and Jahangir, granted to their subjects the right of direct petitioning (which was only won in England after a hard fight). The latter allowed a chain with bells to be hung outside his palace to enable petitioners to bring their grievances to the notice of the Emperor.

The *Qazi'-ul-Qazat* or the Chief *Qazi* was the principal judicial officer in the realm. He appointed *Qazis* in every provincial capital. The *Qazi's* made investigations into, and tried, civil as well as criminal cases of both the Hindus and the Muslims; the *Muftis* expounded Muslim Law; and the *Mir Adis* drew up and pronounced judgments. The *Qazis* were expected to be "just, honest, impartial, to hold trials in the presence of the parties and at the court-house and the seat of government, not to accept presents from the people where they served, nor to attend entertainments given by anybody and everybody, and they were asked to know poverty to be their glory". But in practice they abused their authority, and, as Sir J.N. Sarkar observes, "the *Qazi's* department became a byword and reproach in Mughul times". There were no primary courts below those of the *Qazis*, and the villagers and the inhabitants of smaller towns, having no *Qazis* over them, settled their differences locally "by appeal to the caste courts or *panchayats*, the arbitration of an impartial umpire *(salis)*, or by a resort to force". The *Sadr-us-sudur* or the chief *Sadr* exercised supervision over the lands granted by the Emperors or princes to pious men, scholars and monks, and tried cases relating to these, Below him there was a local *sadr* in every province.

Above the urban and provincial courts was the Emperor himself, who, as the "*Khalif* of the Age", was the fountain of justice and the final court of appeal. Sometimes he acted as a court of first instance too. Fines could be imposed and severe punishments, like amputation, mutilation and whipping, could be inflicted by the courts without any reference to the Emperor, but his consent was necessary in inflicting capital punishment. There was no regular jail system, but the prisoners were confined in forts.

7. The Revenue System

The revenues of the Mughul Empire may be grouped under two heads—central or imperial and local or provincial. The local revenue, which was apparently collected and spent without reference to the finance authorities of the central government, was derived from various minor duties and taxes levied on "production and consumption, on trades and occupations, on various incidents of social life, and most of all on transport". The major sources of central revenue were land revenue, customs, mint, inheritance, plunder and indemnities, presents, monopolies and the poll-tax. Of these, land revenue formed, as in old days, the most important source of the State income.

The important revenue experiments of the Surs were undone in the period of confusion and disorders following, the reigns of Sher Shah and Islam Shah. But the old machinery of government and the time-honoured customs and procedures must have been inherited by Akbar, who found at his accession three kinds of land in the country—the *Khalsa* or crown-lands, the *Jagir* lands, enjoyed by some nobles who collected the local revenues, out of which they sent a portion to the central exchequer and kept the rest for themselves, and the *Sayurghal* lands, granted on free tenure. After securing his freedom from the influence of Bairam and that of the ladies of the harem, Akbar realised the importance of reorganising the finances of his growing empire, which were in a hopelessly confused state. Thus in 1570-1571, Muzaffar Khan Turbati, assisted by Raja Todar Mall, prepared a revised assessment of the land revenue, "based on estimates framed by the local *Qanungoes* and checked by ten superior *Qanungoes* at headquarters". After Gujarat had been conquered, Todar Mall effected there a regular survey of the land, and the assessment was made "with reference to the area and quality of the land". In 1575-1576 Akbar made a new and disastrous experiment by abolishing the old revenue areas and dividing the whole of the Empire, with the exception of the provinces of Gujarat, Bengal and Bihar, into a large number of units, each yielding one *Kror* (crore) a year, and placed over each of them an officer called the *Krori*, whose duties were to collect revenues and encourage cultivation. But the *Kroris* soon grew corrupt and their tyranny reduced the peasants to great misery.

Their offices were, therefore, abolished and the old revenue divisions were restored, though the title of *Krori* continued to survive at least till the reign of Shah Jahan.

Important revenue reforms were introduced in 1582, when Todar Mall was appointed the *Diwan-i-Ashraf*. Hitherto assessments were fixed annually on the basis of production and statistics of current prices, and the demands of the State thus varied from year to year. Todar Mall established a standard or "regulation" system of revenue-collection, the chief features of which were (i) survey and measurement of land, (ii) classification of land, (iii) fixation of rates. Lands were carefully surveyed, and for measurement the old units, whose length fluctuated with the change of season, were replaced by the *Ilahi Gaz* or yard, which was equal to about thirty-three inches, *tanab* or tent-rope, and *jarib* or bamboos joined by iron rings, which assured a constant measure. Land was classified into four classes according to "the continuity or discontinuity of cultivation": (i) *Polaj* or land capable of being annually cultivated, (ii) *Parauti* or land kept fallow for some time to recover productive capacity, (iii) *Chachar* or land that had lain fallow for three or four years, and (iv) *Banjar* or land uncultivated for five years or longer. Only the area actually cultivated was assessed, and, in order to ascertain the average produce of land belonging to each class, the mean of the three grades into which it was divided was taken into consideration. The demand of the State was fixed at one-third of the actual produce, which the ryots could pay either in cash or in kind. The cash rates varied according to crops. This revenue system, as applied to Northern India, Gujarat, and, with some modifications, to the Deccan, was *rayatwari*, that is, "the actual cultivators of the soil were the persons responsible for the annual payment of the fixed revenue". In the outlying portions of the Empire, this system was not applied, but each of these was dealt with as local circumstances required.

For purposes of administration and revenue collection, the Empire was divided into *subahs*, which again were subdivided into *sarkars*, each of which in turn comprised a number of *paraganas*. Each *paragana* was a union of several villages. The *amalguzar* or revenue-collector in charge of a district was assisted by a large subordinate staff. Apart from the village *Muqaddam* (headman) and the village *Patwari*, who were servants of the village community and not of the State, there were measurers and *karkuns*, who prepared the seasonal crop statistics; the *Qanungo*, who kept records of the revenue payable by the villages; the *Bitikchi* or accountant; and the *Potdar* or district treasurer. These officers were instructed to collect revenue with due care and caution and "not to extend the hand of demand out of season". The Emperors were for ever "issuing orders to their officers to show leniency and consideration to the peasants in collecting the revenue, to give up all *abwabs* and to relieve local distress". There are instances in the reigns of Shah Jahan and Aurangzeb of extortionate revenue officials and even provincial governors being dismissed on complaints being made against them by the subjects to the Emperors. Though the lower revenue officers, especially those in the outlying provinces and districts, were not above corruption and malpractices, "the highest were, on the whole, just and statesmanlike" with few exceptions.

The success or failure of the revenue system thus organised must have depended on the quality and nature of the administration at the centre, and evils could not but appear when the administrative machinery was getting out of gear in Aurangzeb's reign. But on the whole its principles were sound and "the practical instructions to the officials all that could be desired". The ryots got a certain amount of security and the fluctuations of the State revenue were prevented, or at least minimised. Further, the ryots were not evicted from their holdings for default of payment, and the " custom of payment by the division of the crop ", on the basis of the actual produce of a year, was better than the modern money rent system by which one has to pay the fixed amount irrespective of the harvest of the year. The demand at the rate of one-third, though rather high, as compared with one-sixth prescribed by Hindu law and custom or with what a modern landowner gets, was not a heavy burden on the peasants, who were compensated by the State with the abolition or remission of various cesses and taxes.

8. The Provincial Government

In 1579-1580 Akbar divided his Empire into twelve provinces, the number of which rose to fifteen[2] towards the close of his reign, to seventeen in the reign of Jahangir and to twenty-one in the time of Aurangzeb. "The administrative agency in the provinces of the Mughul Empire was an exact miniature of the Central Government." The Governor (styled the *Sipah Salar*, Commander-in-Chief, or *Sahib Subah*, Lord of the Province, or simply *Subahdar*, and officially described as the *Nazim)* was the head of the civil as well as military administration of each *subah*. He had a staff of subordinate officers under him, like the *Diwan*, the *Bakhshi*, the *Faujdar*, the *Kotwal*, the *Qazi*, the *Sadr*, the *Amil*, the *Bitikchi*, the *Potdar* and the *Waqa-i-navis*. The *Diwdn* or revenue-chief of a province often acted as the rival of the *Subahdar*. Each was enjoined "to keep a strict watch over the other" so that none of them could grow over-powerful.

9. The Army

No large standing army was maintained by the State, but theoretically "all able-bodied citizens of the empire were potential soldiers of the imperial army". The history of the Mughul army is largely the history of the *Mansabdari* system, the principal features of which have already been noted. Besides the *Mansabdars*, there were the *Dakhilis* or supplementary troopers placed under the command of *Mansabdars* and paid by the State, and *Ahadis* or a body of "gentleman troopers, a special class of horsemen, who were generally round the Emperor's person, and owed allegiance to no one else". The *Mansabdari* system was not free from corruption. "False musters," writes Irvine, "were an evil from which the Mughul army suffered in its most palmy days. Nobles would lend to each other the men to make up their quota, or needy idlers from the bazars would be mounted on the first baggage pony that came to hand and counted in with the others as efficient soldiers". Steps were taken by Akbar's Government to remove these evil practices. Regulations were introduced for periodical musters, a *chihrah* or descriptive roll of a *Mansabdar* was drawn up, "showing his name, his father's name, his tribe or caste, his place of origin, followed by details of his personal appearance"; and the system of branding horses, known as *Dagh-o-mahalli* or simply *Dagh*, was revived. But these measures could not effectively check the evils.

To express it in modern terms, the Mughul forces were composed of (i) cavalry, (ii) infantry, (iii) artillery and (iv) navy. The cavalry was the most important of all these branches. The infantry was largely composed of men drawn from ordinary townsmen and peasants; and "as a part of the fighting strength of the army it was insignificant". Guns, manufactured within the country and also imported from outside, were used in wars by Babur, Humayun, and Akbar, but "the artillery was much more perfect and numerous in 'Alamgir's reign" than before. The artillery was wholly state-paid. There was nothing like any strong navy in the modern sense of the term, but Abul Fazl writes of an "Admiralty Department", the functions of which were (i) to build boats of all kinds for river transport, (ii) to fit out strong boats for transporting war-elephants (iii) to recruit expert seamen, (iv) to supervise the rivers, and (v) to impose, collect or remit river duties and tolls. A fleet of 768 armed vessels and boats was stationed at Dacca to protect the coast of Bengal against the Mugs and the Arakanese pirates. But the naval establishment of the Mughuls does not seem to have been very formidable.

The Mughul army, though not so inefficient as some writers would ask us to believe, was not, however, without certain defects. Firstly, it was not a national army, but was a mixture of diverse elements, each trying to follow its own peculiar methods and manoeuvres. Thus, though its numerical strength increased as years went on, it grew cumbrous and hard to be controlled and managed. Secondly, the soldiers did not owe direct allegiance to the Emperor, but were more attached to their immediate recruiters and superiors, whose acute jealousies and bitter rivalries often destroyed the chances of success in campaigns. Lastly, the pomp and display of the Mughul army in camp, and on the march, were largely responsible for marring its efficiency. Akbar could at times depart from this practice. But generally the imperial army looked like "an unwieldy moving city" and was "encumbered with all the lavish paraphernalia of the imperial court, including a proportion of the harem and its attendants, mounted on elephants and camels, a travelling audience-hall, musicians' gallery, offices, workshops, and bazars. Elephants and camels carried the treasure; hundreds of bullock-carts bore the military stores; an army of mules transported the imperial furniture and effects ". Referring to the grand camp of the Emperor Aurangzeb at Ahmadnagar, Grant Duff comments that "it proved a serious encumbrance to the movements of his army, while the devouring expense of such establishments pressed hard on his finances, and soon crippled even the most necessary of his military and political arrangements". This sort of camp life naturally produced luxury and indiscipline in the army. The inevitable deterioration set in under Jahangir and Shah Jahan and manifested itself fully in the time of Aurangzeb. The army became incapable of "swift action or brilliant adventure". In this respect, the then light cavalry of Shivaji, maintained by him under strict discipline, was far better than the Mughul army.

NOTES

1. Making deductions for the monthly expenses of maintaining troops and other incidental expenses, Moreland calculates that a *mansabdar* of "5,000" received a net monthly salary of at least Rs. 18,000, one of "1,000" at least Rs. 5,000, and "a commander of 500" at least Rs. 1,000 a month, Moreland, *India at the Death of Akbar,* pp. 66*ff*.
2. Agra, Allahabad, Oudh, Delhi, Lahore, Multan, Kabul, Ajmer, Bengal, Bihar, Ahmadabad, Malwa, Berar, Khandesh, Ahmadnagar.

3

Administration in British Territories in India: 1707-1818

Bengal

The history of the evolution of British administrative institutions in Bengal from 1707 to 1818 may be roughly divided into two periods. The first period in this history may be said to have come to an end in 1774 with the coming into force[1] of what is popularly known as Lord North's Regulating Act of 1773.[2] The second period began in 1774 with the coming into operation of the Regulating Act, and continued for our present purposes, till 1818.

First Period: 1707-1774

Before, however, we actually deal with the English political institutions in Bengal during this period, we consider it necessary to say, by way of introduction, a few words in regard to two preliminary matters, namely, (i) when Bengal first became a Presidency under the English, and (ii) what was the manner in which the affairs of the East India Company—or, to be more precise, of the United Company of Merchants of England Trading to the East Indies —were administered in England during this period.

(i) Bengal: A Presidency:[3]

Roughly speaking, before 1682 Bengal had been subordinate to Fort St. George (Madras). In 1682, however, it became, although for a brief period, independent of the latter. One Mr. William Hedges was appointed to be the first independent Agent and

Governor of the (first East India) Company's "affairs and factories in he Bay of Bengal".[4] His commission of appointment was dated 14 November, 1681. He landed at Hoogly on 24 July, 1682, and held office as Agent and Governor of the Company's "affairs in the Bay of Bengal", from that date till 30 August, 1684, when he was superseded[5] by one Mr. William Gyfford (Gifford) who had previously been appointed Agent and Governor of the Company's affairs in the Bay of Bengal, in addition to his duties as Agent and Governor of Fort St. George, Madras. Thus, Bengal once more became subordinate to Madras, and continued to be in this state of subordination from September, 1684 to December, 1699, when one Sir Charles Eyre was appointed Governor of Fort William at Calcutta, and President of all the Company's "Settlements and Affairs in the Kingdoms of Bengal and Behar in the East Indies".[6]

Sir Charles Eyre actually assumed office as Governor of Bengal on 26 May, 1700.[7] Thus Bengal again became independent of Madras, with Sir Charles Eyre as its Governor. This, in brief, is the history of the origin of the Presidency of Bengal.

(ii) Home Administration of Indian Affairs:[8]

Briefly speaking, the constitution, rights and privileges of the East India Company—or, to be very precise, of the United Company of Merchants of England Trading to the East Indies[9]—*practically* during the whole of the period with which we are now concerned,[10] were in essence based upon, and derived from, the Charter which King William III had granted on 5 September, 1698, to the bulk of the subscribers to a loan of two millions sterling to the State, incorporating them as a New East India Company under the denomination of 'The English Company Trading to the East Indies". The King had granted this Charter under the authority conferred upon him by an Act of Parliament.

Under this constitution, there were two bodies for the administration of the affairs of the Company in England: a General Court of Proprietors and a Court of Directors. The supreme authority for the administration of those affairs was, however, vested in the General Court of Proprietors. The Chairman of the Court of Directors of the Company was its "*ex-officio* Chairman", and consequently presided over the meetings of its General Court.

The Court of Directors consisted of twenty-four members who were annually elected by the General Court of Proprietors from among its own members by a majority of votes. The election was held "on some day or days, time or times, between the twenty-fifth day of March and the twenty-fifth day of April in each year". After the constitution of a new Court of Directors at the end of a year, it would, at its first meeting, elect by ballot, from among its own members, its Chairman and Deputy Chairman for the next succeeding year. Although the number of Directors was twenty-four, any thirteen of them would be sufficient to constitute a Court. This number, therefore, was the quorum for all purposes of the Court, and any action taken by any thirteen Directors would be an action of the Court.

The Court of Directors was 'the executive body' of the Company. It was empowered "to act according to such Bye-Laws, Constitutions, Orders, Rules, or Directions, as shall from time to time be made and given unto them by the General Court (of Proprietors) of the Company". In the absence of any such bye-laws, etc., it would, subject to the constitution of the Company as based upon the Act of Parliament and the Royal Charter previously referred to, "direct and manage all the affairs and business of the Company"; choose and appoint its agents or servants from time to time; 'allow and pay reasonable salaries and allowances' to them, or 'remove or displace them, if necessary; and generally do such other business as it would judge necessary for the well ordering and managing of the Company and the affairs there of'. Lastly, it would, subject to the same restriction as noted above, "do, enjoy, perform, and execute all the powers, authorities, privileges, acts, and things in relation to the Company as fully, to all intents and purposes, as if the same were done by the whole Company, or by a General Court (of Proprietors) of the same".

It may be noted here that only a holder of "five hundred pounds, or more, share or interest, in the stock" of the Company would have a vote in the General Court of Proprietors, but that no person could act as a Director till he had taken an oath that he possessed £ 2,000 of the Company's stock, or, if a Quaker, made a declaration to that effect. Nor could a person be "chosen a Director of the Company" who would not, "at the time of such choice, be a natural born subject of England or naturalised, and have in his name or in his own right, and for his use two thousand pounds, or more", of the Company's stock.

The Charter of King William III provided for the appointment of sub-committees by the Court of Directors from among its own members, for the execution of the business of the Company. Actually, however, the term used was "committee" and not "sub-Committee". There were several such committees which would be formed by the Court of Directors at its first meeting after its reconstitution at the end of a year, and amongst which its business would be divided: namely, the Committee of Accounts, the Committee of Buying, the Committee of Correspondence, the Committee of Law-suits, the Committee of Shipping, the Committee of Treasury, the Committee of Warehouses, and the Committee of Private Trade. In April, 1771, a new Committee for the management and application of the Military Fund instituted by Lord Clive, was added. The Chairman and the Deputy Chairman of the Court of Directors were ex-*officio* members of all the Committees.[11]

There was another Committee of the Court of Directors to which we find frequent reference in contemporary letters from the Court to the President and Council in Bengal. This Committee was styled the Secret Committee of the Court. Like its other Committees, it used to be formed by the Court from among its own members, after its own reconstitution by the General Court of Proprietors at the end of a year. It consisted of the Chairman of the Court of Directors, its Deputy Chairman, and some other members thereof, not less than two, or more than seven in number. Any three members of the Committee would constitute a quorum. Any "instructions, orders, and directions" which the Committee or any three members thereof might think fit to issue to any person or persons in the service of the Company in Bengal (or, for the matter of that, in the East Indies), had to be "duly observed and complied with" by them.[12]

English Administrative Institutions in Bengal: 1707 to 1774:

Broadly speaking, during the whole of this period the affairs of the Company in Bengal were ordinarily administered, subject to the control of its Court of Directors and, ultimately, of its Court of Proprietors in England, by a President and Council[13] consisting of its superior servants. The President was also known as Governor. Moreover, there would often be appointed, during the later part of this period, a Select Committee to help the President and Council in the administration of the affairs of the Company in Bengal. The principal settlement of the Company in Bengal was at Fort William in Calcutta. Under this principal settlement, there were several minor settlements[14] of the Company in this side of India. They were referred to either as 'subordinates' or as factories. This nomenclature, however, was not always strictly adhered to, and a 'subordinate' would often be referred to as a factory.[15] A factory would ordinarily be under a 'subordinate'. Subject to the control and direction of the President and Council at Fort William, the affairs of a 'subordinate' were originally managed by a Chief and Council, and those of a factory by a Resident. Later on, the heads of 'subordinates' were also sometimes designated Residents. It may be mentioned here that there were two other principal settlements of the Company in India during the period with which we are now concerned: one at Bombay, and another at Fort St. George, Madras. All these three settlements were also called Presidencies, probably because at the head of each of them there was a President. Broadly speaking, the affairs of the Company in the Presidencies of Bombay and Fort St. George were administered in the same way, and subject to similar control from England, as in the case of the Presidency of Fort William. It may also be noted here that, although the three Presidencies often acted, as a matter of fact, on the principle of mutual help and co-operation in relation to one another, they were, constitutionally speaking, absolutely independent of one another. The President (or Governor) and Council at each Presidency were responsible to the authorities of the Company in England for the proper execution of their duties in India.

The principal settlements of the Company at Bombay and Fort St. George at Madras also had minor settlements under them, as in the case of Fort William at Calcutta.

We shall now deal with the position and powers of the President, Council and the Select Committee at Fort William.

The Governor

The Governor[16] of Fort William in Bengal was appointed by

the Court of Directors of the Company. This was also the case with the Governors of Fort St. George in Madras, of Bombay and of Fort Marlborough at Bencoolen, Sumatra. It was an invariable usage of the Company that the post of Governor and President in a Presidency should be filled by one of its civil servants. In the later part of the period now under consideration, the Governor was required to take an oath and to enter into a penalty bond that he might be "restricted in points of trade and private interest". Moreover, he was required to give a security of £ 10,000 for the faithful performance of his Covenant regarding the non-acceptance of any presents from, any person.

Powers of the Governor:

In his *Memoirs of Warren Hastings.*[17] Gleig has stated in connection with the office of President (i.e., the Governor) that he "may be regarded as bearing to his Council no other relation than that of *primus inter pares*". This statement is substantially correct, as the President and Governor did not possess in those days the power of overriding the majority of his Council or Select Committee and acting on his own authority and responsibility in special cases.[18] As a matter of fact, the power to override the majority of their Council and to act on their own responsibility "in cases of high importance" in the executive sphere was first conferred upon the Governor-General of Bengal, and also upon the Governors of Madras and Bombay, by a Parliamentary enactment of 1786.[19] Technically, therefore, the President was the first among, usually, nine to sixteen 'equals'[20] and every question brought before a meeting of the President and Council was decided, if the whole Council had been duly summoned, by a majority of the Council.[21] And a mere change in its personnel would not affect the system of the Company's Government at Port William. This will be evident from the following extract from a letter of the President and Council of Fort William[22] to the Nawab of Murshidabad:[23]

> "That as the Nabob seems to conjecture there is a total suspension of our Government until Lord dive's arrival. It becomes necessary to explain to him that the system of our Government *is* always the same and can never lose its force by the change of individuals—and that *whoever be President*[24] he does the duties of his office, until a succeeding President

takes the Chair and jointly with the Council conducts all the Company's business with the same authority."

The President and Governor had, however, certain special powers and privileges which contributed much to the dignity, prestige and the influence of his office. For instance, he alone was empowered to carry on correspondence with 'the Country Powers' in India. Again, the Governor of Bengal was also, under the terms of his appointment, the Commander-in-Chief of all the Company's forces in the Presidency of Bengal. And we find in a General Letter from the Court of Directors to the President and Council at Fort William, dated 30 June, 1769:

> "We are much surprised at the many questions which arose in the disputes[25] between our President Mr. Verelst and General Smith concerning their respective Military Authorities. As a full answer to the whole, in a few words, you are to understand that our Governor is to all intents and purposes the Commander in Chief of our Forces and *whatever orders he sends* to *any officer, must be obeyed.*[26] He is answerable to us for the use he makes of this power, and if he takes upon himself to give orders without the consent of the Council or Select Committee upon points belonging to their management he will suffer our severest resentment."

It is evident from all this that the President and Governor of Fort William occupied a very important position in the early governmental system of the Company in Bengal. Indeed, he was considered as 'the supreme Magistrate in Military as well as in Civil Affairs', and as 'the head of both civil and military establishments', because of his 'pre-eminence in all Departments'. His general position as the head of the Company's affairs in Bengal and the duty of the Council at Fort William towards him, had been explained by the Court of Directors in one of its earlier letters of 31 January, 1755 to the President and Council at Fort William, as follows:

> "All the rules and directions we can lay down will be of no effect nor can we ever expect to see our affairs properly conducted unless the President for the time being agreeable to his situation and the real intention of his post is a *General Inspector and Supervisor of 'the whole machine;*[27] in that light we look upon the President and we expect Mr. Drake[28] will exert

himself accordingly. We shall then find that the several important posts which have been hitherto conducted too independently will be properly checked and controlled and our servants in general will likewise be in all respects kept to their duty. Whenever therefore the President shall lay before you[29] any complaints or observations upon the conduct or management of our servants of any rank or degree or proposes any regulations for the better management of our affairs in general or any particular branches of them, you are seriously to attend to and consider them and apply such remedies as the nature of them requires."

The Court also directed in the same letter that, in consequence of the authority vested in the President, he was 'to call upon the several persons employed to see in what manner their business' was executed, so that it itself might have fewer occasions for complaints against the way in which they performed their duties.

We may also note in this connection what Lord Clive stated in the course of a parting message to Mr. Verelst who was to succeed him in the office of President and Governor of Bengal, and to the other members of the Select Committee at Fort William:[30]

"The people of this country have little, or no idea of a divided power: they imagine all authority is vested in one man. The Governor of Bengal should always be looked upon by them, in this light, as far as is consistent with the honour of the Committee and Council. In every vacant season therefore, I think it expedient that he take a tour up the country in the quality of *Supervisor General.*[31] Frauds and oppressions of every sort, being by this means laid open to his view, will in great measure be prevented, and the natives preserve a just opinion of the importance and dignity of your President, upon whose character and conduct much of the prosperity of the Company's affairs in Bengal, must ever depend."

In the exercise of his powers, however, the President and Governor was subject to the control and direction of the Select Committee and the Council at Fort William, and to that of the Court of Directors in England, and he was accountable to them for the manner in which he executed the duties of his office.

Such, in brief, were the position, powers and responsibilities of the Governor of Bengal as these had been, before what is known as the Regulating Act of 1773 came into force. We may observe, however, that, apart from the specific powers vested in him, much depended upon personal factors. If the Governor happened to be a man of strong character and personality, and he himself was above temptations—and there were many in his way in those days—he would certainly be able to maintain the dignity of his office and exercise a considerable influence over men and affairs. But things would be otherwise if the Governor happened to be a weak man or if he was not himself above temptations.[32]

The Council

The constitution of the Council differed from time to time, the number of Councillors including the President and Governor, varying, ordinarily, from nine to sixteen.[33] The views of the Court of Directors on the question whether the Commanding Officer of the army in the Presidency of Bengal should have a constant seat on the Council, also varied from time to time. Members of the Council also varied from time to time. Members of the Council were, like the President and Governor, ordinarily appointed by the Court of Directors. But vacancies would often occur in the membership of the Council either as a result of the death, going away, dismissal or the suspension of its members, or otherwise. If any such vacancies occurred, the President and Council were empowered to fill them provisionally, pending the approval of the Court, by appointing some superior servants of the Company in Bengal. It should, however, be noted here that seniority alone was not to be a ground for such appointments. In its General Letter to Bengal, dated 24 December, 1765, the Court of Directors directed the President and Council "to be extremely careful .... not to admit any one into Council" unless they were fully satisfied that his "abilities, integrity, circumstances and good character in general" rendered him fit for so important a station as the membership of the Council.

We have stated before that the President and Council were empowered provisionally to fill vacancies in the Council by appointing some superior servants of the Company from within Bengal. But sometimes such vacancies would be filled by the appointment of civil servants from other Presidencies. For instance, in 1765-66 four vacancies in the Council were filled by the appointment of four civil servants from the Presidency of Madras.

Public and Secret Departments

The Council would sometimes form itself into two Departments, Public and Secret, for the transaction of its business. For example, it did so at a (Public) Consultation, held at Fort William on 3 November, 1763.

The Select Committee

The Select Committee at Fort William generally consisted of five persons including the President and Governor there. Sometimes, however, it consisted of six persons and sometimes only of four (and even three) persons in certain circumstances. Although it was an almost invariable practice on the part of the Court of Directors to include a military officer—generally the Commanding Officer, for the time being, of the Company's army in Bengal—in the Select Committee, yet it would often lay it down as a general principle that the Commanding Officer should not be allowed to have a constant seat on the Committee.

Select Committees were ordinarily constituted from time to time by the Court of Directors, but casual vacancies therein were filled by their members themselves under the authority vested in them in this regard by the Court. Further, the President (at Fort William) would sometimes himself appoint senior servants of the Company available at Fort William, to be temporary members of the Select Committee. The usual quorum for the Select Committee was three, although "the Select Committee did not lay down any rules for themselves".

The Select Committee constituted by the order of the Court of Directors, dated 1 June, 1764, resolved at its first meeting held at Fort William on 7 May, 1765, that the following oath should be taken by its members:—

> "I, A.B., do swear that I will not reveal to any person whatever, any of the proceedings of this Committee, until the same be laid before the Council or until this Committee be dissolved."

And we find from subsequent records of the Proceedings of

the Select Committee that every person who became a member of the Committee later on, had to take this oath of secrecy before entering upon the duties of his office.

Powers of the Council and the Select Committee:

Briefly speaking, except during a short period in which the Select Committee was, as will be shortly noticed, endowed by the Court of Directors with extraordinary powers and was, therefore, to quote the words of Malcolm,[34] 'the real engine of government', and except during such an emergency as will be referred to hereinafter, the powers of the Council were really immense, since it was vested with 'a general supervising power' over the administration of the Company's affairs in Bengal. Thus we find the Court of Directors laying down in a letter, dated 23 March, 1758, that the Council should have the power of "ordering, governing and managing all the Company's affairs at Fort William in Bengal, and all its depend-dent places and settlements with as full power and authority as the Presidents and Councils in Bengal have been usually invested with". And in a previous letter, dated 11 February, 1756, the Court had directed that the Council constituted thereby would have the power of presiding over and managing "all the Company's affairs at Fort William in Bengal, and all the several dependencies thereunto belonging". In another letter, dated 8 February, 1764, the Court stated: "We have appointed the following gentlemen to be the Council for managing and conducting the Company's affairs at our Presidency of Fort William to whom all obedience is to be paid," etc. Again, shortly afterwards, in reconstituting the Council at Fort William by its letter of 1 June, 1764, the Court described its power as "managing and conducting all our affairs at the Presidency of Fort William in Bengal to whom all obedience is to be paid". Lastly, we may mention that in the Court's commissions appointing a President and Council at Fort William, dated, for instance, 11 February, 1758, and 31 May, 1764, we find that the Council was vested with the power of "governing and managing all the Company's affairs in Bengal and the places and provinces thereunto belonging". Although the Court of Directors vested such extensive powers in the Council as shown above, yet it directed[35] in 1758 that, if ever Fort William were attacked by an enemy, the powers of its Governor and Council were, so far as its defence was concerned, to be suspended, and that the sole authority therefore was to be exercised by a Military Government consisting of the "President, the Major, the Engineer, the Master Attendant for the time being and the next most capable military officer to be appointed by the said persons". This direction of the Court regarding the setting up of a Military Government at Fort William in the event of its being attacked by an enemy, was in essence repeated by it in its General Letters to Bengal, dated 13 March, 1761, 1 June, 1764, and 23 March, 1770, although the Military Government itself was ordered to be constituted differently on different occasions.

It may also be noted here that the President and Council were empowered by a Royal Charter, dated 8 January, 1758, to make bye-laws for the good government and regulation of the Mayor's Court and other Courts erected under the same Charter "for the town of Calcutta at Fort William" and places subordinate thereto, and of the inhabitants thereof. These bye-laws, however, were not to have 'any force or effect' until they were 'approved and confirmed' by the Court of Directors. The President and Council were also vested by the same Charter with certain powers relating to the administration of justice at Fort William and at places and factories subordinate to it.

It will be clear from all this that the President and Council of Fort William were vested at the same time with executive, legislative and judicial powers, and that the principle of separation of powers was not followed in framing the governmental system of the Company at Fort William.

Powers of the Select Committee

The powers of the Select Committee varied from time to time; but except during emergencies when it would be invested by the Court of Directors with extraordinary powers, it was the Council, and not the Select Committee, which was vested with 'a general supervising power' over the administration of the affairs of the Company in Bengal. During an emergency, however, the Select Committee would be vested with special powers. Thus we find that in its General Letter to Bengal, dated 1 June, 1764, the Court stated that the intention of the General Court of Proprietors in desiring Lord Clive to go to Bengal, in view of the critical situation of the Company's affairs in the Province was:

"That by His lordship's character and influence, peace and tranquility might be the easier restored and established in that Subaship.

"In order therefore to answer these purposes in a manner that we apprehend may prove most effectual, we have thought proper to appoint a Committee on this occasion consisting of his Lordship, Mr. Wm. Brightwell Sumner, Brigadier General Carnac, also Messrs. Harry Verelst and Francis Sykes to whom we do hereby give full powers to pursue whatever means they shall judge most proper to attain those desirable ends; but however in all cases where it be done conveniently, the Council at large is to be consulted by the said Committee, though the power of determination is to be in that Committee alone."

As a consequence of the conferment of these special powers upon Lord Clive and his Select Committee, the Council at Fort William became, for the time being, a factor of secondary importance in the administrative system of the Company. This state of things continued till the "general superintending power" which had been vested in the Select Committee by the Court of Directors by its General Letter to Bengal, of 1 June, 1764, and which had been confirmed by its General Letter to Bengal, of 17 May, 1766, was withdrawn from the Committee by the Court by its General Letter to Bengal, of 12 January, 1768.

Considerations of space do not permit here any detailed reference to the prolonged controversy which took place in 1770 between the Council and the Select Committee over the question of their respective jurisdictions.[36] The matter was referred, however, to the Court of Directors both by the Council and by the Select Committee, for its decision thereon. In reply, the Court upheld the contention of the Council as against that of the Select Committee.[37] With its powers thus defined by the Court, the Select Committee continued to function till October, 1774, i.e., practically till the introduction of the new system of Government constituted under what is popularly known as Lord North's Regulating Act of 1773.

Judiciary before 1774

We shall now briefly[38] notice the system of judiciary which the Company set up in Bengal before 1774. In the first place, there were established in each district two "Courts of Judicature; one by the name of *Mofussal Dewannee Audawlut,* or provincial Court of *Dewannee,* for the cogniz(ance) of Civil Causes; the other by the name (of) *Phoujdarree Audawlut,* a Court of *Phoujdarree,* for the trial of all crimes and misdemeanours". Over the first the Collector of the district presided 'on the part of the Company in their quality of King's *Dewan'*. He was 'attended by the provincial *Dewan* appointed by the President and Council' and some other officers. No cause could be 'heard or determined but in the open Court regularly assembled'. In the second the *Cauzee* and *Muftee* of the district and two *Maulavis* would 'sit to expound the law and determine how far the delinquents shall be guilty of a breach thereof.' The Collector of the district, however, was required to 'make it his business' to attend to the proceedings of this Court "so far as to see that all necessary evidences are summoned and examined, that due weight is allowed to their testimony, and that the decision passed is fair and impartial according to the proofs exhibited in the course of the trial". He was thus 'to exercise a sort of general superintendence' over the procedure of this Court. Here also no causes could be 'heard or determined but in the open Court regularly assembled.'

Secondly, two 'Superior Courts of Justice' were established at Calcutta: "one under the denomination of the *Dewdnnee Sudder Audawlut* and the other the *Nizamut Sudder Audawlut*". The President with two members of the Council at Fort William presided over the *Dewannee Sudder Audawlut,* "attended by the *Dewan* of the *Khalsa,* the head *Canongoe* and other officers of the *Cutcherry*". In the absence of the President a third member of the Council might sit along with the other two members. That is to say, not less than three members of the Council were to 'decide on an Appeal'. But the whole Council might sit if it so thought fit.

A 'Chief Officer of Justice appointed on the part of the Nazim' presided over the *Nizdmut Audawlut* by the title of Darogo-*Audaulut* (*Daroga-Audawlut*). He was assisted by the Chief *Cauzee,* the Chief *Muftee,* and three capable *Maulavis.* Their duty was "to revise all the proceedings of the *Phoujddrree Audawlut,* and in capital cases by signifying their approbation or disapprobation thereof with their reasons at large, to prepare the sentence for the Warrant of the Nazim, which shall be returned into the *moffussil* and then carried into execution". With respect to the proceedings of this Court a power of control was vested in the President and Council at Fort William similar to what was vested in the Collectors in the Districts over the *Phoujddrree Audawluts*, so that "the Company's administration in the character of king's *Dewan*", might be satisfied that the "decrees of justice on which both the welfare and safety of the country so materially depend, are not injured or perverted by the effects of partiality or corruption".

Thirdly, with a view to preserving 'the dignity and importance of the Two Superior Courts' just referred to, there were established 'Two Courts of *Audawlut*' at Calcutta, 'exactly on the same plan as those of the Districts'. A member of the Council at Fort William presided over 'the *Dewannee*' Court, and another member of the Council exercised the same kind of control over the *Phoujdarree* Court as was exercised by the Collector over the *Phoujddrree Audawlut* in a district. These duties were to be performed by the members of the Council in rotation. These two inferior courts of justice at Calcutta superseded in 1772 what had previously been known as the *Zamindari* Courts in Calcutta. As *Zamindar* of Sutanati, Calcutta and Govindpur, the Company used to exercise criminal, civil and religious jurisdiction in these places through these *Zamindari* Courts.[39]

Lastly, mention may be made here of the Courts of law existing in Calcutta which owed their origin to a Charter of Justice granted to the Company by the King of England on 8 January, 1753 —we mean the Courts known as the Mayor's Court, the Court of Appeals, the Court of Requests as well as certain, other Courts, such as the Court of Quarter Sessions, for the administration of justice in criminal cases. The Mayor's Court consisted of a Mayor and nine Aldermen. An appeal could be made from the judgment of the Mayor's Court to the President and Council of Fort William. And in certain circumstances a further appeal might be made to the King in Council from a judgment given on appeal by the President and Council.

Such, in brief, was the system of judiciary which the Company had set up in Bengal before a Supreme Court of

Judicature was established at Fort William under a Royal Charter, dated 26 March, 1774. We shall have an occasion to refer to this Court of Judicature later on.

English Administrative Institutions in Bengal: 1774-1818: The Regulating Act of 1773:

Many things contributed to the awakening of the conscience of the people of England to what had been happening in India, and to the consequential enactment by Parliament[40] of the Regulating Act of 1773 with a view to a better regulation and management of the affairs of the Company both in India and in England. Among these we may mention the heavy drain of the wealth of Bengal following the acquisition by the Company of the *Dewani* of Bengal, Bihar and Orissa on 12 August, 1765; the impoverished and miserable condition of the people of Bengal 'since the accession of the Company to the *Dewannee*'; stories of various abuses and iniquities on the part of the Company's servants in this country and of 'colossal fortunes' acquired by many of them, often by unscrupulous means; unhealthy influence exercised by many of these people on English public life on their return to England; war in south of India with Haidar Ali and its financial implications; the terrible famine of 1770 in Bengal and its dreadful consequences; revelations made by the Select and the Secret Committee of the House of Commons, appointed in 1772, in regard to the affairs of the Company; payment of ever increasing dividends to the share-holders of the Company and also of a tribute to the British Exchequer of an annual sum of £ 400,000; and ultimately, financial embarrassments of the Company which practically brought it to the verge of bankruptcy and compelled it to apply to the British Government for a loan for enabling it to get out of its difficulties.

It appears from the Report of a Parliamentary Committee that the authors of the Regulating Act had "five fundamental objects" in view. They were, briefly speaking, as follows:[41]

"1stly: The reformation of the Court of Proprietors of the East India Company.

2ndly: A new model of the Court of Directors, and an enforcement of their authority over the servants abroad.

3rdly: The establishment of a Court of Justice capable of

protecting the natives from the oppressions of British subjects.

4thly: The establishment of a General Council to be seated in Bengal, whose authority should, in many particulars, extend over all the British Settlements in India.

5thly: To furnish the Ministers of the Crown with constant information concerning the whole of the Company's correspondence with India, in order that they might be enabled to inspect the conduct of the Directors and servants, and to watch over the execution of all parts of the Act; that they might be furnished with matter to lay before Parliament from time to time, according as the state of things should render regulation or animadversion necessary".

It need hardly be pointed out here that we are concerned in this chapter mainly with the last three objects of the Regulating Act.

Salient features of the Regulating Act

We shall now notice some of the salient features of the Regulating Act. In a preamble the Act stated that, whereas the powers granted to the Company by Charters had been 'found by experience not to have sufficient force and efficacy to prevent various abuses' which had prevailed in the government and administration of the affairs of the Company, 'as well at home as in India', it had therefore become highly expedient that certain further regulations, better adapted to its then circumstances and conditions, 'should be provided and established'. Accordingly, the Act laid down, in the first place, that, 'at the next ensuing general election', instead of twenty-four Directors being all elected for one year only, six should be elected 'expressly' for one year; six for two years; six for three years; the remaining six for four years; and that "at the expiration of every year, six new Directors, and no more, should be chosen", "in the place of such Directors whose term shall have expired and who are hereby declared incapable of being then re-chosen". In effect, this meant that the members of the Court of Directors, should, instead of being annually elected as before, ordinarily hold office for four years, one-fourth of their number[42] being elected annually. The object of this provision was to strengthen 'the authority of the Court of Directors' and to prevent 'instability in the Councils and measures' of the Company.

Secondly, the Act declared that no person employed in any civil or military office or capacity in the East Indies should be eligible for appointment as a Director until such person should 'have returned to and been resident in England for the space of two years'.

Thirdly, the Act forbade, on pain of severe penalties, any collusive transfer of any stock of the Company for the purpose of voting at any election. Moreover, it raised, with effect from 1 October, 1774, the qualification for a vote at any General Court of Proprietors from £ 500 to £ 1,000 stock, and declared that no person would ordinarily be entitled to such a vote unless he (or she, etc.) had previously possessed the stock for 'twelve calendar months'. The Act also provided for a plurality of votes in certain circumstances up to a maximum" of four votes for any proprietor.[43]

Fourthly, the Act declared that, for the government of the Presidency of Fort William in Bengal, there should be 'appointed a Governor-General, and four counsellors'; and that the whole civil and military government of this Presidency and also the management and government of all the territorial acquisitions and revenues in the kingdoms of Bengal, Bihar and Orissa, should, during such time as the territorial acquisitions and revenues remained in the possession of the Company, be vested in the said Governor-General and Council of the Presidency of Fort William, 'in like manner as the same now are, or at any time heretofore might have been exercised by the President and Council, or Select Committee in the said kingdoms' In case of any difference of opinion on any question proposed at any consultation, the Governor-General and Council were, to be bound 'by the opinion and decision of the major part of those present'. And in case of an equality of votes on any question, as a result of the death or removal or the absence of any member of the Council, the Governor-General, or, in his absence, the eldest counsellor present at the consultation, was to 'have a casting voice', and his opinion was to be 'decisive and conclusive'.

Warren Hastings was to be the first Governor-General under the Act,[44] and Lieutenant-General John Clavering, the Honourable George Monson, Mr. Richard Barwell and Mr. Philip Francis were to be 'the four first counsellors'. They were, subject to what follows, to hold 'their respective offices' for five years 'from the time of their arrival at Fort William in Bengal, and taking upon them the Government' of the Presidency. They could not be removed from office in the meantime, except by the Crown on a representation made by the Court of Directors. If a vacancy occurred in the office of the Governor-General during these five years as a consequence of his death, removal, or resignation, it was to be filled, 'during the remainder of the term aforesaid', by the member of the Council who stood next in rank to the Governor-General. And if a vacancy occurred, during the same time, in the office of a member of the Council, as a result of his death, removal, resignation, or promotion, it was to be filled, for the unexpired portion of the said term of five years, by the Court of Directors with the consent of the Crown. The Governor-General and Council were empowered to act in spite of any vacancy in the Council. At the expiration of the said term of five years 'the power of nominating and removing the succeeding Governor-General and Council' was to be vested in the Court of Directors of the Company.

Fifthly, the Act took the first step towards the centralization of the governmental system of the Company in India. It laid down that the Governor-General and Council were to have 'power of superintending and controlling the government and management of the Presidencies of Madras, Bombay, and Bencoolen',[45] 'so far and in so much as' that it would not be lawful for any President and Council of Madras, Bombay, or Bencoolen, 'to make any orders for commencing hostilities, or declaring or making war, against any Indian princes or powers, or for negotiating or concluding any treaty of peace, or other treaty, with any such Indian princes or powers' without the previous consent of the Governor-General and Council, except in such cases of imminent necessity as would render it dangerous to postpone such hostilities or treaties till the arrival of such orders, and except in such cases where the said Presidents and Councils had received special orders from the Company. Any President and Council who would offend against these provisions of the Act would be liable to be suspended from office by the order of the Governor-General and Council. Moreover, every President and Council of Madras, Bombay and Bencoolen were required by the Act to pay due obedience to such orders as they might receive 'touching the premises' from the Governor-General and Council, and 'constantly and diligently to transmit' to the Governor-General and Council 'advice and intelligence of all transactions and matters whatsoever' that would come to their knowledge, relating to the government, revenues, or interest of the Company. The Governor-General and Council in their turn were required by the Act to pay due obedience to all such orders as they might receive from the Court of Directors, and 'constantly and diligently' to communicate to the Court 'an exact particular' of all matters that would come to their knowledge, 'relating to the government, commerce, revenues, or interest' of the Company. The Court of Directors, too, was required by the Act to transmit, within fourteen days of its receipt of any 'letters or advices' from the Governor-General and Council, (i) to the Treasury 'a true and exact copy of such parts of the said letters or advices' as would relate to the management of the revenues of the Company, and (ii) to a Principal Secretary of State 'a true and exact copy of all such parts' thereof as would relate to the civil or military affairs and government of the Company.

Thus a chain of connection was established by the Act between the administrative machinery set up by the Company in India and His Majesty's Government in England.

Sixthly, the Act declared that, as the Royal Charter, dated 8 January, 1753, which, amongst other things, constituted and established courts of justice at Fort William, did not sufficiently "provide for the due administration of justice in such manner as the state and condition of the Company's Presidency of Fort William in Bengal" required, it "shall and may be lawful" for the Crown to erect and establish by charter a Supreme Court of Judicature at Fort William. This Supreme Court was to consist of a Chief Justice and three other judges who were to be barristers in England or Ireland, of not less than five years' standing, and were to be appointed by the Crown from time to time. It was to have full power and authority to exercise all civil, criminal, admiralty, and ecclesiastical jurisdiction, and to appoint such clerks and other ministerial officers, with such reasonable salaries, as would be approved of by the Governor-General and Council. Further, it was empowered to 'form and establish' such rules of practice, etc., and to do all such other things as might be found necessary for the administration of justice, and for the due execution of powers to be vested in it by the Charter. It was to "be, at all times, a court of record, and . . . a court of Oyer and Terminer, and Gaol Delivery, in and for the said town of Calcutta, and factory of Fort William and the limits thereof, and the factories subordinate thereto". Moreover, the jurisdiction of the Supreme Court was to extend to "all British subjects" residing in the kingdoms or provinces of Bengal, Bihar, and Orissa, or any of them, under the protection of the Company. And it was to "have full power and authority to hear and determine all complaints against any of His Majesty's subjects for any crimes, misdemeanours, or oppressions, committed, or to be committed; and also to entertain, hear, and determine, any suits or actions whatsoever, against any of His Majesty's subjects in Bengal, Bihar, and Orissa, and any suit, action or complaint against any person employed by, or directly or indirectly in the service" of the Company or of any of His Majesty's subjects.

The Supreme Court was not, however, to be competent to hear, try or determine any indictment or information against the Governor-General or any member of his Council, for any offence, not being treason or felony, which they might be charged with having committed in Bengal, Bihar and Orissa. Nor could the Governor-General, any member of his Council, or the Chief Justice or any puisne judge be arrested or imprisoned upon any action, suit or proceeding in the Supreme Court. An appeal would lie to His Majesty in Council from a judgment of the Supreme Court, subject to such conditions as might be laid down in the royal charter establishing the Supreme Court.

Seventhly, the Act directed the Company to pay, during such time as its territorial acquisitions remained in its possession, the following annual salaries to the Governor-General and others as shown below:

The Governor-General	£ 25,000
Each member of the Council at Fort William	£ 10,000
Chief Justice of the Supreme Court	£ 8,000
Each puisne judge	£6,000

In view of these salaries, the above-mentioned persons were forbidden by the Act to accept any other fee, perquisite, emolument or advantage whatsoever. They were also forbidden to accept, from any person on any account whatsoever, any present or reward, pecuniary or otherwise, or any engagement for any present or reward; or to be concerned in any traffic or commerce, except the trade and commerce of the Company itself. A similar restriction was imposed by the Act upon every person holding any civil or military office under the Crown or the Company in the East Indies. Further, the Act laid down that it would not be lawful for any Collector, Supervisor, or any other of His Majesty's subjects, employed in the administration of justice, or their agents or servants, to be concerned in any trade in Bengal, Bihar and Orissa, except on account of the Company. These provisions were inserted in the Act, obviously with a view to ensuring purity and efficiency in the administration of the Company.

Eighthly, the Act empowered the Governor-General and Council "to make and issue such rules, ordinances, and regulations for the good order and civil government" of the Company's settlement at Fort William and other factories and places subordinate thereto, as might be deemed just and reasonable and would not be repugnant to the laws of the realm, and "to set, impose, inflict, and levy, reasonable fines and forfeitures for the breach or non-observance" thereof. But these rules, ordinances, etc., were not to be valid until they were duly "registered and published" in the Supreme Court to be set up under the Act, with the consent and approbation of the Court. And it would be lawful for any person or persons in India "to appeal therefrom" to the King in Council, who was empowered by the Act to set aside any such rules, etc. Moreover, the Governor-General and Council were required by the Act to transmit copies of such rules, ordinances, and regulations to a Principal Secretary of State; and it would be lawful for the King to signify to the Company his disapprobation and disallowance thereof.

Ninthly, the Governor-General and Council and the Chief Justice and other judges of the Supreme Court were empowered by the Act to act as Justices of the Peace for the Company's settlement at Fort William and for several settlements and factories subordinate thereto.

Finally, the Act adequately provided for the trial in England, by His Majesty's Court of King's Bench, of any Governor-General, or any other person employed in the service of the Company in any capacity, or of the Chief Justice or any Puisne Judge of the Supreme Court, or of any of His Majesty's subjects residing in India, who might commit any offence against any of its provisions, or might be guilty of any crime, misdemeanour, or offence, committed against any of His Majesty's subjects, or any inhabitant of India within their respective jurisdictions.

We have given above a summary of what appear to have been the principal provisions of the Regulating Act of 1773. The three new Councillors, namely, John Clavering, George Monson and Philip Francis arrived at Fort William from Europe on 19 October, 1774. The first meeting of the new Council under the Regulating Act was held at Fort William on 20 October, 1774, under the Presidentship of Warren Hastings, (now) Governor-General.[46] The other members who attended this meeting were the three new Councillors from Europe, namely, Clavering, Monson and Francis. Richard Barwell could not attend this meeting, as he came to Calcutta two days later. At this first meeting, the Regulating Act was read, together with the Instructions which the Court of Directors had sent to the Governor-General and Council on 29 March, 1774, in connection with the Act. Besides, it was resolved at this meeting that *a* Proclamation should be made at the Court House by the Sheriff (of Calcutta) at 7 on the next morning. Among other things, this Proclamation was to announce that the powers vested by the Act in the Governor-General and Council were to "commence and take place from the date of the Proclamation" obviously from 21 October, 1774. The new Council also executed some other business at its first meeting.

As authorized by the Regulating Act, a royal Charter was issued by the Crown on 26 March, 1774, providing for the establishment of a Supreme Court of Judicature at Fort William in Bengal. It was to consist of, as stated before, a Chief Justice and three Puisne Judges. Sir Elijah Impey was appointed to be the first Chief Justice, and Messrs. Robert Chambers, Stephen Caesar LeMaistre,, and John Hyde, the first three Puisne Judges. The Charter also ordered the abolition of the Mayor's Court at

Calcutta, without prejudice, however, to the judgments already pronounced by the Court.

Some serious difficulties were experienced in the actual working of the Regulating Act. This was largely due to what were considered to have been defects in its provisions. The first difficulty occurred owing to the absence of any power in the Governor-General to override his Council. As we have seen before, under the Regulating Act, if there arose any difference of opinion on any question brought before a meeting of the Governor-General and Council of Bengal, they were to be bound "by the opinion and decision of the major part of those present at the meeting". Only in case of an equality of votes, the Governor-General, or, in his absence, "the eldest counsellor present" at the meeting, was to have a casting vote, and his opinion was to "be decisive and conclusive". As a consequence of this provision in the Act, Warren Hastings who had been appointed to be the first Governor-General of Bengal by the Act, was often powerless and helpless before his Council, as three of his four councillors, namely, Clavering, Monson, and Francis generally acted together in opposition to him. His difficulties disappeared, however, with the rather 'timely' death of Monson in September, 1776, as he could now have his own way by means of his casting vote; but the lesson taught by them was there. And it may be noted here that when Lord Cornwallis was appointed to the office of Governor-General of Bengal in 1786, he made it a condition of his acceptance of the office that he "should be given the constitutional power to overrule his Council", if necessary. Accordingly an Act[47] was passed by Parliament in 1786 which in effect empowered the Governor-General to overrule, "in cases of high importance, and especially affecting the public interest and welfare", the majority of his Council and to act on his own authority and responsibility.[48] Ever since 1786 this overruling power had been retained, in one shape or another, ever down to the last days of British rule, as a feature of the Indian Constitution.

A second difficulty experienced during the working of the Regulating Act arose from the inadequacy of the power of control and superintendence vested by it in the Governor-General and Council of Bengal over the subordinate Presidencies of Madras and Bombay. And we particularly notice this in the following observations of Warren Hastings, made in the course of a letter to Lawrence Sulivan, dated at Fort William 22 March, 1776:[49]

> "You long ago knew my wish to see a control given to this government over the other Presidencies, but I never meant such a control as is now exercised; nor did the Parliament mean it. The Act gives us a mere negative power, and no more. It says the other Presidencies shall not make war nor treaties without the sanction of this government, but carefully guards against every expression which can imply a power to dictate what the other Presidencies shall do. . . . Instead of uniting all the powers of India, all the use we have hitherto made of this Act of Parliament has been to tease and embarrass."

The third great difficulty experienced during the actual operation of the Regulating Act, arose from the absence of a precise definition by it of the jurisdiction of the Supreme Court to, be established thereunder, and also of the relationship to subsist between the Supreme Court and the Governor-General and Council. This difficulty took the form of serious conflicts between the Governor-General and Council on the one side and the Supreme Court on the other.[50] And it was perhaps inevitable. As James Mill has rightly observed by way of a comment on this aspect of the Regulating Act:

> "They (i.e., the British Parliament) saw not, that they were establishing two independent and rival powers in India, that of the Supreme Council, and that of the Supreme Court; they drew no line to mark the boundary between them: and they foresaw not the consequences which followed, a series of encroachments and disputes which unnerved the powers of government and threatened their destruction."[51]

However, an amending Act was passed by Parliament in the year 1781, which removed some of the difficulties arising from the Regulating Act. Among other things, the Act of 1781 laid down, in the first place, that the Governor-General and Council of Bengal were not to be subject, jointly or severally, to the jurisdiction of the Supreme Court "for or by reason of any Act or Order, or any other matter or thing whatsoever, counselled, ordered, (or) done by them in their public capacity only, and acting as Governor-General and Council."

Secondly, no action for wrong or injury was to lie in the Supreme Court against any person whatsoever exercising a judicial office in the country courts, for any judgment, decree, or order of the said Court, or against any person for any act done by or in virtue of the order of the said Court.

Thirdly, the Supreme Court "was not to have or exercise any jurisdiction in matters concerning the revenue, or concerning any act done in the collection thereof, according to the usage and practice of the country", or the regulations framed by the Governor-General and Council.[52]

Fourthly, the Act of 1781 declared:

> "And whereas the Governor-General and Council, or some Committee thereof or appointed thereby, do determine on appeals and references from the Country or Provincial Courts in Civil Causes; be it further enacted that the said Court shall and lawfully may hold all such pleas and appeals, in the manner and with such powers as it hitherto hath held the same, and shall be deemed in Law a Court of Record; and the judgments therein given shall be final and conclusive, except upon appeal to His Majesty, in civil suits only, the value of which shall be five thousand pounds and upwards."

The said Court[53] was also declared to be "a Court to hear and determine on all offences, abuses, and extortions, committed in the collection of revenue, or on severities used beyond what shall appear to the said Court customary or necessary to the case, and to punish the same according to sound discretion, provided the said punishment does not extend to death, or maiming, or perpetual imprisonment".

Judicial and discretionary powers vested in the Governor-General and Council by these provisions are worthy of note.

Fifthly, the Act of 1781 indemnified the Governor-General and Council and the Advocate-General at Fort William as well as all persons acting under their orders, from any action, suit or prosecution whatsoever, for or on account of any disobedience to, or resistance to the execution of any process or order of the Supreme Court.

Finally, this Act empowered the Governor-General and

Council to frame, from time to time, regulations "for the Provincial Courts and Councils", and directed .them to transmit, within six months after the making of these regulations, copies thereof to the Court of Directors and to a Secretary of State. These regulations might be disallowed or amended by His Majesty in Council, and would come into "force and authority", if not disallowed within two years, subject to such amendments as might be made therein.

As Ilbert has observed, the decision of Parliament, as embodied in the Act of 1781, was substantially in favour of the Governor-General and Council and against the Supreme Court on all points.[54]

Pitt's India Act:

We shall now pass on to what is popularly known as Pitt's India Act, 1784. This Act introduced some important changes into the system of Indian administration. Its object was to provide "for the better regulation and management of the affairs of the East India Company, and of the British possessions in India; and for establishing a Court of Judicature for the more speedy and effectual trial of persons accused of offences committed in the East Indies". Space does not permit us to deal here with the Parliamentary history of this measure.[55] It may, however, be noted here that its enactment had been preceded by elaborate inquiries by two Parliamentary Committees into the affairs of the Company in India, and that the reports submitted by these Committees were largely responsible for it.

We may now notice some of the principal provisions of the Act of 1784. In the first place, this Act empowered the Crown to appoint, for the better government and security of the British territorial possessions in the East Indies, a Board of Commissioners for the Affairs of India, not exceeding six in number, as it might think fit, who were all to be members of the Privy Council, and of whom one of the Principal Secretaries of State and the Chancellor of the Exchequer for the time being, were to be two. Any three members of the Board would form a quorum "for executing the several powers" to be vested in the Commissioners. The Secretary of State, or, in his absence, the Chancellor of the Exchequer, or, in the absence of both of them, the senior of the other Commissioners, "according to his rank in seniority of appointment", was to "preside at, and be President" of the Board. In case of an equality of votes at any meeting of the Board, the President was to have a second or casting vote. The Commissioners were invested by the Act "with the superintendence and control over all the British territorial possessions in the East Indies, and over the affairs of the Company", as shown hereinafter.

This Board of Commissioners for the Affairs of India was generally known as the Board of Control, and will be so referred to by us hereinafter.

Secondly, the Act fully empowered the Board "to superintend, direct, and control, all acts, operations, and concerns, which in any wise relate to the civil or military government or revenues of the British territorial possessions in the East Indies". And, in view of this, all the members of the Board were, at all convenient times, to "have access to all papers and muniments" of the Company, and to be furnished with such extracts or copies thereof as they might require from time to time. The Court of Directors of the Company were "required and directed" by the Act to deliver to the Board of Control, "within eight days after the holding of such respective courts", copies of all minutes, orders, resolutions, and other proceedings of all general and special Courts of Proprietors of the Company as well as of the Court of Directors itself, so far as they related to the civil or military government or revenues of the British territorial possessions in the East Indies. Further, the Court of Directors was required to deliver to the Board copies of all dispatches which it itself, or any of its Committees, might receive from any of its servants in the East Indies, immediately after the arrival thereof; and also copies of all letters, orders and instructions whatsoever which it itself, or any of its Committees, might think of dispatching to any of its servants in the East Indies. Moreover, the Court of Directors was required by the Act to pay due obedience to, and be "governed and bound" by, such orders and directions as it might, from time to time, receive from the Board of Control, touching the civil or military government and revenues of the British territorial possessions in the East Indies.

Within fourteen days after the receipt of such copies as mentioned above, the Board of Control was to return the same to the Court of Directors with its approbation thereof, or its reasons at large for disapproving the same, together with its instructions in respect thereto. And the Court of Directors, thereupon, was to dispatch the letters, orders, and instructions so approved or amended, to its servants in India without any further delay, unless, on any representation made by it, the Board directed any alterations to be made therein. But no letters, orders, or instructions were at any time to be sent by the Court of Directors to the East Indies, on any account or pretence whatsoever, until after such previous communication thereof to the Board of Control as shown above.

If, however, the Court of Directors ever neglected to transmit to the Board of Control its intended dispatches on any subject within fourteen days after requisition made, then it would be lawful for the Board to prepare and send to the Directors any orders or instructions concerning the civil or military Government of the British territories and possessions in the East Indies. And the Court of Directors was required to transmit in effect the said orders and instructions to the Governments and Presidencies in India concerned, unless on any representation made by the Directors to the Board, the latter directed any alteration to be made therein. It would be permissible, however, for the Court of Directors to apply by petition, in certain circumstances, to His Majesty in Council, touching such orders and instructions. The decision of His Majesty in Council on the application would be final and conclusive.

Thirdly, the Court of Directors was required by the Act to appoint, from amongst its own members, a Secret Committee, consisting of not more than three persons. And if, in the opinion of the Board of Control, any matter required secrecy, then it would be lawful for it to send secret orders and instructions to the Secret Committee of the Court, which was thereupon required, without disclosing the same to any other Director, to transmit the said orders and instructions to the Governments and Presidencies in India. And these Governments and Presidencies were directed to pay a faithful obedience to such orders and instructions, and return their answers to the same, to the Secret Committee, which was to communicate forthwith such answers to the Board of Control.

Fourthly, the Board of Control was not to have any power of nominating or appointing any of the servants of the Company. The power of filling a vacancy in the office of Governor-General, Governor, any member of Council, or any Commander-in-Chief was vested by the Act in the Court of Directors. It would, however, be lawful for the Crown as well as for the Court of Directors to "remove or recall" from office any Governor-General, or Governor, or Member of Council, or any other person holding any office, civil or military, under the Company in India.

Fifthly, the Government of the Presidency of Fort William in Bengal, also referred to in the Act as the Supreme Government, was to "consist of a Governor-General and three Supreme Counsellors only", of whom the Commander-in-Chief of the Company's forces in India for the time being, was to be one and to have "voice and precedence in Council next after the Governor-General."[56] And the Government of each of the Presidencies of Fort St. George, and Bombay was to consist of a Governor or President and three Counsellors only, of whom the Commander-in-Chief of the Presidency was to be one, "having the like precedence in Council as in the Presidency of Fort William in Bengal", unless the Commander-in-Chief of the Company's forces in India happened to be present in the Presidency; and in that case the latter was to be one of the Counsellors, instead of the local Commander-in-Chief who would, however, have during such time only a seat, but no voice in the local Council. No resignation of the office of Governor-General, Governor, Commander-in-Chief, or Member of Council in any Presidency was to be deemed "legal or valid" unless it was "made by an instrument in writing under the hand of the officer or person resigning the same".

Sixthly, the Governor-General and Council of Fort William were empowered "to superintend, control, and direct, the several presidencies and governments now or hereafter to be erected or established in the East Indies" by the Company, "in all such points as relate to any transactions with the country powers, or to war or peace, or to the application of the revenues or forces of such presidencies and settlements in time of war, or any such points as shall, from time to time, be specially referred by the Court of Directors of the said Company to their superintendence and control". And the said presidencies and settlements were bound to obey the "orders and directions" of the Governor-General in Council "in all cases whatever, except only where" they had received positive instructions from the Court of Directors, or from the Secret Committee of the Court, "repugnant to the orders and instructions" of the Governor-General and Council, and not known to the latter at the time of dispatching their orders and instructions. Thus the controlling authority of the Supreme Government at Fort William over the subordinate governments of Madras and Bombay was increased and the process of centralization of power commenced by the Regulating Act of 1773 was carried a step further by the Act of 1784.

Seventhly, if "any act, order, resolution, matter, or proceeding" of the Court of Directors had once received the approval of the Board of Control, it could not be revoked or rescinded by the General Court of Proprietors.

Eighthly, the Act of 1784 declared that, "whereas to pursue schemes of conquest and extension of dominion in India are measures repugnant to the wish, the honour, and policy of this nation", it would not be lawful for the Governor-General and Council of Fort William, "without the express command and authority" of the Court of Directors or of its Secret Committee, "to declare war or commence hostilities, or enter into any treaty for making war, against any of the country princes or States in India, or any treaty for guaranteeing the possessions of any country princes or states", except where hostilities had actually been commenced, or preparations actually made for the commencement of hostilities, against the British nation in India, or against some of the princes or States dependent thereon, or whose territories the Company had agreed to defend or guarantee in accordance with any existing treaty. Similarly, it would not be lawful for the Governor and Council of Madras or Bombay or of any other subordinate settlement to issue any order for commencing hostilities or levying war, or to negotiate any treaty with any Indian prince or State (except in cases of sudden emergency or imminent danger, when it might appear dangerous to postpone such hostilities or treaty), unless in pursuance of express orders from the Governor-General and Council, or from the Court of Directors, or from its Secret Committee. And every such treaty was, if possible, to "contain a clause for subjecting the same to the ratification or rejection of the Governor-General and Council". Further, every such Governor and Council were required to pay due obedience to all such orders as they might from time to time receive from the Governor-General and Council concerning the above. Any Governor and Council who would wilfully refuse to pay due obedience to such orders and instructions as they might receive from the Governor-General and Council were liable to be suspended from office by order of the latter. Moreover, Governors and Councils of subordinate presidencies were required constantly and diligently to transmit to the Governor-General and Council at Fort William exact copies of all their "orders, resolutions, and acts", and "also advice and intelligence of all transactions and matters" which would come to their knowledge, or which the Governor-General and Council might from time to time require.

Finally, the Act of 1784 made "elaborate provisions for the prevention and punishment of corruption, misgovernment or disobedience' on the part of the Company's servants in India. For instance, the demanding or receiving of any sum of money, or other valuable thing, as a gift or present by any British subject holding any office under His Majesty or the Company in the East Indies, was to be deemed to be extortion, and to be proceeded against and punished as such. The offender was also to forfeit to His Majesty the whole gift or present so received, or the full value thereof. It was provided, however, that the Court of Justice before which every such offence would be tried, would have full power and authority to direct the said present or gift, or the value thereof, to be restored to the party who had given the same, or "to order the whole, or any part thereof, or of any fine" which the Court might impose on the offender, to be paid or given to the prosecutor or informer, as the Court might think fit

The Act was to come into force in Great Britain immediately after it had received the royal assent, and in India with effect from 1 January, 1785.

We have given above a summary of what appear to us to have been the principal provisions of the Act of 1784. It will be evident from what we have stated that; except in respect of the power of appointment to offices in India and the management of the Company's trade, the Act virtually made the Board of Control the supreme authority in regard to the affairs of the Company in India and placed the Company, to quote the words of Ilbert, "in direct and permanent subordination to a body representing the British Government".[57] This Board of Control which was really to form a part of the Ministry in England, was to be the machinery which would "enable the Ministry to control the proceedings of the Company".[58] As a matter of fact, subject to the superintendence of the Board of Control, the Court of Directors "conducted the correspondence with the Company's officers in India".[59] The Court of Directors exercised, however, the rights of patronage in regard to appointments in India. The Board of Control was, as Pitt had intended it to be, strictly a Board of Control;[60] it had no power of appointment, nor any patronage. The functions of the Board were in practice exercised by its President,[61] who "occupied in the Government (of the day) a position corresponding to some extent to that of a modern Secretary of State for India",[62] and would thus always be a member of the British Cabinet.[63] So far as the home administration of Indian affairs was concerned, this state of things practically continued down to 1858.

Another noticeable feature of the Act of 1784 was its attempt to produce, to quote the words of Pitt, "a unity of system" in the Indian part of the Company's administration, "by investing the supreme government to be seated in Bengal, with an effectual control over every other presidency, and by investing the supreme government with executive power".[64] Particularly, the power of suspension vested in the Bengal Government in relation to other Presidencies gave it a considerable controlling authority over them. It is quite true that this controlling authority could not always be effectively exercised in actual practice, owing to the difficulties of "communication between different capital towns" in those days. Nevertheless, its very existence went a long way towards producing a unified and a centralized system of Government in this country.

We have already referred to an Act of 1786, and also to the particular provision thereof, which empowered the Governor-General of Fort William in certain circumstances to override his

Council and act on his own responsibility.[65] This "discretionary power of acting without the concurrence" of his Council, "or of forbearing from any action according to its opinion, "in cases of high importance, and specially affecting the public interest and welfare", was conferred upon the Governor-General, with a view to giving "energy, vigour and dispatch to the measures and proceedings of the Executive Government". But the practical result of this discretionary authority was, as Chesney has observed, "to render the power of the Governor-General supreme".[66] This Act of 1786 also enabled the offices of Governor-General and Commander-in-Chief to be united in the same person if this was considered necessary.[67]

Before we conclude this chapter we should like to refer to one or two more Acts of Parliament relating to India. None of these Acts, however, introduced any institutional change of a really constitutional importance into the administrative system of the Company in Bengal. Let us take, for instance, what is popularly known as the Charter Act of 1793. It was practically a consolidating measure. Among other things, it provided that the Board of Control to which we have referred before, was to consist of "such members of the Privy Council (of whom the two Principal Secretaries of State, and the Chancellor of the Exchequer were always to be there) and such other two persons as the Crown might think fit to appoint." The first-named Commissioner in the letters patent appointing the Board, was to be its President. As before, three members of the Board were to form a quorum. And for the first time, provision was made for the payment of salaries to the members of the Board.

This Act also declared that when the office of Governor-General and the office of Commander-in-Chief of all the forces in India were not combined in the same person, such Commander-in-Chief might be a member of the Council at Fort William if he was "specially authorized for that purpose" by the Court of Directors, but not otherwise.

An Act of 1797 reduced the number of judges of the Supreme Court at Calcutta to three—a Chief Justice and two Puisne Judges.

What is known as the Charter Act of 1813, the enactment of which had as usual been preceded by elaborate Parliamentary inquiries into the affairs of the Company in India, provided, among other things, for the continuance of the Company, for a further period of twenty years, the enjoyment of its territorial acquisitions and revenues, "without prejudice to the undoubted sovereignty of the Crown of the United Kingdom of Great Britain and Ireland in and over the same". Further, it retained to the Company its monopoly of trade with China and also its trade in tea, but threw open to all British subjects the rest of the trade with India, subject to some conditions.[68] Thirdly, this Act provided for the separation of the commercial accounts of the Company from its territorial accounts.[69] Fourthly, it laid down that the appointments to offices of Governor-General, Governors, and Commanders-in-Chief were to be made by the Company, subject to the approval of the Crown. Finally, the Act empowered the Governor-General in Council to direct "a sum of not less than one lac of rupees in each year" to be "set apart and applied to the revival and improvement of literature, and the encouragement of the learned natives of India, and for the introduction and promotion of a knowledge of the sciences among the inhabitants of the British territories in India".[70] This provision of the Act of 1813 is interesting as it represents the first attempt on the part of the British Government at imposing an obligation on the Company of fostering education in this country.

NOTES

1. The first meeting of the Governor-General and Council under the Regulating Act of 1773 (13 Geo. III, c. 63) was held at Fort William on 20 October, 1774. It may, therefore, be held that the Act came into force on this date. *See* the General Letter to the Court of Directors, dated at Fort William 21 November, 1774, Para, 2.
2. The East India Company Act, 1773 (13 Geo. III, c. 63).
3. For a detailed history of the origin of the Presidency of Bengal, *see*, D. N. Banerjee, *Early Administrative System of the East India Company in Bengal*, Vol. I, 1765-1774, Appendix 4. For further references in this connexion also *see* the same, p. 629n.
4. It may be noted here that, according to C. R. Wilson (*The Early Annals of the English in Bengal*, p. 83), the "Commission which made Hedges Governor, associated six others with him in the Council of the Bay, Job Charnock, John Beard, John Richards, Francis Ellis, Joseph Dodd, and William Johnson".
5. Mr. William Hedges appears to have been dismissed from the

service of the Company.

6. For the relevant documentary evidence, *see* D. N. Banerjee, *op. cit*, pp. 631-32.
7. With, according to C. R. Wilson (*op. cit*, p. 157), the following four gentlemen as the members of his Council at Calcutta: "John Beard, second, and accountant; Nathaniel Halsey, third, and warehouse-keeper; Jonathan White, fourth and purser marine; (and) Ralph Sheldon, fifth, and receiver of revenues". Thus, altogether the Calcutta Council consisted of five members including the President and Governor.
8. For details in this connection, *fee* D. N. Banerjee, *op. cit.*, pp. 104-116 and note.
9. The history of this name is as follows: There were two English East India Companies at the beginning of the eighteenth century: one, incorporated by Queen Elizabeth by a Charter, dated 31 December, 1600, was designated "The Governor and Company of Merchants of London Trading into the East Indies"; and the other, incorporated on 5 September, 1698, by a Charter of King William III, was styled "The English Company Trading to the East Indies". They were also referred to as the first and the second East India Company; the Old and the New Company; and as the London and the English East India Company, respectively. These two Companies had become serious rivals to each other in their East Indian trade, and this rivalry had naturally been proving disastrous to the interests of both. Their rivalry, however, was brought to an end in 1702 by an Indenture Tripartite, dated 22 July, 1702, "between Queen Anne of the first part; the Old Company of the second part; and the New Company of the third part". This indenture was the first substantial step towards the ultimate amalgamation in 1709 of the two Companies into a United Company. One of the terms of this indenture was that "in two months after the expiration of seven years from its date, the Old Company would surrender their Charters.... into the Queen's hand", and that the Queen would "accept of such surrender". Further, "from thenceforth the New Company" was "to be called *The United Company of Merchants of England trading to the East Indies* whose affairs" were to be conducted by its "own sole" Directors, *agreeably to the provisions of its Charter granted by King William III on 5 September, 1698. The* indenture also provided for some transitional arrangements for the carrying on of their East Indian trade by the two Companies during the said seven years from its date. This is how the name of the *United Company of Merchants*, etc., originated.

We may add that by a deed, dated 22 March, 1709, the Old Company surrendered its "Charters, and Corporate Capacity" to Queen Anne, and the Queen accepted the surrender on 7 May, 1709, "by patent under her great seal of this date;" and that, previously to this, the Old Company had, by a deed, dated 22 July, 1702, conveyed to the New Company the island of St. Helena as well as all its forts, lands, factories and other territorial and other possessions in the East Indies (i.e., lying between the Cape of Good Hope and the Straits of Magellan), and the Earl of Godolphin, the Lord High Treasurer, had "in pursuance of an Act of the sixth year of Queen Anne" (6 Anne, Chap. XVII) given, on 29 September, 1708, an award on certain points of dispute still subsisting between the two Companies. Thus the union of the two rival Companies was actually effected in 1709 in accordance with the terms of the Indenture Tripartite previously referred to, and the provisions of the award of the Earl of Godolphin. For further details in this connection, *see* D. N. Banerjee, *op. cit.*, pp. 104-06 and note as well as the authorities referred to therein.

10. Technically speaking, between 1709 and 1774. As shown in the preceding footnote, the union of the Old and the New East India Companies was actually effected in 1709. During the short period between 1707 and 1709—or rather, between 1702 and 1709, there were some transitional arrangements for the carrying on of their East Indian trade by the two companies. For the purpose of this Chapter, we can ignore those arrangements between 1707 and 1709.

11. *See* Peter Auber, Analysis *of the Constitution of East India Company,* 1826, p. 182. For further details and references, *see* D. N. Banerjee, *op. cit.*, pp. 113- 16 and note.

12. For further details, *see* D. N. Banerjee, *op. cit.*; pp 114-16 and note.

13. It may be interesting to note here that during the period from 1 February, 1704, to 20 July, 1710—presumably, pending the arrival at Calcutta of the information of the actual union of the Old and the New East India Companies and consequential arrangements thereafter—there were "no less than three Councils" functioning at Calcutta. "In the first place", writes C.R. Wilson, "there was the Council for the management of the separate affairs of the Old London Company, at the head of which was John Beard. Then there was the Council for the separate affairs of the new English Company, which left Hoogly for Calcutta in May, and at the head of which was Sir Edward Littleton. And lastly, there was the Establishment Council for

the management of all the United Company's affairs in Bengal". This last body consisted of eight per sons, including Mr. Robert Hedges and Mr. Ralph Sheldon: "four members of the Old and four members of the New Company's Service". "It was presided over in alternate weeks by Hedges and Sheldon. . . . The 'rotation government', as it was called, came into power on 1 February, 1704. *This* state of affairs came to an end with the assumption, on 20 July, 1710, of the office of Governor and President of Fort William by the Hon'ble Antony Weltden, with Mr. Robert Hedges and seven others as members of his Council. Obviously, the new Government had been ordered to be so formed by the United Company after the *actual* union of the Old and the New East India Companies in 1709. *See* C. R. Wilson, *op. cit.*, pp. 161-63, 186-87, 227-28 and 337-38. It may also be interesting to note here that in 1757-58 another attempt was made by the Court of Directors of the United Company to establish a Rotation Government in Bengal. Actually, however, it was not established. *See* for details in this connection, D, N. Banerjee, *op. cit.*, pp. 136-39n.

14. Such as Cossimbazar, Dacca, Patna, Maldah, Luckeypore, etc.
15. It appears that a factory of considerable importance would be designated a 'subordinate'.
16. For a detailed treatment of the position, remuneration and the powers of the Governor, *see* D.N. Banerjee, *op. cit.*, Chapter II.
17. Vol. I, p. 23 (Ed. 1841).
18. Thus we find Henry Vansittart, President and Governor of Fort William, writing to the Court of Directors in 1763: The powers of the President, the Select Committee and the Council require to be settled and better distinguished. I think they might be so regulated as to check and balance, each other, and render the administration of your affairs more steady than it can be at present In the last disputes I found myself, without the least authority beyond and other Members of the Council, nor could I prevent or put a negative upon the most unjust and improper Resolution of the majority. I was obliged to be myself the channel for conveying those Resolutions to the Nabob (Cossim Ali Khan), otherwise instead of threatening him with a rupture they would immediately have declared a rupture and ordered the Army to march against him so that upon the present footing it is in the power of any majority of the Council to engage the Company in new wars, whenever a Party shall be inclined to make new demands Most of the members of the Board (i.e., the Council) have been taught by those who were at the head of the party against the late government that everyone had a

right to equal authority with the President in the management of all affairs with the Country Powers, consequently they have all formed plans of their own and if your Honors do not take effectual care to prevent it, you may very soon hear that the present system is voted injurious to the Company's interests or insufficient for the management of the Court.

From Henry Vansittart's letter to the Court of Directors, dated (presumably) 8 October, 1763. (For a discussion about the date of this letter, *see* D. N. Banerjee, *op. cit.*, p. 149n.)

We also find in a letter from Warren Hastings to the Court of Directors, dated at Fort William 11 November, 1773:

The powers of the Governor, although supposed to be great, are, in reality, little more than those of any individual in his Council. Their compliance, his own abilities, or a superior share of attention and the opinion that he possesses extraordinary powers, may give him the effect of them, and an ascendant over his Associates in the Administration; but a moment's consideration is sufficient to discover the nakedness of his authority, and to level him with the rest.

The Fifth Report from the Committee of Secrecy, appointed (by the House of Commons) to enquire into the causes of the war in the Carnatic, and *of the* condition *of the* British Possessions in those parts, printed in the year 1782, Appendix 5; also Gleig, *Memoirs of Warren Hastings,* Vol. I, p. 370.

19. 26 George III, Chap. XVI, Sections VI & XI.

This special power was "not to be exercised by any Governor-General or Governor or President who would *casually* succeed to such office as a result of death or resignation of any Governor-General, Governor or President, unless he was provisionally appointed to succeed to the office by the Court of Directors or unless he was confirmed in the office by the said Court", ibid., Section X.

20. In certain circumstances, even seventeen. *See* D. N. Banerjee, *op. cit.*, pp. 192 and note.

21. And apparently, not by the majority of those present at any meeting. *See* ibid., p. 149, in. 1, and pp. 243-44 and note.

22. Presumably, dated at Fort William, 10 November, 1764, as the letter occurs in the Proceedings of the Consultation, Secret Department, held at Fort William on 10 November, 1764.

23. (At that time) Jaffer Ali Khan, i.e., Mir Jaffar.

24. The italics are ours.

25. For details in regard to these disputes, *see* D. N. Banerjee, *op.*

cit., pp. 154-68 and notes.

26. The italics are ours.
27. The italics are ours.
28. Mr. Roger Drake Junior, the then President of Fort William.
29. That is, the Council at Fort William.
30. *See* Lord Clive's letter, dated at Calcutta, 23 January, 1767, addressed to Harry Verelst Esqr., and Members of the Select Committee, entered in the Proceedings of the Select Committee, Fort William, of 11 February, 1767.
31. Hie italics are ours.
32. *See* in this connection D. N. Banerjee, *op. cit.*, pp. 185-91 and note.
33. For detail in this connection see Ibid., Chapters III & IV. Under an order of the Court of Directors, dated 1 June, 1764, the maximum number might even be seventeen for certain purposes. *See* ibid., pp. 192-93 and note.
34. Sir John Malcolm, *The Life of Robert, Lord Clive,* Vol 'III, p. 152.
35. *See* the Company's General Letter to the President and Council of Fort William in Bengal, dated 12 May, 1758, para 20.
36. For details, see Banerjee, *op. cit.*, pp. 293-313.
37. *See* the Court's General Letter to Bengal, dated 10 April, 1771, and its additional General Letter to Bengal, dated 25 April, 1771.
38. For details, see Banerjee, *op. cit.*, Chaps. VII & VIII.
39. Known as the *Phoujdarree* Court 'for the trial of crimes'; the 'Court of Cutcherry for civil causes'; the 'Collector's Court for matters of revenue'; and according to some writers, a Caste cutcherry for taking 'cognizance of all matters relative to the several caste (sic) tribes of the Hindoo religion'.
40. The East India Company Act, 1773 (13 George, III, C. 63). *See* Keith, *Speeches and Documents on Indian Policy* (The World's Classics) Vol. I, pp. 45-60.
41. Ninth Report from the Select Committee, House of Commons, appointed to take into consideration the state of the Administration of Justice, etc., printed in the year 1783.
42. The total number of members of the Court of Directors was twenty-four.
43. Thus the possession of £ 3,000 stock would entitle a proprietor to two votes; that of £ 6,000 stock to three votes; and that of £ 10,000 stock or more to four votes.
44. He had previously been appointed. Governor of Bengal with

effect from 13 April, 1772.

45. That is, Fort Marlborough in Sumatra.

46. *See* the General Letter to the Court of Directors, dated at Fort William 21 November, 1774; also Appendix 44 to the Fifth Report from the Committee of Secrecy, appointed to enquire into the causes of the war in the Carnatic, etc., printed in the year 1782.

47. 26 George III, Chap. XVI.

48. This "discretionary power" of the Governor-General to overrule his Council was not however to be exercised in regard to judicial or legislative matters. It was only to operate in the executive sphere. See ibid.

49. *See* Gleig, *Memoirs of Warren Hastings,* (1841), pp. 41-42.

50. For details, *see* in this connection, among other works, James Mill, History *of* British India, Vol IV, Wilson's Edition, Book V, Chap. VI; also Firminger, *Historical* Introduction *to the Fifth Report* (1812), Chap. XIII.

51. *See* James Mill, *op. cit.,* p. 309.

52. *See* Ilbert, *The Government of India,* 3rd Ed., p. 55; also Peter Auber, *Rise and Progress of the British Power in India* (1837), pp, 588-89; also the Act of 1781 itself.

53. That is, "The Governor-General in Council. 54. Ilbert, *op. cit.,* p. 58.

55. *See* in this connection James Mill, *op. cit.,* Chap. IX; also Peter Auber, Vol. I, Chap. XII, and Vol II, Chap. I

56. It may be noted here that the Act of 1786 (26 George III, Chap. XVI), "enabled the offices of Governor-General and Commander-in-Chief to be united in the same person." *See* Ilbert, *op. cit.,* p. 67.

57. Ilbert, *op. cit.,* p. 62; also *Report of the Committee on the Home* Administration of Indian *Affairs,* London (1919), James Mill, op., cit., pp. 559-60 says:

"Of two bodies, when one has the right of unlimited command, and the other is constrained - to unlimited obedience, the latter has no power whatsoever, but just as much, or as little, as the former is pleased to allow. This is the relative position of the Board of Control and the East India Company. The powers of the Board of Control convert the Company's Courts into agents of its will. The real, the sole governing power of India is the Board of Control, and it only makes use of the Court of Directors as an instrument, as a subordinate office, for the management of details, and the preparation of business for the cognizance of the superior power".

58. *See* Chesney, Indian Polity, pp. 41-42.
59. *See The Report of the Committee on the Home* Administration of Indian *Affairs,* 1919.
60. *See* Pitt's speech on the India Bill on July 6, 1784; Mukherji, Indian Constitutional Documents, *1600-1918,* Vol. I, p. 53.
61. *The Report of the Committee on the Home Administration of Indian Affairs,* 1919.
62. See ibid.; also Ilbert, *op. cit.,* p. 66.

    "In point of fact", writes James Mill, "the whole business of the Board of Control rested with the senior member of the Board other than the Secretary of State and the Chancellor of the Exchequer; the other Commissioners being seldom called to deliberate, or even for form's sake to assemble. The senior is known by the name of the President of the Board of Control, and is essentially a new Secretary of State; a Secretary for the Indian department" James Mill, *op. cit.,* p. 558.
63. Chesney, *op. cit.,* p. 360.
64. Pitt's speech on the India Bill on July 6, 1784, P Mukherji, *op. cit.,* p 53.
65. A similar power was also conferred by the Act of 1786 (26 George III, Chap. XVI) upon the Governors of Fort St. George (Madras) and Bombay to override their respective Councils in certain circumstances.
66. *See* Chesney, *op. cit.,* p. 45.
67. Ilbert, *op. cit.,* p. 67; also Peter Auber, *op. cit.,* Vol. II, p. 13.
68. Ilbert, *op. cit.,* pp. 75-77; also Auber, *op. cit.,* Vol. II, pp. 488-91.
69. Ilbert, *op. cit.,* pp. 78-79; also Auber, *op. cit.,* Vol II, pp. 488-91
70. Ramsay Muir, *The Making of* British India, pp. 296-97

4

Public Administration in India: The British Legacy

Until the nineteen forties, the frame of reference for the study of public administration in India was largely British and continental. Its parameters were set within the framework of constitutional law. American textbooks of Willoughby and White were not unknown but their influence was limited. The fifties saw the opening of the floodgates of Americanism in Indian studies, where Wilson's essay "The Study of Administration" or Goodnow's thesis on the "Dichotomy between Politics and Administration" became a Bible for the newly initiated. The movement for "efficiency and economy" became so potent a factor that other considerations of statecraft became a trivia. It was assumed that "administration" was a value-free factor and a key for all achievements. Attempts were made to create a "Science of Administration". In spite of Simon's warning against "scientism" in the forties the broad-liberal base of public administration continued to shrink.

It should be pertinent to remember that public administration is "administration by state" and it covers the entire gamut of state activity which in turn is influenced by the nature of state itself. How could ideological commitments ever be ignored by administration? Roscoe Martin's paper on "Relationship between Political Science and Public Administration - A State of Union" prepared for the American Political Science Association and, subsequently, published in the *American Political Science Review* shows its deep concern for the schism between "efficiency and economy" movement and the continuous search by state for a value-based management. Frank Marini's call for a "new public administration" was really nothing new but just a re-confession of the eternal concern of ethics for public affairs.

Once we assume that public administration is a study, of state activity, its "ecology" becomes the most important element. In *New Frontiers of Public Administration*, John Gaus emphasized its importance to American scholars. But the message is much more relevant to the Indian scene. It is the oldest human activity which involved even step from planning to action and final appraisal Aristotle was examining the forms of government only with a view to identifying proper administrative action appropriate to each form of government Montesquieu in his spirit of the Laws was stressing the same point. In the Indian context, our concern for parliamentary government secularism and development affects the mode of administration. For understanding their contours, a reading of the Indian constitutional history becomes indispensable.

Having accepted that public administration is basically nation-based it becomes essential to go into the roots of political organisation and administrative institutions of a country. Thus, it may be imperative to delve into the history of the organisations and institutions as they emerged. It remains of interest to understand how a small body of traders were able to establish an empire and became a successor state to the great Mughals. They developed a system which lasted more than two centuries and is serving even today.

The British empire in India was the largest ever known to our history. How were the forces of anarchy tamed? How was everyone's war against everyone contained? The replacement of personal, despotic rule, full of conspiracies, intrigues and treacheries by a concern for a public weal and rule of law in themselves provide fascinating enquiry. The consolidation of the Indian empire, checking of many social evils, initiating a system of education and laws and developmental works in irrigation, transport and communication involved big decisions. We could profit immensely by studying their decisional process.

The concept of the greatest good of the greatest numbers, growth of representative institutions at the national, state and local levels and the system of laws are the great achievements of Indian administration. Many facets of their evolution could be examined only in a historical perspective. We, in India, have not shown enough interest in pursuing the study of administration from such an angle. Strangely, much more interest has been shown by foreigners in the study of Indian administration after independence from an ecological perspective. An analysis of the administrative system during the last two centuries should have been primarily the concern of Indian scholars, but somehow, we have failed to do adequate justice to it. Proper insight into the past is always helpful in understanding the present and chartering a course of action for the future.

The British conquest of India cannot be explained solely in terms of superiority of arms. The arms were available with Indian rulers too. The rival European forces were there to help them against the British. But what happened? Robert Clive, no professional soldier, with a poor supply line, and an outnumbered army, shone at Arcot. Again, at Plassey with hardly four thousand soldiers, out of which just one-third being European, with no cavalry and a limited supply of arms and ammunition, he routed the ten times stronger forces of Siraj-ud-daula. I visited Plassey and Murshidabad and stood before the granite column in awe which records that" ...from this point... Robert Clive commanded the troops on 23rd of July 1757". Orme records for posterity that two days before the battle of Plassey, Clive, for a moment thought of abandoning the fight and retiring to Calcutta.

The battles of Karamnasa in 1761 or Buxer in 1764 were fought in similar circumstances. A number of dedicated commanders, with a small European contingent and largely Indian soldiers, fought and won against vastly superior forces. The fall of Tipu and later of the Marathas displays remarkable resourcefulness of diplomacy and military organisation. These developments led to the emergence of modern Indian administration.

During the first Sikh war (1846-48), Lord Hardinge was the Governor-General and Lord Gough the Commander-in-Chief. Hardinge who was an ex-army officer, thought the war with the Sikhs most important. He volunteered to work under Lord Gough, who did not give him any independent command, but throughout kept him by his side. At one time, when the morale was not too high. Hardinge and Gough kept their chin up and head high and never allowed troops' morale to suffer. This and like instances could serve as excellent subject for study in leadership and administration.

The representative institutions in India, the constitution, parliament, state administrative machinery, the entire ethos of nationhood (in a political sense), and the local government systems were evolved over a period of two centuries. The Westminster model has been the guiding spirit of Indian constitutional developments. A large number of our nationalist leaders drew inspiration from the British educational system. Its universities showed them a new vista and ideas generated there became the forerunner of the Indian renaissance. Mahatma Gandhi, the father of the nation, had his education in England. He was deeply influenced by Ruskin and the pacifists and it moulded his ideas about the Indo-British relations. Our first Prime Minister Jawaharlal Nehru had his education at Harrow and Cambridge. The influence of European struggle for freedom and democracy and the Fabians in his early life was sustained throughout his struggle for freedom and during the formative period of our republic.

Relations between India and Britain have been long and deep, encompassing more than three and a half centuries. From the arrival of Hawkins in 1608, till August 15, 1947, when it became independent, India witnessed a cataclysmic march of history. From simple trading interests, the East India Company turned into an empire builder. By the middle of the 19th century, peace was brought to the country and anarchy contained. Fields were mapped and lists of every man's agrarian rights were prepared. The task of building roads, bridges and railways, of harnessing the rivers for irrigation had started. It is notable in Indo-British relations that the English did not come as invaders. There was no plunder or taking of slaves. There have been charges of economic exploitation; but there are also encomiums of economic regeneration. The charges of economic exploitation are true and understandable but contributions to industrialisation and modernisation of agriculture are there for everyone to see. The rule of law took precedence over arbitrariness.

The scepticism towards authority, which swept Europe following the French Revolution, influenced India as well. But coming through the milder climate of England, moderated first by Burke, and later by Bentham, it brought human happiness as *raison d'etre* for any civil or political institution. The induction of this philosophy found much to question in India, when our own civilization had ceased to grow and when our pity for human suffering seemed to be used up and finished. Utilitarianism created a new reaction in Indian life and it began to grow with vigour. The Englishmen of the 1820s and 1830s had expected that western education might help the growth of Christianity; but it did not happen. However, it stirred the Indian minds deeply and changed the concept of their own religion.

There is a parallel between the servants of the East India Company and the Roman Emperors and their pro-consuls. They amassed power and pelf, abused it and then grew into a body of men "minutely just, inflexibly upright." The names of Athens and likewise of England are associated in men's minds with freedom. Athenians fought at Salamis and Marathon for it, yet they denied freedom to their own colonies. The English were unwilling to grant freedom to the Americans. But the lessons of Yorktown and Saratoga dawned on them. During the 19th century they were moving towards a society where liberty was cherished. Gradually, cautiously, they brought Reform Bills doing away with restrictions based on privilege. In India, the ideas of Bentham and Mill did come over time. But to begin with, the stress was more upon peace and unity rather than upon freedom. The efforts were directed to equal justice for all and the building of roads, railways, canals and bridges. The historians, political scientists and students of administration may find fascinating the analysis of Indo-British relations in terms of Christian doctrine that "a man must be judged not by his worst so much as by his best, and in the end, not even by his best but by what he aimed at."

The administrative organisations and institutions in India, as pointed out earlier, were greatly influenced by the Whig philosophy with its central belief and conviction that "political power was essentially corrupting and inevitably abused; that power was to be exercised with safety, must be reduced to a minimum, and even then kept divided and counter-balanced." The landed property was the kernel of the Whig concept of political society. To them, landed property appeared as the agency affecting reconciliation of freedom with order. Cornwallis maintained that "from a system of landed property flowed a natural ordering of society into ranks and classes, nowhere more necessary than in India." He tried to give concrete form to the rule of law in the Bengal Code of Regulations of 1793. It resulted in the separation of the judiciary and the executive. The early administration of the Company succeeded the despotic powers of the Indian rulers. The policy initiated by Cornwallis was carried forward by Wellesley with his imperial vision. His subordinates, Munro, Malcolm, Elphinstone and Metcalfe, however surprisingly, resisted the policy of applying British constitutional principles to Indian administration. Out of their efforts emerged a new and conscious alternative to an anglicised form of administration.

The Maratha War finally terminated in 1818 and with it came a political transformation in India. The sword was to be exchanged for the pen and the soldier diplomat gave way to the administrator and judge. At this stage the group that controlled and directed Indian administration was moving away from Whigism and was imbued with Burke's notion of history which regarded human society as a continuous community of the past, present and future. It rejected the view that a political society could be constructed anew on the basis of abstract principles based on an alien tradition. This thinking was now and forever reflected in the growth of administrative organisations and institutions. Thus, though the virtue of rule of law and division of powers is accepted, it is also stressed that they must be modified to suit the Indian condition. This trend led to a paternalistic emergence in administration. There also comes a caution and moderation in their approach to institution-building as seen in Munro's letter to Elphmstone:

> It is too much regulation that ruins everything. Englishmen are as great fanatics in politics as Mahomedans in religion. They suppose that no country can be saved without English institutions. The natives of this country have enough of their own to answer every useful object of internal administration,

and if we maintain and protect them, the country will in a few months settle itself.

In contrast to the abstractions of the rule of law, and the blind, automatic operation of an impersonal bureaucracy. Munro's school looked to a continuation of the Indian tradition of personal government. This group felt that for the general public, government must be represented simply; there should not be a multiplicity of officers and a multiplicity of forms. There should be a single officer, who had powers to inquire, to judge and to punish, without the delay and intricacies of the western legal process. In practical terms, it meant a union of powers, at least at the district level. They all agreed that the collector should be accorded magisterial powers, which would give him control of the district police and the power of summary punishment. The collector's office was to be the great executive office of local government.

The great administrative foundations of law, revenue and the form of government had been settled in Bentinck's time. The early civilians from Haileybury were greatly influenced by Bentham and grew with a belief in the greatest happiness of the greatest numbers. James Mill simplified the Indian question to three issues: (i) the form of government; (ii) the nature of the laws; and (iii) the mode of taxation. Macaulay had declared about the Charter Act of 1883, that to the last day of his life he would be proud of having assisted in framing the Bill which contained "that noble clause, which exacts that no native of our Indian empire shall, by reason of his colour, his descent, or religion, be incapable of holding office." Long after the Utilitarians had ceased to be a distinctive party, and only their rigorous logic was remembered, administration was finally made uniform under a system which harmonized strong executive with the rule of law. Many have characterised the period of 1798-1858 as the golden age of British rule in India during which the basic foundation of administrative oragnisations and institutions were laid down. Mutiny came as an Interruption. There was not much in the assumption of direct responsibility by the crown which followed it; Government of India Acts, in 1813, 1833 and 1853, had asserted a little more clearly the sovereignty of the parliament. All that happened in 1858 was the final extinction of a corporation through which sovereignty had once been exercised. After mutiny, there was not much change in administrative organisations or institutions. But Lord Rippon's local self-government acts, and the enlargements of the legislative councils in 1893 did indicate that India was one day to be governed by Indians themselves.

Before the arrival of Curzon, the administration was based more upon individual character of men and less on system. Curzon enforced a system and with him came the end of an era. The years between 1909 and 1947 saw the demission of power. The Morley-Minto and Montague-Chelmsford reforms and the act of 1935 affected the institutions, which, in substance and form, exist till date. It may be pertinent to underline the role of the first Governor-General of India, who did yeoman's service in reviving the Indian learning. The important project which Hastings encouraged and patronised was a Code of Gentoo Laws by Nathaniel Halhed, Warren Hastings and Nathaniel Halhed have commonly been depicted as having designs on strengthening the British hold on India through study of the laws and languages of the natives. What is less known, however, is that Halhed, besides being the author of the code, also translated the *Puranas* and *Mahabharat* into English. Francis Gladwin (one of the founder-members of the Asiatic Society) compiled monumental works like English-Persian vocabulary and the *Ain-e-Akbari*. The most prominent of this early group of orientalists was Charles Wilkins who translated the *Bhagvad Gita* into English. He was the first non-missionary European to master Sanskrit, and whose work inspired Sir William Jones, the greatest orientalist of his time. Hastings' approach to oriental studies is indicated by his quoting *Gita* in letters to his wife, discussing the Indian classics with Halhed, and in the midst of troubles on the political front, learning both Persian and the common dialects of Bengal. While Hastings represented the new approach to colonialism, contemporary scholars who took up Indian studies were products of the age of enlightenment in Europe and especially in England. The year 1784 saw the establishment of Asiatic Society in Calcutta by Sir William Jones. The opening lines of Jones's inaugural address to the Society gave a vision and real content to what other historians and philosophers had merely talked about. Referring to his journey to India on appointment as a judge in

Bengal, Jones said:

> When I was at sea last August, I found one evening, on inspecting the observations of the day, that India lay before us, and Persia on the left, whilst a breeze from Arabia blew nearly on our stern . . . it gave me inexpressible pleasure to find myself in the midst of so noble an amphitheatre, almost encircled by the vast regions of Asia, which has ever been esteemed the nurse of sciences, the inventoress of delightful and useful arts, the scene of glorious actions, fertile in the productions of human genius, abounding in natural wonders, and infinitely diversified in the forms of religion and government, in the laws, manners, customs, and languages, as well as in the feature and complexions of men. I could not help remarking how important and extensive a field was yet unexplored, and how many solid advantages unimproved.

Many of us, associated with India's struggle for freedom, had developed somewhat an unappreciative attitude towards the British. However, this was not quite true of Mahatma Gandhi or Jawaharlal Nehru. About the British influence over the Indian mind, I can do no better than quote a passage from Nehru's autobiography: "Personally I owe too much to England in my mental make-up ever to feel wholly alien to her, and do what I will, I cannot get rid of the habits of mind and the standards and the way of judging other countries as well as life generally, which I acquired at school and college in England." The Jawaharlal Nehru Memorial Trust was founded in 1966 on the initiative of Lord Mountbatten, with him as its first chairman. The first memorial lecture in honour of Nehru was delivered by Lord Butler, who was a contemporary of Nehru at Cambridge. In his opening remarks, Lord Butler felt that as Master of Nehru's old college. Trinity, he had been invited for the first honour. He hoped that the lecture might help tie closer bonds between Cambridge and India and, what was of even greater importance, the friendship between Britain and India. He cited Nehru from a broadcast made in London in January 1951:

> You will remember the magnificent examples of which both England and India have reason to be proud. Both of us, in spite of long continued conflict, approached our problems with this basic temper of peace and we not only resolved

> them but produced, at the same time, abiding understanding and friendship. That is a great example which we might well bear in mind whenever any other crisis in the relations of nations confront us. That is the only civilized approach to problems and leaves no ill-will or bitterness behind.

Meredith Townsend's *Europe and Asia* had influenced both Nehru and Lord Butler and makes a common allusion to the precarious nature of the British hold on India long before it was threatened:

> The Indian Empire is not a miracle in the rhetorician's sense, but in the theologian's sense. It is a thing which exists and is alive, but cannot be accounted for by any process of reasoning founded on experience. It is a miracle, as a floating island of granite would be a miracle, or a bird of brass which flew and sung and lived on the mid-air. It is a structure built on nothing, without foundations, without buttresses, held in its place by some force the origin of which is undiscoverable and the nature of which has never been explained.

Lord Butler also acknowledges that Nehru drew his attention to the following short passage: "The clearness of the European's brain never tells him when the revolt of the Asiatic is near at hand, and all the subtlety of the Asiatic never tells him when a threat will make the European halt, and when it will pass him like the idle wind." By the middle of this century India stood at a trijunction of social, political and industrial revolutions. So it was not enough to remember that the former rule was just, impartial, benevolent and considerate. In the 1820s, for Indians, the memory of anarchy was fresh. So they felt respect, even affection, for Tod and Sleeman, for Malcolm and Munro. Now the time had come, as envisaged by Munro and Elphinstone themselves, that a change must come from a government *for* Indians to a government *by* Indians. However, Indians shall cherish the fondest memory of British times, which was regenerating and recuperating. As to the ultimate value of the whole incursion, perhaps it will take centuries to judge properly as in the case of Greeks and Romans.

5

Secretariat

The word *Secretariat* means the Secretary's office. The Secretary, being the principal adviser to the Minister, needs to be equipped with an office to assist him in performance of his functions. This term is the origin of the time when what we had in India was really the secretaries' government. After Independence the power of governance came into the hands of popularly elected Ministers, and, thus, the Ministry, not the Secretary, became the real fount of authority. In the altered political and constitutional situation, thus, the term Secretariat has come to be a synonym for the Minister's office. The label is of ancient vintage, but its complexion has undergone a basic change since Independence.

Let us now turn our attention to the term *Government*. This, too, carries multiple meanings depending upon the context in which it is used. It may mean (i) totality of operating employees, (ii) any individual governmental agency empowered to take any decision, (iii) headquarters organization of the government, (iv) the Council of Ministers, which is the final body to decide on policies and to take decisions, (v) President/Governor, who is head of the State. In the parliamentary system of government the President/Governor is the constitutional head; the Council of Ministers is the ultimate repository of authority, and, therefore, in this chapter Government is used in this sense.

Role and Objectives of Secretariat

The Secretariat, being an office, is the organization to assist the Government in the fulfilment of its responsibilities. As a concept, the Secretariat has an important role to perform. In the first place, it assists the Ministers in the formulation of governmental policies. The Ministers have come into power on the basis of broad programmes of action promised to the electorate. These broad programmes need to be provided with content and shape in order to be made workable. This apart, Ministers have got to finalize policies on various emerging problems not quite anticipated in the party manifesto. As policies can be framed on the basis of adequate data, precedents and other relevant information, the Secretariat makes these available to the Minister, thus enabling him to formulate policies. In the second place, the Secretariat assists the Ministers in their legislative work too. As is obvious, the legislative leadership, today, rests with the Government. The Secretariat prepares drafts of legislations to be introduced in the legislature. It engages in the collection of relevant information for answering parliamentary questions, and, also, for various parliamentary committees. Thirdly, the Secretariat acts as an institutionalized memory to enable the Government to examine the emerging problems in the light of precedents and past practices. Such an examination is necessary for ensuring objectivity, consistency and continuity. Fourthly, it carries out a detailed scrutiny of a problem bringing to bear an overall comprehensive viewpoint on it, getting approval, if required, of other lateral agencies like the Ministry of Law and the Ministry of Finance; and consulting, also, other organizations concerned with a particular matter. This Is part of the necessary decision-making process in the Government. In other words, the Secretariat is the clearing house preliminary to governmental decisions. Fifthly, it functions as the main channel of communication between one government and another one or agencies like the Planning Commission, Finance Commission, etc. And lastly, the Secretariat also ensures that field offices execute, with efficiency and economy, the policies and decisions of the Government.

It follows that, as a concept, the Secretariat, is an essential institution in the public administration of the country, being both inevitable and desirable. Indeed, no one can seriously question its indefinite continuance in the system of the Government in India.

The Secretariat is, thus, the highest office of the Government, indeed, its nerve centre. The secretariat system in India owes its existence to two strands of administrative philosophy:

1. The task of policy-making must needs be separated from that of its execution.
2. A transitory cadre of officers operating on the tenure system of staffing controlling a permanent office is a prerequisite to the vitality of the administrative system as a whole.

"The existence of a Secretariat in the government organisation arises from the need for separating questions of policy from current administration so that the latter is entirely handed over to a separate agency which enjoys a certain amount of freedom in the field of execution."[1] If the same persons are charged with the functions of policy-making as well as of day-to-day administration, the former task is most likely to suffer. As L.S. Amery says "Routine business is always more urgent and calls for less intellectual effort than sitting down to think seriously about something that may happen 'next year, sometime, never'. It is only by the creation of a separate policy department, a general staff, freed from administration as a whole, that it is possible to secure forethought and effective planning."[2] Such is the administrative belief which is the basis of the secretariat system both at the Centre and in the States. It may be of interest, here, to note that no such distinction exists in Great Britain. In that country a Ministry is an integrated entity embracing within the single organisation both policy-making and implementing agencies. In this respect India and Sweden might be held to be comparable: Sweden has two separate and quite distinct sets of organizations, one for policy-making and another charged with the responsibility of implementation of the policies.

Many advantages are claimed in favour of the present 'split' system that exists in India:

(i) Freedom from operational involvements makes policy makers forward looking and plan in terms of the overall national requirements and objectives.

(ii) The Secretariat is the disinterested adviser to the minister, examining the proposals coming from the executive agencies in an objective way—from the larger point of view of the Government as a whole. The Secretary in the Secretariat is the Secretary, not to his minister, but to the government as a whole.

(iii) This separation keeps the Secretariat to a smaller size.

(iv) This system also avoids over-centralization, for the executive agencies are given freedom in the implementation of policies and in the areas allotted to them.

The Secretariat, generally, performs the following functions:

1. Policy-making.
2. Framing rules and principles of procedure.
3. Exercise of financial control.
4. Work connected with legislation.
5. Guiding and directing the executive agencies in the performance of their tasks.
6. Evaluation of the work done by the executive agencies.

The Secretariat is a policy-making body and should not undertake work of an original nature. Where, however, there are no field agencies to perform certain tasks, the latter continue to be executed by the Secretariat. To this extent, the functions of the Secretariat become 'original'. The Secretariat performs the following functions:

(1) Assisting the Minister in policy-making and in modifying policies from time to time, as and when necessary.

(2) Framing legislation and rules and regulations.

(3) Sectoral planning and programme formulation.

(4) (a) Budgeting and control of expenditure in respect of activities of the Ministry/department; and

(b) According or securing administrative and financial approval to operational programmes and plans and their subsequent modifications.

(5) Supervision and control over the execution of policies and programmes by the executive departments or semi-autonomous field agencies, and evaluation of the results.

(6) Coordination and interpretation of policies, assisting other branches of the Government and maintaining contact with State Governments.

(7) Initiating measures to develop greater personnel and organisational competence both in the ministry/department and its executive agencies.

(8) Assisting the Minister in the discharge of his parliamentary responsibilities.

Tenure System

The superior positions in the Secretariat are as a rule manned by officers who come from the States (and also from certain central services) for a specified period and who after serving their 'tenure' would (or, should) revert to their respective states or services. In official parlance, this arrangement is known as the tenure system. It has been a sacred principle of secretariat staffing since 1905. The father of the tenure system was Lord Curzon who never forgot 'the men in the districts,' and this system originated from his firm belief: "India may be governed from Simla or Calcutta; but is administered from the plains." Lovat Fraser, his biographer, writes: "It is largely . . . Lord Curzon's influence that the type of officer, once very prevalent, who had practically no experience of district work is fastly disappearing from the Indian Civil Service."[3]

Staffing of the Secretariat by officers drawn from the States has been commended by a succession of committees and commissions and has been the avowed policy of the Government. In reply to the recommendation of the Secretariat Procedure Committee (Llewellyn Smith) that the tenure office of Secretaries and Deputy Secretaries should be extended from the existing 3 to 4 years,[4] the Government of India categorically stated in 1919:

> "The Government of India concur in the Committee's remarks that the posts of Secretary and Deputy Secretary must be temporary, since it is necessary that the Secretariat should be in living contact with the administrative work in the Provinces. For the same reason they hesitate to adopt the committee's recommendation, for each year spent by an officer in the secretariat materially weakens that contact. Moreover it is desirable to enlarge the category of officers who had

experience of secretariat work. The field to draw upon is already inconveniently small and the Government of India fears that any lengthening of the tenure of office might result in the further contraction of this field. On those grounds, the Government of India have decided to maintain the existing arrangements whereby, except in the Foreign and Political and Legislative Departments, the tenure of office is limited to 3 years, though in the case of any officer, it may be extended beyond that period by order of the Governor-General."

The Simon Commission (1930) too commended the continuance of this practice of rotation of officers between the Secretariat and the field. It remarked: "It is an accepted principle that efficient secretariat service, both in the provinces and at Delhi, depends upon a constant interchange of personnel between the districts and the Secretariat, the provinces and the centre. . . . Experience gained with the Central Government or at the Provincial secretariat is, in the system of Indian administration, as much an asset to the provinces or districts as recent and intimate knowledge of the districts and provinces is invaluable in the local (provincial) and Central Secretariats. Circulation between them makes for vigour of the whole."[5]

The Maxwell Committee (1937) also lent its support to this practice. According to the Committee, 'The officers of a permanent cadre at the Secretariat would lose touch with the life of India', which will be a positive handicap in the performance of their task, and secondly "the presence in the (then) provincial secretariat of officers who had experience in the Central Secretariat and *vice versa* helped to provide a link between the Central and Provincial Governments."[6] The Committee concluded, "all these considerations make it most desirable that stay at headquarters should be separated as far as possible by periods to be spent elsewhere, which will increase an officer's touch with reality, widen his vision and if possible add to his technical equipment. Further, there are obvious advantages in ensuring that a substantial number of officers serving in other fields than the Secretariat should possess a secretariat training and acquaintance with the outlook, methods and the difficulties of the Central Government and the Central Legislature."[7]

The arguments both in favour of the tenure system and against it are summed up below:

Arguments for

(1) The civil servants governed by a regular system of rotation between the Central Government and the State Governments exercise a wholesome and steadying influence on the functioning of the federal system of governance in the country. The tenure system performs this function with an exceptionally silent eloquence. Such a role is of crucial significance in view of the stresses and strains to which the centre-state relations in the country are subjected consequent on the different political parties coming into power at the central and the state levels.

(2) The superior posts in the Secretariat should be manned by the persons possessing experience of district administration. It is vital that the officers rotate between Line and Staff work.

(3) The officers of the Secretariat should have living contact with the actual facts of administration. A longer stay at the Secretariat is apt to disrupt this contact. Further, in order to have an idea of the practical bearing of policies, determined in the Secretariat, upon the lives and interests of the people, it is necessary that they do not get completely immersed in mere paper discussions.

(4) The tenure system benefits the states as well. They are enabled to have officers possessing a wide range of experience and familiar with the national approach to problems.

(5) A very long stay at the Secretariat is apt to make a man stale. The tenure system obviates this possibility.

(6) As the Secretariat has a number of special advantages to confer upon officers, an unbroken stay of the same officers would create two classes of 'have gots' and 'have nots' in the bureaucracy, which would be unfair and detrimental to morale in the civil service.

(7) Under the tenure system most officers are promised a spell of stay at the Secretariat, thus equalizing opportunity for all.

(8) The Secretariat can easily get rid of incompetent persons, for the man comes only on *tenure*.

(9) It is indicative of, and strengthens, the administrative unity of the country.

(10) It strengthens the independence of the civil service. It is a check against too complete a subservience to the higher levels of functionaries—both official and political.

ARGUMENTS AGAINST

(1) Work in Ministries is fast becoming specialised in nature. The tenure system does not ensure specialization.

(2) District experience is really not necessary in many areas of activities being undertaken at present by the Central Government.

(3) The tenure system has strengthened the Office at the expense of the officer. A new officer inevitably depends too much on the Office. We are too well familiar with the evils of "office-dominated administration".

It is necessary here to point out that at no point of time was the tenure system prevalent in all the departments of the Government of India. Foreign and Political, Indian Audit and Accounts, Posts and Telegraphs, Customs and Income-tax Departments had been the well-known exceptions even during the British period. The creation of the Central Secretariat Service has, even in departments where tenure system officially operates, thrown a new challenge to this practice. Today, the personnel borne on this service are manning a substantial number of posts of Under Secretaries and a fairly significant proportion of posts of Deputy Secretaries. Their impact has been felt up to the level of Joint Secretaries. The specialists who are recruited in the Secretariat in increasing numbers are also not subject to rotation to areas away from the Secretariat. The area of operation of the tenure system has further shrunk. The creation, in 1938, of the Finance-Commerce Pool, and, in 1957, of the Central Administrative Pool has brought about significant modifications in the tenure system. The former was created to meet the specialised needs of the economic departments (Finance, Commerce, etc.). It was created mainly from the Indian Civil Service but had also a sprinkling of officers drawn from other Central services like Indian Audit and Accounts Service, Customs, Income-tax and Military Accounts departments. The Central

Administrative Pool was 'established' by the selection of officers from the Indian Administrative Services, Central Services and State Services. There are two categories of posts in it —general purpose and specialized. The 'Pool' device is an attempt to overcome the uncertainty, both in the matter of supply and quality of officers—inherent in the tenure system. And, even where it operates, it appears to be more observed in the breach than in the observance. Although the tenure system is still officially in existence, there are numerous officers in the Secretariat who have never been reverted to their original moorings. The Indian Civil Service and its replacement, the Indian Administrative Service, have been essentially out-door services but with the unannounced whittling down of the tenure system, these services have become, in reality, or are on the way to becoming, largely secretariat services.

Mention must be made here of the Bengal Administration Enquiry Committee (Rowlands Committee), which recommended an important modification in the existing tenure system.[8] The committee said that the secretariat positions should be occupied by officers of a certain minimum years (12 years) of field experience. The officers who possess this necessary experience may be asked to opt for either the Secretariat or the field. Those who opt for the Secretariat should spend the rest of their career in the Secretariat.

The tenure system is an origin of the period when the country was unitarily governed and when, therefore, the Central Government 'was a Government of the Governments in India rather than a Government of India'. As Maxwell Committee had said:

> "It was this factor more than any other which provided both the need and the justification of a system whereby the officers were lent for short periods by the provinces to the Government of India, which possessed hardly any permanent officials in the higher ranks. The officer coming from a province brought administrative experience and practical knowledge of subjects with which the Central Government was concerned and, when his tenure was completed, he was able to return to administration with a deeper insight into those subjects and better understanding of the purposes, which his administrative duties were intended to fulfil."[9]

The base has fundamentally changed with the replacement of the Unitary Government by a largely federal one. Now, the line of demarcation between the Centre and the States is, to a considerable extent, a vertical one. In the changed context it is doubtful if the tenure system continues to serve its original intentions. Even the original intentions might well have outlived their utility under the altered political and administrative conditions. This does not mean, however, that the tenure system is likely to be discarded. On the contrary, one can prophesy that it will continue indefinitely—of course in a distort form. In the first place, this is conductive to the administrative unity of the country—a factor of paramount importance. Secondly, the system has created powerful vested interests around itself. The I.C.S. and I.A.S. have virtually ceased to be the outdoor services as they were during the British period. They are tending to become secretariat services. Under the tenure system the members of these services (and certain other central services) are enabled to come to the Secretariat which confers numerous benefits and advantages on the personnel working within it. In the first place, a stay in the Secretariat assures an existence which is singularly free from those strains and stresses to which the personnel in the field are continually exposed. What have come to be called 'professional hazards' characteristically confront the public personnel posted in the field and not those occupying positions in the Secretariat. Secondly, a posting in the Secretariat means stay in the national capital with all its civil, social and cultural amenities. This becomes an especially powerful attraction, as such amenities are as a rule not available, alteast in such amplitude, at non-capital places. The availability of better and more diversified educational facilities for children 'pulls' the civil servants to the Secretariat. Thirdly, the Secretariat postings carry with them special monetary allowances, which itself acts as a powerful inducement to seek posting in the Secretariat and prolong one's stay in it, Fourthly, a posting in the Secretariat gives limitless opportunities to a civil servant to come into close contact with his senior colleagues including the political masters, and this enables him to 'catch' their eye more quickly, This, in its turn, enhances the prospects of his promotions as compared to those posted away from the Secretariat. Finally, as it is the Secretariat which conducts dealings with various international organizations and foreign governments, its personnel necessarily come to get more opportunities of foreign visits, by no means an ordinary attraction in this country.

No class which enjoys so many privileges would agree to surrender them easily. As an administrative leadership securely rests with the I.C.S. and I.A.S., the latter tend to operate the tenure system in a unidirectional fashion, that is, for coming to the Secretariat—not always going away from it.

The tenure for different grades at present are as follows:

1.	Under Secretary	3 years.
2.	Deputy Secretary	4 years.
3.	Joint Secretary	5 years.
4.	Secretary	5 years.

Department and Ministry

The distinction between 'department' and 'Ministry' may be explained by referring to 'Ministry' as the Minister's charge and 'department' as the secretary's charge. The word 'Ministry' is not entirely free from confusion and ambiguity. It first came into vogue in 1947 when a decision was taken to substitute Ministry for department. Although a Ministry stands for the minister's charge, its administrative component is not uniformly defined. A Ministry may not have a department; may have one or more than one departments in which it is formally and completely divided; or it may have, in addition, a department (or more than one), thus leading the use of 'Ministry' both for the whole and part (or parts). Of course, the word 'Ministry' is also used collectively for the political executive.

While a department may be referred to as the secretary's charge, all secretaries, although they get the same salary,[10] are not necessarily of equal 'rank'. A Ministry may have two or more secretaries, each in charge of a specified segment of the Ministry's work, or of a department in it, but there is, in addition, one Secretary who is head of, and represents, the entire Ministry. Although all of them are secretaries, the former are subordinate to the latter who, in addition to his own work, coordinates the work of these secretaries of departments/segments of work within the Ministry. This needs To be illustrated. The Ministry of Defence, comprising two departments, has three secretaries —Defence Secretary, Secretary of Defence Production

Department, Secretary of Defence Supply Department, All these three Secretaries get the same salary but the latter two have a 'rank' lower than that of the Defence Secretary who, in addition to his normal work, coordinates the work of these two Secretaries. In the Ministry of Education, on the other hand, there were, until recently, two Secretaries who enjoyed equal and independent status. Such an arrangement (which obtains in some of the Ministries as well) is not suited to an efficient and harmonius function of the Ministry, for the coordination between the two secretaries is to be elected at the level of the Minister.

The Secretariat, as mentioned earlier, is a collective noun standing for the complex of departments or Ministries whose administrative heads are designated as Secretaries and whose political heads are Ministers. But all Ministries and departments are not considered to be equally important or prestigious. Once, the Ministry of Home Affairs enjoyed an obviously higher prestige, and a position in it was eagerly sought. This is no more so. Under the impact of the successive five-year plans, the Ministries dealing with economic matters have shot into prominence and not unoften civil servants mobilise lobbies to seek and retain their postings in them. The reasons for this general craze are not far to seek. Civil servants in these Ministries have necessarily to take decisions on matters vitally impinging on the economic development of the country, and as such they feel a sense of their importance both in the clientele groups and in the bureaucratic circles. They travel very widely and international travels are no less extensive. They have to sign contracts and agreements with foreign countries and their nationals and to issue permits and licences to Indians. The economic leverage which civil servants in Ministries such as Ministries of Finance; Commerce; Industry; Petroleum, Chemicals and Fertilizers have come to wield tend to put them apart from the rest. No where in the Secretariat do so many look to so few for so much. Much lower in the social ranking would perhaps be placement in Ministries dealing with welfare and cultural affairs. Such Ministries lack glamour and power commanded by the first category of civil servants, and are generally rated as backyard postings generally going to those either genuinely interested in such matters or without much influences.

A department during the British period, was normally of a manageable size, with only three tiers of hierarchy—Secretary, Deputy Secretary, and Under Secretary or Assistant Secretary. Later, with increase in complexity of some departments, the Secretary began to be assisted by Joint or Additional Secretary who functioned as Secretary in relation to the subject allotted to him in a department. The prevailing official opinion, nevertheless, was consistently unfavourable to the creation of this post. In 1946 there were in all 25 Joint Secretaries and only 5 Additional Secretaries. After independence the size of the departments/Ministries began increasing considerably, making it almost impossible to adhere to the three-tier hierarchy. The organization showed a tendency to grow both vertically and horizontally. Today, there are a score of Additional Secretaries while the Joint Secretaries number more than one hundred,

Functions of different grades

At present the grades of officers are as follows:

1. Secretary
2. Additional Secretary
3. Joint Secretary
4. Deputy Secretary
5. Under Secretary

The first 3 grades constitute what may be called 'Top Management' while the grades of Deputy Secretary and Under Secretary, the 'Middle Management'. These different grades function on the principle of the 'filter'. It is the duty of each grade of officer to dispose of as much work as he can, and see that only the more important cases reach the top officer.

The functions of the Secretary are quite well-defined and well-known. He is the administrative head of the Ministry/department and the principal adviser to the Minister. He represents his Ministry/department before the committees of Parliament. As Gopalaswami Ayyangar has observed,

> "A Secretary should not be immersed in files and burdened with routine. It is essential that he should have time to grasp the overall picture, size up the problems facing Government in the field allotted to his charge, and think and plan ahead.

All these are his proper functions and must be efficiently performed. Failure to make adequate provision in this respect cannot be compensated by mere increase in the establishment under the control".[11]

The Secretary, however, is free to give general or specific instructions for certain cases or types of cases to be submitted to him directly. He keeps—or should keep himself fully informed of the work of his Ministry/department by demanding weekly summaries on the nature of cases disposed of by lower levels and the manner of their disposal.

Where the charge of a Secretary is too large, he may be assisted by a Joint or Additional Secretary who formally functions as Secretary in relation to the subject allotted to him in the Ministry/department. The function of the latter is to relieve the Secretary of a bloc of work and to deal, where necessary, direct with the Minister. The Secretary, however, is invariably kept informed on all these direct dealings with the Minister, for he is not formally relieved of his responsibility as head of the Ministry/department. This manner of giving relief to the Secretary is not very satisfactory, for it does violence to the theory that the Secretary is in complete charge of his Ministry/department. The Joint and Additional Secretaries should, therefore, be appointed only sparingly. Their appointment may be justified only in Ministries/departments such as the Ministry of Finance where the total work is too large for a single Secretary but which, at the same time, cannot be divided because it is not separable. At present, many of them, however, report directly to the Secretary, thus giving the latter virtually no relief. They function, in fact, as glorified Deputy Secretaries. Sir Richard Tottenham had warned: "Additional and Joint Secretary should not be either cheap Secretaries or expensive Deputy Secretaries".

The Deputy Secretary is an officer who, as his designation implies, acts on behalf of the Secretary. He should dispose of as many cases as possible of his own volition. Only on more important cases he should—in fact must—seek the Secretary's instruction either by referring to him in writing or discussing with him orally. The oral communication has, of late, fallen into disuse and needs to be encouraged as often- as possible. The role of the Deputy Secretary in policy-making has suffered considerably, so much so that, today, he stand on the outer edge of the decision-making apparatus. This process had begun during the Second World War and has been significantly accelerated after the attainment of Independence. Richard Tottenham said in 1945:

> "The grade of Deputy Secretary is at present debased—again perhaps for unavoidable reasons. Many Deputy Secretaries now are doing the kind of work that Under Secretary should do, if Under Secretary were available; but their paper 'status', I think, deters from exercising that personal control over the office which is one of the proper functions of an Under Secretary. In my opinion, the Deputy Secretary should be an officer of considerable seniority competent to dispose of a very large amount of work on behalf of the Secretary and able, as his title implies, to deputize for him when the need arises, He should, in fact, be nearer to the present incorrect conception of a Joint Secretary."[12]

The Under Secretary should dispose of minor cases of his own volition. Ordinarily, it is the Under Secretary who should initiate action on all inward communications. He should submit more important matters to the. Deputy Secretary in such a form that the latter is enabled to deal with them quickly. As the Maxwell Committee observed:

> "Under Secretaries also should attempt to reduce as far as possible the number of files to be formally submitted to the Deputy Secretary by taking the latter's verbal orders in appropriate cases. We consider that one of the great losses in recent years in the working of Secretariat departments is the practical disappearance, due to various cases, of the summary and draft of the efficient Under Secretary."[13]

It is necessary here to point out that the functionaries at these different levels perform their functions, keeping in mind the interests of the Government of India as a whole. The Secretary in other words, is the Secretary to the Government of India, not to his Minister alone. This is true of lower levels as well. Unfortunately, however, there is too much of departmental thinking and the Secretary, today, ordinarily thinks in terms of his Ministry/department only, which is apt to hamper overall efficiency and coordinational efforts. This thinking does not end at the Secretary's level: it has to an extent percolated downwards in the department. The Deputy Secretary often thinks only in terms of his division; the Under Secretary, of his branch. All this is certainly not conductive to the attainment of organizational goals and organizational harmony or happiness, organization being defined in the broadest term, comprehending the Government of India as a whole.

Officer on Special Duty

The practice to appoint officers on Special Duty (O.S.D.) dates from the British period of rule in India. While justifying the practice of appointing officers on special duty, a governmental spokesman told the Central Legislative Assembly in 1931:

> "I want to tell the House that when we place officers on special duty we do so on two different criteria. Firstly, we only place officers on special duty if we are convinced that the officer, by his proposals and by the action he takes under our orders, brings about economy very much greater than the money we spend while we employ him on special duty, The other class of appointments that we make of officers on special duty is when we are convinced that it is an obligation on our part to take certain action in the interest of the large staff that we employ. There are certain service conditions of employees which require complete overhaulIng for instance. Usually this work cannot be done unless heaps of details relating to facts are got out and these can only be got out from first hand information by an officer who will tour about and get it for us. That is the second class, and there are sometimes officers who are put on a combination of both duties."[14]

There is a justification for appointing an Officer on Special Duty under certain situations. When some work is considered of quite obvious importance and it is decided that it could be better performed if one individual is made responsible for it, an O.S.D. is appointed, normally from among the existing personnel, to attend to that particular work. Also, if some work is of a purely temporary character, it, instead of being spread over existing numerous units, may be meaningfully concentrated in one hand. This arrangement offers the following advantages:

1. It facilitates coordination, for one man has been assigned specific responsibility.
2. It imparts a sense of importance and urgency to that work.
3. The work starts receiving concentrated whole-time attention of one individual.
4. It permits quicker implementation.

The post of O.S.D. is not necessarily indicative of any status, O.S.Ds. may have a status ranging between that of the Secretary and of Under Secretary. Even some Section Officers have been known to be appointed as O.S.Ds, The according of appropriate status depends upon the nature and type of the work.

The Government has been, however, appointing O.S.Ds. with greater ease and higher frequency, There appear to be too many O.S.Ds. (their number is about 30) in the Central Secretariat than is strictly necessary in terms of the nature of work given to them, Secondly, the O.S.Ds. usually continue on their posts rather indefinitely. The post of O.S.D. is, strictly speaking, a temporary one. If a person continues as an O.S.D rather indefinitely, it cannot be said that his duty is of a special nature.

In the rigid hierarchy of the Secretariat the designation 'O.S.D.' has a distinctiveness, all its own, which has an attraction for many. Further as the post of O.S.D. is not necessarily indicative of any status, the holder of it—particularly if he belongs to the middle management level—could probably look more important before those uninitiated in the mysteries of the secretariat hierarchy.

Because of its innate flexibility (i.e., not committed to a particular hierarchial level and temporary in nature) the post of O.S.D. ideally lends itself to use as a training post. When an official is being promoted to a higher post he may be required to work first as an understudy to the present incumbent of the higher office, and, thus, get initiated into the responsibilities and duties of this level. He may be given the designation of O.S.D. and attached to him. After completing this period of apprenticeship and grooming he gets formally inducted into the new position shedding, in the process, that fossil of O.S.D. This post came handy when S. Ranganathan was nominated as Comptroller and Auditor-General-designate. First appointed as an O.S.D. he worked as understudy to the outgoing Comptroller & Auditor General, A.K. Roy, and afterwards succeeded him.

Office

Below this "transitory cadre of a few superior officers" exists—and flourishes—"a permanent but less qualified office", to quote from the Wheeler Report (1937). But the importance of the "Office" is, in the present set up, unquestioned. The efficiency of the higher level functionaries is, to a large extent, conditioned by the competence of the office. The latter is the foundation sustaining the entire super-sturcture. It serves as the organisational 'memory', being the repository of specialised knowledge and precedents. This 'memory' function is important in the context of the tenure system which makes the officers birds of passage.

The functions of the office may be enumerated as following:

(i) To link all the previous papers quoted in the 'Fresh Receipt';

(ii) To see that all the facts, so far as they are open to check, are correct;

(iii) To draw attention, Where necessary, to the statutory or customary procedure and to point out the law and rules and where they are to be found;

(iv) To supply other relevant facts and figures available in the Ministry and to put up the standing guard file on the subject, if any, or other papers containing precedents or previous decisions of policy;

(v) To state the question or questions for consideration and to bring out clearly the points requiring decisions; and

(vi) To suggest a course of action, wherever possible.

The office comprises:

I. Section Officer (Class I and Class II)

II. Assistant

III. Upper Division Clerk

IV. Lower Division Clerk

The work of the Section Officer is mainly of a supervisory nature. He presides over the office which normally has, in addition to him, four assistants, one Upper Division Clerk, and two/three Lower Division Clerks. At the lowest rung of the ladder stands the Lower Division Clerk whose task is to perform purely routine duties such as collection of previous papers, maintenance of files and registers, despatch of mail, etc. The Upper Division Clerk has a similar set of functions to perform, but, in addition to these, he notes on simple cases and assists in-their disposal. The Assistant's function is to collect the precedents, examine relevant rules, and orders on the subject and make 'suggestions' for disposal. The Section Officer supervise those under him and ensure that the notes prepared by his subordinates are factually correct. He is the first line supervisor in the secretariat hierarchy. In addition, he is expected to settle minor cases of his own volition, but, in practice/this is rather rare.

A word may be said about the method of recruitment at these levels.[15] The Lower Division Clerk is recruited directly through a competitive examination which, since 1976, is organised by the Staff Services Commission. Direct recruitment to the level of Upper Division Clerks has of late been stopped and these posts are now filled by promoting Lower Division Clerks. The posts of Assistants are filled partly by direct recruitment from the open market through a competitive examination and partly by promotion of Upper Division Clerks. The posts of Section Officers are filled partly by direct recruitment through a competitive examination and partly through promotion of Assistants. As a result of the combination of direct recruitment and promotion, two distinct age-groups reflecting two distinct sub-cultures are represented at these levels in the Secretariat', The office, as constituted at present, suffers from several shortcomings. Sir Richard Tottenham gave a succinct account of them in the following words:

> "The disadvantages of the system can be summed up in the two phrases—'excessive noting' and 'file shifting', the combined effect of which is 'delay' and 'inefficiency'. These evils have been recognised by every committee and every special officer who has ever dealt with the subject, and probably by every officer who has ever been in the Secretariat. Yet they persist. Why? Partly because they are inherent in the

system itself. If consistency and continuity of government policy are held to be essential (as they must be within reason) and if the element of continuity has to be supplied by the 'office' (as it must largely be if the officers are continually changing), the need for the 'office note' immediately appears. The 'office', if it is to justify its existence (and incidentally, perhaps, its expansion) must play for safety. It must put its officers—and especially its newly joined officers—fully into the picture; and the inevitable tendency is to make 'heavier weather' over this business than is really necessary. The newly joined officer, on the other hand, is forced to rely on the 'office' for guidance. He gets caught up in the machine; and soon he has so much work to do that he cannot afford the time to reflect whether he is doing it in the best way. The tradition dies hard that a man's career may be made, or marred, by the length of his notes on those collections of paper which have been described as the 'Kensal Green of greatness'. Moreover there is the rule, which the 'office' is careful to bring to his notice, that other departments concerned must be consulted and it is fatally easy to form the habit of postponing or avoiding a decision by marking the file to some other department. Finally, with the increase in the number of departments, the device of sending the file to all who may be interested or concerned ceases to be a simple and convenient process and becomes a source of intolerable delay."[16]

These defects appear to be quite ancient in origin and were serious enough to provoke Lord Curzon's thinking. He laments the practice:

"Under which everybody solemnly paraphrases, initials, notes or recommends and is handed down to posterity in print. . . . The present system has the following obvious drawbacks. Firstly, people write who have no Business to write. Secondly, a case is delayed for days and sometimes for weeks (!) in a department (and *a fortiori* still longer in cases of inter-departmental reference) while it is passing through this dismal ordeal of irresponsible loquacity. Thirdly, in the wilderness of diverse opinions, it's original proportions and points are eventually lost to view, until no one is able to say what is the issue, or what is the stage at which it has arrived. I have myself had to pick out unsolved cases, which have been literally buried under the super-incumbent mass of writing, and would, unless disturbed, have lain mummified in the departmental tomb, until one day accidentally unearthed by a later generation. Fourthly, all these opinions, disquisitions, trivial departmental stages, and even initials of clerks, preserved as they are in print, swell the volume of our official records to a point at which the notes far exceed the official proceedings in bulk and length; and must, in the long run, require a library like that of the British Museum to contain them."

Expanding Secretariat

In 1946 there were in all twenty departments, some of which had been created during the war, and were of a temporary character. On 15 August 1947 there were 18 Ministries—a new designation of the department. This number has ever been on the increase—a reflection of the increase in governmental work load, and partly also of the political necessity to provide ministerial offices to an increasing of number of aspirants. The following table traces an evolution of Departments/Ministries in the Central Government since 1858:

A	B
1858	**1909**
Secretariat of 4 Departments	Secretariat of 9 Departments
—Foreign Department	—Home
—Home	—Foreign
—Financial	—Militant
—Military	—Finance
	—Public Works
	—Legislative
	—Revenue & Agriculture
	—Commerce & Industry
	—Army & Military Supply
C	**D**
1919	**1939**
Secretariat of 9 Departments	Secretariat of 10 Departments
—Army	—Defence
—Foreign & Political	—External Affairs
—Finance	—Finance

—Home
—Legislative
—Education
—Commerce & Industry
—Revenue & Agriculture
—Public Works Department

—Home
—Legislative
—Education, Health & Lands
—Commerce
—Labour
—Railways
—Communications

E
1945

Secretariat of 21 Departments
—War
—Defence
—External Affairs
—Finance
—Civil Defence
—Home
—Information & Broadcasting
—Legislative
—Commonwealth Relations
—Agriculture
—Education
—Health
—Supply
—Food
—Industries & Civil Supplies
—Commerce
—Labour
—War Transport
—Ports and Air
—Planning & Development
—Railways

F
1946

19 Departments
—War
—External Affairs
—Commonwealth Relations
—Finance
—Home
—Legislative
—Legislative Assembly
—Agriculture
—Education
—Health
—Commerce
—Labour
—Food
—Industries & Supplies
—Information & Arts
—Ports & Air Transport
—Railway Department
—War Transport Department
—Works, Mines & Power

G
15 August 1947

Secretariat of 18 Ministries
—Defence
—External Affairs & Commonwealth Relations
—Finance
—Home
—States
—Information & Broadcasting
—Law
—Agriculture
—Education

H
June 1952 (Present Constitution)

Secretariat of 20 Ministries
—Defence
—External Affairs & Commonwealth Relations
—Finance
—Home
—States
—Information & Broadcasting
—Law
—Food & Agriculture
—Education

—Health
—Food
—Industries & Supplies
—Commerce
—Labour
—Transport
—Railways
—Communications
—Works, Mines & Power

—Health
—Industry & Commerce
—Labour
—Transport
—Railways
—Communications
—Works, Housing & Supply
—Production
—Irrigation & Power
—Relief & Rehabilitation
—Parliamentary Affairs

The Secretariat Consisted of 53 Departments in 1978

1-5 Ministry of Agriculture and Irrigation:

(i) Department of Agriculture
(ii) Department of Food
(iii) Department of Rural Development
(iv) Department of Agricultural Research and Education
(v) Department of Irrigation

6-7 Ministry of Commerce, Civil Supplies and Cooperation:

(i) Department of Commerce
(ii) Department of Civil Supplies and Cooperation

8 Ministry of Communications

9-11 Ministry of Defence:

(i) Department of Defence Production
(ii) Department of Defence Supplies

12-13 Ministry of Education and Social Welfare:

(i) Department of Education
(ii) Department of Social Welfare

14-15 Ministry of Energy:

(i) Department of Power
(ii) Department of Coal

16 Ministry of External Affairs 17-19 Ministry of Finance:

(i) Department of Economic Affairs
(ii) Department of Expenditure
(iii) Department of Revenue

20-21 Ministry of Health and Family Welfare:

(i) Department of Health

(ii) Department of Family Welfare

22-24 Ministry of Home Affairs:

(i) Department of Official Language

(ii) Department of Personnel and Administrative Reforms.

25-26 Ministry of Industry:

(i) Department of Industrial Development

(ii) Department of Heavy Industry

27 Ministry of Information and Broadcasting

28 Ministry of Labour

29-32 Ministry of Law, Justice and Company Affairs:

(i) Department of Legal Affairs

(ii) Legislative Department

(iii) Department of Justice

(iv) Department of Company Affairs

33-34 Ministry of Petroleum, Chemicals and Fertilizers:

(i) Department of Petroleum

(ii) Department of Chemicals and Fertilizers

35-36 Ministry of Planning:

(i) Department of Statistics

37 Ministry of Railways/Rail Board

38 Ministry of Shipping and Transport

39-40 Ministry of Steel and Mines

(i) Department of Steel

(ii) Department of Mines

41-42 Ministry of Supply and Rehabilitation:

(i) Department of Rehabilitation

(ii) Department of Supply

43 Ministry of Tourism and Civil Aviation

44 Ministry of Works and Housing

45 Department of Atomic Energy

46 Department of Culture

47 Department of Electronics

48 Department of Parliamentary Affairs

49 Department of Science and Technology

50 Department of Space

51 Cabinet Secretariat

52 President's Secretariat

53 Prime Minister's Office

Even when the labels continue unchanged, the contents have materially altered. This point may be illustrated with the help of Department of Agriculture.

Till 1942 the Central Government took little interest in agricultural matters. It maintained institutes for advanced training and research in agricultural, veterinary, dairy and forestry matters. After the declaration of war by Japan, the Centre found in 1942 that it had to launch a campaign for the growing of more food, and necessary funds were provided for the same. The work continued to be tackled by the composite Education, Health and Lands Department. But in 1944 a separate section was created under an Additional Secretary for dealing with Agriculture, and this became a new department in 1945. On the eve of Independence it was organized in 4 main divisions. One division dealt with crop protection, plant protection and emergency irrigation; the second division with protective foods, i.e. livestock, dairy, fish, fruits, etc.; the third with lands and Survey of India and the fourth with co-operation, rural debt, marketing, etc. In 1967 the department became a huge organization, employing, along with the sister Department of Food, 33,500 persons. Its functions, today include (this list is illustrative, not exhaustive):

1. Liaison with international organizations.
2. Participation in international conferences.
3. Locust control.
4. Plant quarantine.
5. Crop and cattle insurance.
6. Fishing & fisheries.
7. Fundamental research & higher education in agriculture, animal husbandry, dairying, forestry and fisheries.
8. Coordination and determination of standards in research and educational institutes in the field of food and agriculture, animal husbandry and dairying.

9. Agricultural and livestock census.
10. All India Services—Indian Agricultural Service, Indian Forest Service.
11. Commodity committees,
12. Cesses for financing the Indian Council of Agricultural Research.
13. Prevention of adulteration of agricultural products.
14. Agricultural Economics and Statistics.
15. Veterinary practice.
16. Prevention of the extension from one state to another of infectious or contagious diseases or pests affecting animals or plants.
17. Price control of agricultural commodities excluding food grains, sugar, *vanaspati*, jute, cotton and tea.
18. Administration of Land Acquisition Act, 1894,
19. Financial assistance to various state undertakings,
20. All matters relating to foreign aid in so far as agriculture and allied subjects are concerned.
21. Soil and land use survey
22. Extension training.
23. Refrigeration and cold storage facilities.
24. Mechanized farms.

We may now conclude the present discussion by summing up of the chief characteristics of the emergent secretariat system.

(i) Secretariat has witnessed a large and rapid expansion, as would be obvious from the following table:

	1900	1911	1919	1930	1937	1954	1959	1966
Secretary	7	11	12	12	9	23	32	over
Addl. Secretary						8	4	60
Joint Secretary	1	Nil	Nil	12	7	43+7 ex-officio	81	over 100
Dy Secy.	9	9	7	26	13	101+9 ex-officio	230	242
Under Secy.	9	8	8	44	16	275+10 ex-officio	475	448

(ii) One-third of the Secretariat is engaged in work of a housekeeping nature alone.

(iii) It has picked up not an insignificant amount of original work, and, what is more, work of an infructuous nature.

(iv) The principle 'one Secretary for one Ministry' is gradually becoming an exception rather than the rule. The Minister in most Ministries is, today, advised by more than one Secretary. There is emerging, as a consequence, an organization which resembles a many-headed structure.

(v) The office of Joint Secretary has become a regular feature now.

(vi) There are some faint indications of departure from the time honored principles of unity of command, span of control, etc. The norm still is that an employee reports to one and only person, but exceptions to this rule are emerging. In the Ministry of Defence, for example, the Deputy Secretary reports to a number of Joint Secretaries for various categories of work. Similarly, the Under Secretaries in this Ministry is in charge of one section only.

(vii) Although superior positions in the Ministry are staffed by officers belonging to the I.C.S. and I.A.S., the Secretariat, today, suffers from a high degree of departmentalism, and even sectarian thinking.

Criticism of the Secretariat

The Secretariat has, of late, been subjected to severe criticism. Surely, one does not find fault with the Secretariat as a concept, but the manner in which it has been functioning, the attitude it has brought to bear on its task, its size and the style of its staffing have all combined to make it an institution in need of radical reforms. The principal criticisms directed against it are as follows:

(i) The Secretariat is a policy-making body but today it dabbles in the type of work which belongs, essentially, to the executive agencies. What is more, this type of work has been on the increase all these years. This is obviously injurious to administrative efficiency. For, in the first place, the Secretariat is prevented from concentrating on policy-making and, secondly this encroachment has materially weakened the power and authority of the executive agencies,

(ii) The Secretariat itself is a victim of empire building and is engaged in the performance of work which is either out of its province (which is policy-making) or is of an infructuous nature.

(iii) It is an overgrown institution—a typically pampered child. The Secretariat has too many persons in terms of the amount of work (essential as well as non-essential) done. The personnel in the Secretariat either engage in unnecessary work which leads to the hiring of additional staff or remain under worked chanting grievances, which is fatal to morale.

(iv) The personnel in the Secretariat suffer from a certain amount of superiority, even arrogance and vanity vis-a-vis the executive agencies. Instead of assisting and encouraging the latter in the carrying out of their responsibilities, the Secretariat today acts as an inhibiting factor. A policy-making body can perform its functions efficiently if it lives close to the realities of the situation. In other words, the Secretariat can be efficient if it projects, effectively, the experience gathered in the field. This calls for a systematic transfer of personnel between the Secretariat and the field. This is largely lacking in the Secretariat;

(v) The Secretariat is the principal cause of delay. This is the result of a number of factors—lack of adequate delegation of executive agencies, cumbersome procedures of doing work in the Secretariat, a widespread desire to postpone decision, to over-consult, to over-coordinate etc. If the Secretariat is, as it claims to be, the eyes and ears of the Government, it must function with the highest measure of efficiency.

(vi) The Secretariat is accused of being unfair in other matters as well. It is, for instance, said that the Secretariat has concentrated under its roof the best personnel available within the Government. As a result, the executive agencies are suffering from some kind of anemia in terms of both power and qualified manpower.

Each of the above criticisms has an element of truth in it. It is vital that suitable action is taken to purge Secretariat of its weaknesses and impurities that have gathered round it because of bad house-keeping. To this end the following points may be mentioned:

(i) The Secretariat must exist only as a policy-making institution and no more. The non-policy-making matters must constitute the responsibility of the executive agencies. This means that substantial delegation of functions, powers and authority to executive agency is imperative.

(ii) Its functioning too, should be streamlined by getting rid of the dominance of the *Office*. In other words, it must function on the concept of officer-oriented administration. Besides, there must be systematic transfer of people between the Secretariat and the field to keep it in living contact with realities.

(iii) There does not appear to be any valid reason for paying personnel in the Secretariat at a higher level than those outside. The special allowances being paid to the personnel deputed to the Secretariat must cease after a period of one year, The special allowance is given on the assumption that an officer, when he joins his new post, gets dislocated and has to incur additional expenditure to get settled down in the new place. There is, therefore, little justification for continuing it beyond one year,

The Secretariat comprises a number of departments depending upon factors like the total workload, priorities given to certain subjects political exigencies of the time etc. A department has a Minister as its political head and a Secretary as its administrative head. It must be remembered that it is only for the sake of over all efficiency of the Government that the various departments in the Secretariat are created; as Richard Tottenham emphasized, "Departments are after all no more than parts of a single machine, and it is a pity that more emphasis is not laid on the second syllable of word."[17]

It is precisely to emphasize this aspect that the Secretary of the department carries the designation of 'Secretary to the Government of India.' The general principle on which most departments are formed are that subjects which are of an allied nature should be grouped together. The well-known instances of this principle are the Ministries of Home Affairs, Defence, Agriculture, etc. But there are always certain activities in the Government which cut across the fields of other departments, and are grouped into what may be called as 'horizontal' departments. The Ministries of Law, Finance, Information and Broadcasting are organized on this principle.

NOTES

1. *Report of the Administrative Enquiry Committee Bombay*, Government of Bombay, 1948, para 91.
2. Amery, L.S.: *Thoughts on the Constitution*, London, OUP, 1953, Second Edition, p. 88.
3. Fraser, Lovat: *India Under Curzon and After*, New York, Henry Holt, 19H, p. 260.
4. The Committee had noted the 'undoubted disadvantages which result from the present system under which almost all the responsible officers of a Department are mere birds of passage, and practically the whole of the permanent traditions of the Department are the exclusive possession of the Office Establishment'. It, however, did not "propose to disturb the present (tenure) system under which the posts of Secretary and Deputy Secretary are temporary, since we fear that the disadvantages of cutting off the Secretariat from living contact with the higher administrative work of the provinces would in the long run out-weigh the immediate advantage gained through rendering these officers permanent. But we are disposed to think that their present term of office (three years) is unduly short and that it might with advantage be extended to four years." Report of the Government of India Secretariat
5. Report of the Indian Statutory Commission, Vol. 1, Survey, London, H.M.S.O. Cmd. 3568, 1939, para 315.
6. Report on Organisation and Procedure, 1937, paras 51-52. Procedure Committee, 1919, para 72.
7. *Ibid.*, para 53.
8. Report of the Bengal Administration Enquiry Committee 1944-45, Alipur Bengal Government Press, 1945, paras 201-03

9. *Ibid.*, para 45.
10. The Secretary of the Department of Parliamentary Affairs is of a junior rank.
11. *Report on Reorganization of the Machinery of Government*, 1949, para 14.
12. Reports on the Reorganisation of the Central Government, 1945-46, Report No. 4, para 1.
13. *Ibid.*, para 23.
14. *Legislative Assembly Debates*, Vol. II, No. 2, 23 February 1931, 1132.
15. There is also one *daftari* (Rs. 75.90 p.m.) and one peon (Rs. 70-80 p.m. attached to two sections).
16. Reports on the Reorganization of the Central Government, 1945-46 (Richard Tottenham) Report No. 4, para 5.
17. Tottenham, R.: *Report on the Reorganisation of the Central Government*, 1945-46, p. 41.

6

Recruitment

Recruitment is a process which is of vital importance to the administrative system as a whole, for it determines the tone and caliber of the public services, and on it rests the usefulness and relevance of the machinery of government to the society. Recruitment is the key to a strong public service, and, as Stahl puts it, the "cornerstone of the whole public personnel structure."[1] A faulty recruitment policy inflicts a permanent weakness upon the administration, the latter virtually becomes a haven for the dull and the incompetent. No amount of in service training can make faultily recruited persons bright and efficient. The need for a sound recruitment policy is, thus, clearly vindicated. "No element of the career service is more important than the recruitment policy."[2] "Incidentally, it will do well to note that, in the sphere of recruitment, public administration differs so fundamentally from private administration. A recruitment policy in the field of public administration must be reconciled with a country's constitutional requirements and political outlook. No such limitations need necessarily confront the private administration.

The need for a sound recruitment policy was first realized by China centuries ago, and this recognition found reflection in the adoption of the merit principle, based on competitive examinations. Prussia was the first country in modern times to have evolved a sound recruitment system. In India, the merit principle has been in existence since 1853. Britain adopted it in 1857.

The merit principle of recruitment replaced the spoils system. This change has however, been slow and gradual. In Britain, this change could be completed in 1870 though the Government had set up a Civil Service Commission in 1855, to test candidates who had been nominated by the departments, Clearly an element of patronage persisted. In 1870, the present system of open competition was; recognized as the normal method of recruitment. This reform, it must be mentioned, owed itself to the Northcote-Treyelyan Report, published in 1853, which had commended the adoption of the merit system through open competition. In the United States, the spoils system has had a longer history. The merit principle was adopted in the Civil Service Act of 1883, which set up the Civil Service Commission for the first time. The immediate provocation came from President Garfield's assassination (1888) by a disappointed job-seeker.

The maladies of the spoils system were so glaring and deep that the Civil Service Commissions were designed as reform movements to uproot the spoils system. Recruitment was, thus, conceived of in purely negative terms—its task being mainly confined 'to keep the rascals out.' It was naively believed that once this was done, competent persons would come forward for employment in the public services. This was a highly erroneous assumption. J. Donald Kingsley has rightly commented upon this state of affairs: "The rascals have been kept out, perhaps, but so have many men of vision and ability."

What is, therefore, needed is an effort to attract the qualified persons towards the public services. Recruitment policies should be positive and calculated to attract the best and the most competent. This approach is superlatively important in view of the rapidly increasing accumulation of the governmental business. As Pfiffner and Presthus observe: "Personnel recruitment for the second half of the twentieth century will have to be geared to a nuclear physical world in which the solutions of human problems will demand the utmost in human competence. The emphasis will be not only on finding, but on building men who are capable of performing the complex tasks of coordinating institutions growing ever more complex. Clearly, in such a world, emphasis will fall not so much upon 'keeping the rascals out' but on how to induce the best to serve the State and how to so assess their abilities to ensure that each will be placed where he belongs."[3]

The necessity of evolving a positive recruitment policy is no longer left in doubt. The basic elements of such a policy include, or should include, the following :[4]

(i) discovery and cultivation of the employment market for posts in the public services;

(ii) use of attractive recruitment literature and publicity;

(iii) use of scientific tests for determining abilities of the candidates;

(iv) tapping capable candidates from within the services;

(v) placement programme which assigns the right man to the right job; and

(vi) a follow up probationary programme as an integral of the recruitment process.

The problem of recruitment involves a number of elements, which may, thus, be broadly summarized :

(i) Location of the recruitment authority;

(ii) Recruitment from within versus recruitment from without;

(iii) Qualifications of the employees;

(iv) Methods of determining qualifications; and

(v) Administrative machinery for determination of qualifications.

Location of the recruiting authority

The determination of the recruiting authority is one of, his essential features of the personnel system. Indeed, this problem is of such general importance that the recruiting authority is determined by the Constitution of the country itself. Generally speaking, there are two views on this aspect. According, to one, the recruiting power should vest in the electorates who should elect all the important officers of the government. Further, these officers, should be elected for shorter periods. This system is, to be, sure, the elective system, properly speaking. This system is open to criticism. In the first place, people may not make wise choice when a large number of officials have to be elected. Secondly, people are likely to be swayed by personal considerations. Thirdly, only a limited number of governmental officials have policy-determining functions, necessitating a political control over them. An overwhelming number of them are engaged in the implementation of policies. These may, instead, be selected through the process of recruitment. The other view, arguing on these lines, recommends that only the chief executive and the members of the legislatures need be elected and others should be appointed through a system of recruitment. The recruiting power is vested in some organs of the government. Formally, this organ is the Chief Executive; in reality, however it is the Public Service Commission.

Method of recruitment

"There are two methods of recruitment—recruitment from within, and recruitment from without. The first method is, properly speaking, promotion, and the second one is recruitment in the true sense of the term. These two methods are not mutually exclusive and all governments meet their personnel requirements by taking recourse to both of them. Indeed the best solution of the problem lies in a happy blend of the two in the light of administrative experience and the general political outlook. It may, however, be pointed out that direct recruitment should be the rule at lower levels; direct recruitment combined with a liberal system of promotions (recruitment from within) should be the policy for middle levels; and top positions should normally go by well-designed system of promotion. Thus, this problem is chiefly concerned with the middle rungs of the public services.

It will do well to analyze the relative merits and demerits of both these methods of recruitment. The following advantages are claimed in favour of direct recruitment of personnel :

(i) It is in complete accord with the principle of democracy. It provides equal opportunities to all regardless of whether they are already in the public services or not. It is, thus, a fair system which does not practice any discrimination.

(ii) Government has a wider field from which it can meet its personnel requirements. Recruitment from within severely restricts the field to those employees only who are already in the public services.

(iii) Government can continue attracting capable young persons who would otherwise be diverted to other jobs, depriving government of its just share in the country's best products of universities and educational institutes.

(iv) Direct recruitment ensures a continuous supply of fresh men, of abilities and competence. "This is particularly essential in technical and professional fields where new techniques and ideas continue rapidly emerging. Governmental work and practices are thus, enabled to keep pace with advances made in these several fields.

(v) Since direct recruitment ensures a regular induction of young persons into the government, the public services are kept attuned to the changing socio-economic conditions of the country.

This system, thus, arrests stagnation and the development of conservative habits.

The advantages of this system are cited as the shortcomings of the second method, namely, recruitment from, within, and *vice versa.* The system of recruitment from within claims the following advantages (which are cited as the shortcomings of the system of direct recruitment) :

(i) This system ensures that persons who are appointed at higher posts have had sufficient experience of governmental work and administration. This experience helps them in discharging their new responsibilities with both ability and confidence.

(ii) It provides the employees with ample opportunities for advancement. The employees well know that they will work their way up if they continue working efficiently and loyally. This system, thus, provides incentive to the employees to work well. Both the reward and the penalty for efficient work or lack of it are built in this system.

(iii) As persons appointed to higher posts already possess experience and knowledge of governmental work, prolonged training may not be necessary for them. Government has, consequently, spared this additional burden and cost. Also, it reduces the burden of the Public Service Commission and other recruiting authorities, who would otherwise be called upon to examine an army of applicants.

(iv) The employees would like to continue in the public services if they have reasonable chances of promotions. This prospect makes the public services more attractive. The Government may offer lower salaries at lower grades of the services. Yet, people would find these jobs acceptable under the well-defined prospect that they would move up the hierarchy in due course of time. In the United States, where this system does not generally exist, there is a heavy turnover of employees. The Government employees feel, they are up against a dead wall; and as a result of this feeling, migrate to private enterprises. This heavy exodus of employees is hardly conducive to the soundness of the administration.

(v) Under the system of direct recruitment, recourse is necessarily taken to examinations and/or interviews. These devices are not foolproof method of assessing the abilities and personal traits of the applicants. Only work at the desk reveals these qualities. Hence, the system of recruitment from within ensures that the competent persons would be entrusted with higher responsibilities. At any rate, this system is more reliable than the system of direct recruitment. No Government can afford to appoint inexperienced though apparently bright persons to posts of higher responsibilities.

(vi) This system is an indispensable element of the career service, which has been described by White as "an occupation which one normally takes up in youth with the expectation of advancement and pursues until retirement."[5] As the Commission of Inquiry on Public Service Personnel, appointed by the Social Science Research Council of the United States, remarked in its report (Better Government Personnel, 1935), " . . ,a career cannot be said to exist if top positions are generally recruited from outside, from men who do not understand the work, and in such a way as to create an effective bar to advancement from the bottom to the top of the service itself."[6]

The principal shortcomings of the system are as follows:

(i) It narrows down the area of selection by practicing

discrimination.

(ii) It provides for a 'closed' public service, strongly discouraging 'lateral entry', which, ensures a constantly fresh outlook.

(iii) It puts premium on experience, and neglects the brilliant university-trained young persons. This systems may, thus, favour the mediocres.

Neither of these two systems can be exclusively adopted for the selection of personnel in the government. In practice, a good recruitment policy combines both the system in varying proportion, to achieve the best results. In India, direct recruitment is limited to the lowest positions in each service, and to a young group of entrants. A certain proportion of posts is earmarked for being filled up by promotion. The general position is that, as the services or classes become higher, the proportion of direct recruitment too goes on increasing. The position with regard to the Central Services Classes I and II, is, thus, described by the First Pay Commission: "It is necessary to explain that recruitment to Class I is made primarily "through a competitive examination held by the Public Service Commission (and occasionally by selection by them) and to a lesser extent by promotion (with the concurrence of the Public Service Commission) from Class II. Class II also is in many cases recruited through a competitive examination held by the Public Service Commission (or, by selection by them). The proportion of men promoted to Class II from lower rank is, however, larger than in the case of promotions to Class I; in some departments, Class II is entirely filled by promotion."[7] The proportion of direct recruitment and promotion varies from service to service, class to class, and department to department.' In the Income-tax department, for instance, twenty percent of the posts are set aside for being filled up through promotion, and the remaining eighty percent of the posts are filled up by direct recruitment. The posts of the upper division clerks in the Central Government are now all filled up by promotion of lower division clerks, thus, doing away with direct recruitment for these posts. Stoppage of direct recruitment to the grade of upper division clerks was recommended by the Second Central Pay Commission (1957-1959), with a view to improving the prospects of lower division clerks. Recruitment to the All-India Services is made direct by holding a competitive examination, but a certain number of these posts go to promotees. In the case of the Indian Administrative Service, these promotees also come from the executive offices of the States. In pass I Services, there is a system of reservation of 25 to 30 percent of posts for promoting persons from the lower services.

Qualifications required of the employees

The question of qualifications required of public employees is of enormous importance, as on it rests largely the general efficiency of the public services. The qualifications required of them may be divided into two parts General and Special. General qualifications apply to all public employees and are, thus, of universal application. They relate to civil status, domicile, sex, and age. Special qualifications deal with education, experience, technical knowledge, and personal traits. We would briefly discuss these several qualifications in what follows:

General qualifications

(i) Citizenship

An applicant for the public service must be the citizen of the State. Aliens are debarred from holding any public offices. Even when an alien is employed, the employment is strictly for a short duration. In India, the public offices are also open to the subjects of Nepal in view of the well-established historic ties with that country.

(ii) Domicile or residence

Domicile qualification was first prescribed by the United States, where even today the federate States are given due representation in the national service.

In India, the domicile rules were in force till 1957. The States Reorganization Commission had strongly objected to these provisions governing eligibility of State public services. "The desire of the local people for the State services being manned mainly by the sons of the soil" is understandable, but only up to a point. When such devices as domicile rules operate to make the public services an exclusive preserve of the majority language group of the State, this is bound to cause discontent among the other groups apart from impeding the free flow of talent and impairing administrative efficiency.

> "We were greatly concerned to observe that in one State, for instance, domicile rules were applied not only to determine eligibility for appointment to the public services but also to regulate the awards of contracts and rights in respect of fisheries, ferries, toll-bridges, forests and excise shops. . . .
>
> Such stipulations, in our opinion, are not only inconsistent with Articles 15, 16 and 19 of the Constitution, but go against the very conception of an Indian citizenship. We do not feel called upon to pronounce on the purely legal aspects of these restrictions, but we have no doubt whatsoever that their total effect is the exact opposite of what was intended by the; Constitution."[8]

Spurred by the indictment of the domicile rules, the Central Government enacted the Public Employment (Requirement as to Residence) Act, 1957. This Act is, indeed, a landmark in the recruitment policy of the Government, for it does away with domicile restrictions in regard to public appointments. The Act seeks to strengthen the administrative unity of the country, by ensuring equality of opportunity to all citizens in matters of entry into the public services. It must, however, be pointed out that recruitment to certain categories of government posts in the Telengana region in Andhra Pradesh is confined only to the *mulkis*, i.e., the regular residents of the Telengana region in Andhra Pradesh.

(iii) Sex

It was not long ago when the employment of women in the public services was a taboo in most countries. This restriction has, however, disappeared with passage of time, and now most countries permit their employment in the public services. In India, the Constitution expressly lays down that "there shall be equality of opportunity for all citizens in matters relating to employment or appointment to any office under the State."[9] Women are, thus, gaining entry into the public services. In 1973, their number stood at 73,000, thus constituting 2.6 per cent of all the regular Central Government personnel.

(iv) Age

When we come to this aspect, we discern, generally speaking, two practices. Some countries, like India, Britain, etc., recruit young persons for public services. On the other hand, the United States employs more mature men and women. These practices leave indelible impact upon the personnel structure of the government. Kingsley analyzes the impact in the following words: "There are only two feasible systems of public recruitment, although in practice they may be combined in varying degrees. The alternatives are to recruit young people direct from schools and universities upon the basis of academic examinations, or to recruit more mature men and women upon the basis of practical tests related to their work experience. The first alternative has been widely followed in Europe; notably in England; the second, in the United States. The first presupposes the existence of a number of career hierarchies or ladders, upon which the more promising officers move throughout their public lives. The second tends to regard the civil service as a collection of more or less discrete positions to be filled on the basis of technical qualifications for the particular job. The first emphasizes promotion and results in a fluid or mobile service. The second emphasizes techniques at entry and results in a more static service. The first favours the promising youngster; the second too often favours mediocre maturity. The first gears the Civil Service to the educational system. The second gears it to the ebb and flow of employment volume in private industry. . . . Neither one of these systems, considered as extremes, is adequate to the requirement of the modern public service, and any satisfactory schemes of recruitment must combine elements of both."[10]

One of the essential ingredients of a career service is that recruitment should be limited to younger persons who can make the government work their career, and further, who can be moulded and trained for higher administrative responsibilities. However, persons of higher age groups should not be completely debarred from entry into public services, particularly in the background of the expanding functions of the Government. In India, young persons between the ages of 16 and 28 enter the public services, though, to be sure, for specialized jobs, experienced persons in the higher age groups are also appointed.

However, from 1986 the upper age has been brought down to twenty-six.

On the other hand, "the American recruiting system is stacked heavily against the promising youngster and in favour of the mediocre mature person. This is due to the fact that entry to tests requires specific periods of experience in work similar to the position for which the test is given."[11] A salient feature of the American recruiting system is that "one may enter the American public service at almost any level and at almost any age."[12]

Special qualifications

(i) Educational qualifications

Here, too, one comes across two practices. The British system has laid down definite educational qualifications for entry into public services. In Britain, recruitment from open market is restricted to the grades of Higher Executive Officer, Executive Officer (or, Administration Trainee), Clerical Officer, and Clerical Assistant. There are only 3 academic points at which one may enter the British civil service: first, ordinary level General Certificate of Education (G.C.E.), second, advanced level General Certificate of Education, and third, first degree level examination. These three levels of recruitment into the civil service are also linked with different age-groups (between 17-1/2 and 28 years of age, for the Executive Officer, and between 20 and 28 years for the Administration Trainees).[13] In sharp Contrast to the British practice of laying down definite educational qualifications as well as age-limits for entry into the main classes, the American system does not prescribe any minimum educational qualification; here anyone can enter the public service after qualifying in the competitive tests.

The Indian system has the British imprint. Broadly speaking, the essential minimum qualification for entry into the administrative and the executive services in India is a university degree. The minimum qualification for entry into the clerical services (lower division) is matriculation or its equivalent.

The general criticism against the prevailing system of recruitment to public service in India has been that it encourages far too many persons to study for university degree, resulting in over-crowding in the universities and a consequent fall in the academic standards. Moreover, the university education is hardly required for executive, or clerical services. This is waste of time and energy of the young persons. If, on the other hand, persons are enabled to enter these services at a lower educational level, they would acquire while still young, the knowledge and skill needed for work in the service. Indeed, this feeling is so widespread that the Central Government set up, in April, 1953, the Public Services (Qualifications for Recruitment) Committee to examine how far and at what levels the possession of a university degree is necessary for recruitment to public services. Other terms of reference of the Committee were to consider the type of tests which may be instituted to assess the relative merits of candidates in an objective manner in the absence of a university degree; and to consider measures to ensure that the numbers of candidates competing for posts and services under Government are not wastefully large. The Government accepted, with some modifications the recommendations of the Committee. Under the decision taken by the Government a university degree is not an essential requirement for recruitment to all clerical, Central Class III, and State Subordinate non-clerical services. Candidates appearing for the Upper Division clerical and Central Class III non-clerical services need possess Intermediate, Senior Cambridge or Higher-Secondary certificate. A university degree, however, continues to be an essential qualification for other services— All India and Central Class I, Central Class II (gazetted and non-gazetted), State Class II (gazetted) and State Subordinate (gazetted) services. For Central Class II (non-gazetted) and State Subordinate (gazetted) services the age-limit is 20 to 28 years; for State Class II (gazetted) 21 to 28 years. In order to reduce the number of applicants to a manageable size, no candidate was, until recently, permitted to appear more than twice in any open competitive examination. At present, a candidate can take a maximum of three chances.

(ii) Experience

In the United States, where entry to the public services can take place at any age, experience of actual performance of task is greatly valued and demanded. The Indian system recruits young persons fresh from universities and colleges. For technical service, however, experience is considered a desirable qualification.

(ii) Personal qualifications

The public servant must possess executive ability, tact, resourcefulness, integrity, energy, faithfulness and capacity to get along with others. He should be a leader of men, and imbued with a sense of public interest. His conduct should be above criticism and reproach; and like Caesar's wife, above suspicion. He should bear malice towards none. As he is a part of a highly complex administrative organization, he must possess skills which have been listed by Pfiffner and Presthus as follows:

"1. A flexible, but essentially scientific mode of thought, characterized by a recognition of the need for coordination.
2. Familiarity with the subject-matter of organization and management.
3. Facility at problem-solving.
4. A highly developed reading and writing ability.
5. Ability to settle vexing situations through interpersonal contact."[14]

(iv) Technical experience

The Government is now increasingly employing economists, statisticians, accountants, legal advisers, engineers, scientists and similar technical personnel. An expanding government, like ours, has to recruit and train a great number of both generalist administrators and technical administrators. However, their employment raises a question of the proper relationship between these technical and administrative personnel. No satisfactory answer has so far been discovered. Meanwhile, grievances of the 'technocrats' continue mounting. It is probably true that the latter are 'one-idea' men, incapable of taking broader viewpoint on the issues. Nevertheless, the developmental administration like ours cannot afford to neglect or sidetrack them for long. The claims of both—the generalist and the specialist—must be reconciled by giving due recognition to the importance of the latter. It would do well to note the recommendation of the Second Pay Commission (1957-1959) on this aspect: "Where the work of a Department at the headquarters of the Government of India is mainly technical, it is desirable, in our view, that the Secretary should be a person who, while possessing administrative ability and capable of taking a broad Government wide view of matters, has a technical background in the particular field. In a Department which has a considerable amount of technical as well as administrative work, the Secretary may be either a technical officer, with proved administrative capacity, or a generalist administrator; technical officers should not be excluded from the field of choice on *a priori* considerations but should be considered on merits. Further, the top technical advisers or heads of Departments should have full opportunity to have their views considered by the Minister, along with any views which the Secretary of the Department may have; for which a suitable arrangement may be a joint discussion with the Minister, whenever there is an unresolved difference of opinion between the technical head and the Secretary. The basic idea governing the relationship between the two must be the recognition that the former should have an effective share in the forming of policies and programmes at the highest official level."[16] In practice, however, it is the general-purpose administrator who still reigns supreme—an outmoded tradition of Government functioning in an increasingly complex and technologically-oriented environment.

Methods of determining qualifications

Direct recruitment to the administrative and most of the executive services is made broadly speaking on the basis of a competitive examination conducted by the Union Public Service Commission. The examination includes:

(i) a test of intellectual ability and scholastic attainment through a written examination in a certain number of subjects (optional papers);

(ii) a written test, common to all candidates, designed to test capacity for effective thinking, sense of form, power of clear and lucid expression, and general knowledge (compulsory papers); and

(iii) an interview to assess a candidate's personal qualities, including some intellectual qualities which a written examination cannot test.

The scheme of the examination is a combination of three different views about what qualities need be tested for entry into the administrative or executive services. The first view believes in the transferability of academic talent to governmental work. It had been brilliantly propounded by Macaulay in 1853. "It seems to me that there never was a fact proved by a large mass of evidence, or a more unvaried experience than this that men who distinguish themselves in their youth above their contemporaries almost always keep to the end of their lives the start which they have gained."[16] He had further argued: "Men who have been engaged, up to one and two and twenty, in studies which have no immediate connection with the business of any profession, and the effect of which is merely to open, to invigorate and to enrich the mind, will generally be found, in the business of every profession, superior to men who have, at eighteen or nineteen, devoted themselves to the special studies of their calling. Indeed, early superiority in literature and science generally indicates the existence of some qualities which are securities against vice—industry, self-denial, a taste for pleasures not sensual, a laudable desire of honourable distinction, a still more laudable desire to obtain the approbation of friends and relations. We, therefore, think that the intellectual test will be found in practice to be also the best moral test that can be advised."[17] The second view is in sharp contrast to the one just described above. It regards the object of selection as the assessment of the entire personality of the applicant and matching the selected one with the type of work in the Civil Service. An example of this method of recruitment is Method II for recruitment of Administrative Trainees (ATs) in Britain. The third view falls in between these two contrasting concepts, and has shaped the recruitment system in France. This purports to select candidates possessing intellectual ability and training, but whose intellectual training has been in subjects which provide the essential background and knowledge, required for work in the Civil Service. To come back to the scheme of examination in India, the optional papers test the intellectual equipment and scholastic abilities of the candidates. The compulsory papers counteract the ills of narrow academic specialization, and, at the same time, test abilities for work in the Civil Service. And the personality test seeks to examine the personal qualities of the candidate.

It is now proposed to describe briefly the method of recruitment to the administrative and higher services in India. As mentioned earlier, the recruitment is made by the Central Government on the basis of a competitive examination conducted by the Union Public Service Commission.

The examination is a combined one for a number of services like the I.F.S., I.A.S., I.P.S., I.A.A.S., etc. To appear at the examination, a candidate must be between the age of 21 and 26. Till recently, the upper age for entry into public services was 26, but in 1979 it was raised to 28. The upper age has been reduced to 26 since 1986. Only a University graduate (one holding B.A. or B.Sc. or an equivalent degree) can appear at the examination. Engineering graduates are allowed to compete, but medical graduates are not, in the sense that subjects prescribed for medical graduates are not included in' the competitive examination. The examination combines a written test of a high standard with a 'personality test' by the Union Public Service Commission in the form of a personal interview. The former aims at judging the level of intelligence and academic learning and the latter attempts to take a measure of the qualities of personality and character. The examination system is modeled on the British 'general' type rather than the American 'specialized' type.

Till 1978, there used to be a single competitive examination for the higher civil service and there was no screening test, whatever, to judge that only those who showed some intellectual promise were to be allowed to write it. In the absence of any screening, a large number of candidates were being let loose on the written examination. By mid-seventies nearly 40,000 candidates were thus, taking the main test whereas the number of posts to be filled did not exceed 400. It was senseless to administer a competitive examination to such large numbers.

Kothari Committee on Recruitment Policy And Selection Methods

A realization like this induced the Union Public Service Commission to set up a Committee to examine the system of recruitment to the all-India and central services and to recommend such changes in the scheme of examinations and in the selection methods as would give adequate emphasis to knowledge, skills and qualities appropriate to the role and functions of the services in the context of tasks of national development. This Committee was set up in 1975 under the chairmanship of D.S. Kothari and it submitted its Report in 1976.

The Kothari Committee recommended that for recruitment to the I.A.S. and other Class I central services there should be a preliminary screening examination and a post-training test besides the main civil services examination (plus, an interview worth 300 marks). The suggestion for a preliminary objective type test to weed out candidates who are not competent enough to write the main examination is unexceptionable. The Union Public Service Commission is at present more a rejecting body than a recruiting one. The screening test should be of an objective type so that it is easy to identify those who have the requisite range and depth of knowledge.

The Committee has also proposed a 400 mark post-selection test at the end of a year-long foundational course of institutional training which is compulsory for each selected candidate. The assignment to a particular service is to be done on the basis of the total of the marks obtained at the main examination and the post-training test, taking into account the candidates' preferences for the services.

It is to be noted that the post-selection test is an interview by a Selection Board constituted by the Union Public Service Commission. It may, thus, be noted that the Committee accorded more importance to the interview (carrying 700 marks than it has now carrying 400, 300 and 200 marks for the Indian Foreign Service, the Indian Administrative Service, and other services respectively). Since human beings evaluate other human beings, an element of subjectivity cannot be completely ruled out.

The Kothari Committee also recommended that the candidates for the main examination should be allowed to answer all the papers, except the language one, in any language listed in the eighth schedule of the Constitution or English. This, indeed, is a continuation of the official policy first adopted in 1968. The number of those choosing to exercise the option to write in the regional languages had either remained stationary or even declined, the percentage never exceeding 18. This is as much ascribable to the inadequate development of the regional languages as to the snobbish value of English. Also, with uneven development of the regional languages a broadly uniform level of competence is unlikely if not impossible to attain. Besides, this may set into motion rather subjective and political criteria of evaluation, which have to be strictly guarded against.

The recommendations of the Kothari Committee have some features worth noting.. The Committee recommends a single scheme of recruitment common to the I.A.S., I.P.S., and non-technical Class I Central services. What it means is that no service is called upon to take additional examinations thus adding to its ego. This is an egalitarian move and is to be welcomed. At the same time, the Kothari Report is discriminatory. The Committee has compiled a list of subjects for the preliminary test from which candidates are to choose their optional papers. While most subjects currently taught in the universities were included in the list a popular subject like Public Administration was excluded. One ought not to ignore or underestimate the importance of the discipline of Public Administration in an examination designed to recruit personnel for public administration. Of what avail was it to deny the nation a pool of competent candidates who might be willing to volunteer for the civil services ? The injustice was rectified in 1987 when the subject of Public Administration was included in the Preliminary Test.

The basic policy governing recruitment to civil service was first laid down in the year 1854, thanks to the Report on the Indian Civil Service, submitted by Macaulay and his colleagues. Even after over 120 years, Macaulay continues to dominate the system of public recruitment in India. Thus viewed, the Kothari Committee Report may look more like a revised edition of the Macaulay Report reflecting the latter's spiritual philosophy but updating it, primarily, to take care of the vast numbers who now offer themselves for public employment.

The Kothari Committee's is a useful report but it must not be used to divert the nation's attention from the range of reforms necessary in the face of contemporary challenges. The Committee had limited terms of reference, and it did not, or could not, call into question the existing civil service system of the country. Outside the ambit of the Committee lie many basic questions demanding resolution. Is the existing structure of the civil service rational and functional ? Are civil servants given the type of institutional and on-the-job training which is in harmony with the nation's professed goals ? Are the performance appraisal and promotion system fair and objective ? Is the machinery for redressal of public grievances and complaints against maladministration adequate ? This is only an illustrative list; personnel administration includes many more facets, and personnel reform is necessarily to be broadly conceived, designed and executed.

In December 1978, the Central Government accepted the scheme of examination as recommended by the Kothari Committee and, thus, the competitive examination held by the Union Public Service Commission since 1979 marks a significant departure from the pattern hitherto followed. In other words, the competitive examination for the higher civil service held in 1979 and onwards is based on the new scheme.

Scheme of Competitive Examination

The pattern of the present competitive examination is described in the following paragraphs.

Any Indian citizen who possesses a university degree and is in the age-group 21-26 can appear at the competitive examination. There is age-relaxation in the case of the candidates belonging to scheduled castes and scheduled tribes.

There is a single examination for recruitment to the Indian Administrative Service, Indian Foreign Service, Indian Police Service and Group 'A' (erstwhile Class I) central services. This marks a departure from the previous arrangement under which there were three categories of competitive examinations, one for Indian Administrative Service, and Indian Foreign Service, another for Indian Police Service, and a third one for the central services. All the services are, thus, put on the same footing under the present scheme.

The civil service examination consists of two parts, a qualifying Preliminary Examination (objective type), and the Main Examination (written examination and interview). The

Preliminary Examination consists of two papers, one in General Studies and the second in an optional subject out of the following: Agriculture; Botany; Chemistry; Commerce; Economics; Engineering (Civil, Electrical or Mechanical); Geography; Geology; Indian History; Law; Mathematics; Philosophy; Physics; Political Science; Psychology; Public Administration; Sociology; and Zoology,

Both the papers are of objective type. The paper in General Studies carries 150 marks, and the paper in optional subject 300 marks. Only those who qualify in the Preliminary Examination are allowed to appear at the Main Examination, But the marks obtained in it are not considered in the Main Examination. The Main Examination consists of two parts—the written examination and the interview. The written examination consists of eight papers, each carrying 300 marks (all conventional essay type) as under:

(i) One Indian language mentioned in the eighth schedule of the Constitution. (The languages mentioned in this schedule are: Assamese, Bengali, Gujarati, Hindi, Kannada, Kashmiri, Malayalam, Marathi, Oriya, Punjabi, Sanskrit, Sindhi, Tamil, Telugu, and Urdu).

(ii) English.

(iii) & (iv) General Studies.

(v) & (vi) First optional subject, (vii) & (viii) Second optional subject.

A candidate may choose any two subjects from the following:

1. Agriculture.
2. Animal Husbandry and Veterinary Science.
3. Anthropology.
4. Botany.
5. Chemistry.
6. Civil Engineering.
7. Commerce and Accountancy.
8. Economics.
9. Electrical Engineering.

10. Geography.
11. Geology.
12. History,
13. Law.
14. Literature in any one of the following Languages: Assamese, Bengali, Gujarati, Hindi, Kannada, Kashmiri, Marathi, Malayalam, Oriya, Punjabi, Sanskrit, Sindhi, Tamil, Telugu, Urdu, Arabic, Persian, German, French, Russian and English.
15. Management and Public Administration.*
16. Mathematics
17. Mechanical Engineering.
18. Philosophy.
19. Physics.
20. Sociology.
21. Statistics.
22. Psychology.
23. Political Science and International Relations.*

The candidates have been given the choice to write their papers, other than English and the language papers, in any language mentioned in the eighth schedule of the Constitution or in English. However, the question papers both for the Preliminary and the Main' Examination are set only in English and Hindi.

Those who qualify in the written part of the Main Examination alone are called for interview which is conducted by the UPSC. The marks for interview are 250. The marks obtained in the written examination as well as in the interview are added and the final merit list is prepared on that basis.

The candidates are allowed three chances for the civil service examination. The scheduled caste and scheduled tribe candidates are, however, allowed to take the examination without any

* A candidate who takes 'Management and Public Administration is not permitted to take 'Political Science and International Relations'.

restriction on the number of chances, of course, subject to the prescribed age limits.

The Kothari Committee made a recommendation that the selection procedure may include another stage also whereby the allocation to various services is to be made after assessing the performance of the candidates at the Lal Bahadur Shastri Academy of Administration, on the recommendation of the Union Public Service Commission.

The recommendation was not accepted by the Government on the plea that 'this will involve reorganization of the Academy'. The allocation of the candidates to different services is, thus, made on the basis of the Main Examination and interview, taking into consideration their rank in the final examination and preferences. This was the case earlier too. The Kothari Committee's recommendation in favour of allocating the candidates to the various services after they have completed their training is based on the argument that allocation to the services would become more scientific if this is done after watching the candidates' performance during the period of training and in the post-training test.

It is a theoretically sensible recommendation, but in practice would lead to highly undesirable results. The interval between the .main examination and the post-training test is too brief to make the 'servicification' really objective. At the same time, it is long enough for the blue-eyed boys and girls to mobilize support and gain entry into the more prestigious service ! It is, therefore, very proper that servicification is made exactly when the results of the competitive examination are announced.**

The first Preliminary Examination was held in June 1979, and over one lakh candidates applied for it. 70,000 candidates appeared at the Preliminary Examination, out of which 7,000 qualified for the Main Examination. It is to be noted that the

** When we write this, we vividly remember that in the earlier editions of the present book we had ourselves argued for the allocation of candidates to different services after the completion of their training at the National Academy of Administration. Unfortunately, the general level of integrity in the country is presently not very high, and it is not safe to delay the process of servicification.

number of posts to be filled up is around 600, which means that eleven candidates are to compete for each post that is available.

The Main Examination includes a compulsory paper in the regional language, but it is only of the matriculation standard and its marks, moreover, are not counted in the ranking of the candidates. What is more, the candidates in the north-eastern States of India are exempted from this paper.

The list of successful candidates arranged in order of merit is sent by the Union Public Service Commission to the Ministry of Home Affairs. The first choice of selection is given to the Ministry of External Affairs, and after it has chosen the required quota for the Foreign Service, the Home Ministry chooses for the I.A.S. Then come other Departments in a fixed order. Of course, in making the selection, the preferences indicated by the candidates in their application forms are taken into account.

Such a system of examination has come in for a great deal of criticism. In the first place, doubts have been expressed as to the reliability of marks awarded at *viva voce*, and it has to be admitted that there is considerable scope here for the elements of chance and luck. Much depends on the personnel of the interviewing Board, the passing moods of examiners, the differences in the nature of questions put to different candidates, and so on. It is legitimately open to question whether a 15 to 20 minutes' desultory conversation on sundry matters can lead to a correct assessment of the qualities sought for in candidates, and for that matter, a comparative valuation as between different candidates. However, this kind of drawback is by no means peculiar to India. Finer[18] points out that as a result of investigation carried out by the International Institute Examinations Enquiry into the Civil Service Viva Examinations, it was discovered that for the same candidates, but by different boards, difference of as many as 92 and 70 marks was shown in extreme cases, with the average of 37 marks on the basis of 300 being the maximum marks, the marks awarded by individual examiners varied even more than the common results obtained by the Board collectively. One candidate put first by one Board was put twentieth by another, and so on. Suggesting the replacement of the existing interview system in India by psychological tests, A. D. Gorwala points out: "The importance of psychological tests must be realized and they must gradually replace the *viva voce*. A fifteen minutes' conversation with laymen, although possessing the wide experience of the Public Service Commissions, can be no substitute for an expert psychological examination designed to give a scientific insight into the candidates' mental and emotional make-up. The holding of such tests will, of course, cost more, but if thereby the services get better material, and there is no reason to suppose that they will not, the extra money will have been well spent."[19] In India, so far the British 'house party' or 'weekend' type of interview (which includes a series of tests extended over a period of about forty-eight hours) has not yet been adopted except for the selection of officers in the defence forces.

The written examination has also not escaped criticism. Pointing out the weaknesses of the written examination, Gorwaja says, "There are also often complaints about the low standard of some of the papers set for optional subjects, and it is felt that candidates taking those subjects have unfair advantage. This is inevitable from time to time, but in order to give as equal a chance as possible, that part of the examination which is common to all candidates must form a larger proportion of the whole than at present enabling relative merit to be more properly judged."[20] Commenting on the general inadequacy of the system of selection, Appleby remarks: "The criteria by which personnel are selected by the Public Service Commissions are not up-to-date and examining and appraising techniques are far from modern. Selection tends to be by one type, of person, which naturally perpetuates its own type. Selection is too much in terms of academic records and appraisals by experienced academic examiners, too little in terms of many other considerations as are highly important in public administration . . . too little attention in selection is given to any but the most subjective and incidental attention to capacity for growth."[21]

Administrative machinery for determination of qualifications

No description of the public services in India can be complete without some reference to the Union Public Service Commission.

The Royal Commission of Superior Civil Service in India (Lee Commission) wrote in 1924: "Whatever democratic institutions exist, experience has shown that to secure an efficient Civil

Service it is essential to protect it, so far as possible, from political and personal influences and to give it that position of stability and security which is vital to its successful working as the impartial and efficient instruments by which Governments, of whatever complexion, may give effect to their policies. In countries where this principle has been neglected and where the 'spoils system' has taken its place, an inefficient and disorganized Civil Service has been the inevitable result." Every democratic country, therefore, has entrusted the task of recruitment to public services, in general, to an independent body like the Civil Service Commission as in the United States and Britain. In India, it was the Government of India Act 1919 which, for the first time set up a Public Service Commission. The Government of India Act 1935 provided not only for a Federal Public Service Commission but also for Public Service Commissions in the Provinces. The Constitution has continued the arrangement (Art. 315). In fact, the Public Service Commissions in India, created as they are by the Constitution itself, are in a stronger position than the Civil Service Commissions in the U. S. A. and Britain. The U. S. Civil Service Commission was set up under a statute passed by the Congress in 1883, but was recently abolished and replaced by the Office of Personnel Management. The Civil Service Commission of United Kingdom owes itself to an Order-in-Council, and thus, does not have even a statutory base; what is more, it has been made a part of the Civil Service Department and thus does not function as a separate body.

Composition

The Constitution has not fixed the number of members of the Union Public Service Commission, and has left the matter to the President (which means, the Government). At present (in 1983), the Commission has a Chairman and eight members,[22] who are appointed by the President. At least one-half of the members should be persons with a minimum of ten years' experience in Government service. The tenure of office is fixed for 6 years or until the attainment of 65 years of age, whichever is earlier. A member can be removed from office only by an order of the President on the ground of insolvency, infirmity of mind or body, or engagement in paid employment outside the duties of his office. He may also be removed on the ground of misbehaviour, if, following a reference to and inquiry by the Supreme Court, the Court has upheld the cause of removal. The Constitution further provides that any concern or interest in any contract or agreement made by the Government of India, or participation in any way in the profits thereof will be sufficient proof of misbehaviour. The other conditions of service of the members are determined by the President, but these cannot be changed to the disadvantage of the members during their term of office. The entire expenses of the Commission, including the salaries of members, are charged to the Consolidated Fund of India. This means that they are not required to be submitted to the vote of Parliament. In order to ensure the impartiality and independence of the member, the Constitution further provides that, upon ceasing to be member in due time, the incumbent will be ineligible for any further appointment in the same office or in any office under the Government except a higher appointment in the same Commission.

The Commission has its own staff for carrying out its functions. In 1982, the number of personnel on its staff was 1,235 including 226 gazetted officers. Its senior staff includes one Secretary, one Controller of Examinations, one Joint Secretary, eighteen Deputy Secretaries, one Officer on Special Duty, one Director (Data Processing), fortyone Under-Secretaries and one Finance and Accounts Officer, the number registers an increase of 26 in one year's time, which is rather excessive and needs some check. The U.P.S.C. should not allow itself to develop obesity: large-sized organisation is a slow-moving organisation.

Functions

The Functions of the Commission may be summarized as below:

1. To advise the Government on all matters relating to the method of recruitment and principles to be followed in making appointment to Civil Services either directly or by promotion.

2. To conduct examinations for appointments to the All-India and Union Services. Some of the more important of these examinations are—the combined examination for the I.F.S., I.A.S., I.P.S., I.A.A.S., and other Central Services, the Joint Services Wing examination, the Engineering

Services examination, and the Ministerial Services examination. For the various examinations conducted by it in 1981-82, there was a total of some 2,49,000 candidates; of these the Commission interviewed some 17656.

3. To interview candidates for direct recruitment. Reference has already been made above to the emergency recruitment in 1947-1949. Over 20,000 applications were handled in this connection and over 6,000 candidates interviewed to fill some 1,500 posts.
4. To advise the Government on the suitability of candidates for promotion and transfer. Recommendations for such promotions are made by the Department concerned, and the Commission is requested to ratify them. On the average, the Commission handles about 4,000 cases annually.
5. The Commission is also consulted on matters like temporary appointments for periods exceeding one year but not exceeding three years, grant of extension of service, and re-employment of certain retired servants. About 1,000 such cases come up every year.
6. To advise the Government on disciplinary matters affecting civil servants. In 1982, the number, of cases relating to promotion, disciplinary matters, seniority, etc., was 31,509. On an average the disciplinary cases number 300 in a year.
7. The Commission is also consulted on matters like regularization of appointments, claims for the award of pension, claims for reimbursement of legal expenses incurred by Government servants in defending legal proceedings instituted against them in respect of acts done in the execution of their official duties, claims for pension or compensation in respect of injuries sustained while on duty.
8. To advise the Government on any other matter specifically referred to it by the President.

Moreover, there is a provision in the Constitution authorizing Parliament to extend the functions of the Commission.

The Constitution requires the Commission to submit to the President an annual report on the work done by it during the year. The report, accompanied by a memorandum explaining the action taken by the Government on the recommendations of the Commission, is to be placed before the Parliament. The memorandum should explain the reason for the non-acceptance of the recommendations of the Commission by the Government, if there are such cases. It must be observed, however, that the Commission is only an advisory body, and its recommendations are not binding on the Government. Yet, it must be mentioned* that by and large, the Commission's recommendations are accepted by the Government. The following figures reveal the number of cases wherein the Commission's advice was not accepted by the Government:

Year	Number of Cases
1950-51	6 [23]
1951-52	1 [24]
1952-53	2 [25]
1953-54	4 [26]
1954-55	1 [27]
1955-56	1 [28]
1956-57	1 [29]
1957-58	Nil [30]
1958-59	Nil [31]
1959-60	1 [32]
1960-61	2 [33]
1961-62	1 [34]
1962-63	1 [35]
1963-64	Nil [36]
1964-65	1 [37]
1965-66	1 [38]
1966-67	1 [39]
1967-68	2 [40]
1968-69	2 [41]
1969-70	Nil [42]
1970-71	4 [43]
1971-72	2 [44]
1972-73	3 [45]
1973-74	2 [46]
1974-75	Nil [47]
1975-76	4 [48]
1976-77	2 [49]
1977-78	1 [50]
1978-79	Nil [51]
1979-80	1 [52]
1980-81	Nil [53]
1981-82	1 [54]

Concluding observation

Historically, the Public Service Commissions emerged with a negative role—namely, to keep the 'rascals' out. It is only after the 'rascals' have been kept out that a more positive role came to be gradually evolved for them. Talent-hunting marks the second stage in the history of Public Service Commissions in the world. In India, the Public Service Commission has been so designed as to function in the first stage, for the Constitution does not envisage any wider or vital role for the Commission in personnel administration. It is par excellence a recruiting sergeant with purely advisory role, consulted also in certain disciplinary and other matters. Personnel development, in the broad sense of the term, is not its concern.

As said, the Constitution enjoins upon the Government to consult the Public Service Commission in disciplinary matters. The emergence of the Central Vigilance Commission cannot exactly be reconciled with the constitutionally prescribed role of the Public Service Commission. The Central Vigilance Commission may, for instance, recommend disciplinary action of one type against a certain civil servant; Public Service Commission is also to be compulsorily consulted, under the Constitution, in such matters. An embarrassing situation for the Government of the day would emerge if these two bodies fail to agree on the precise advice. Which advice should prevail with the government ? Sanctity and sanction behind the views of the constitutionally created body and the one which is just the creation of an executive resolution are not identical. This potential anachronism could be resolved only by an amendment of the Constitution.

Staff Service Commission

The Union Public Service Commission is the recruitment agency for the higher civil service (i.e., Group A and Group B) in the Central Government. Till 1975, there was no centralized agency in Government to make recruitment to the Group C posts. As more than fifty per cent of the civil servants fall in Group C, an absence of a body to undertake recruitment to this class becomes a serious weakness in the personnel system of the country. On November 4, 1975, therefore, the Central Government set up under an executive resolution, a Subordinate Services Commission, later renamed as Staff Services Commission (SSC).

The S.S.C. has been made responsible for recruiting personnel to non-technical Group C (i.e., Class III) posts in the Secretariat, the attached offices and the subordinate offices in the Central Government. The Railways, the offices of the Comptroller and Auditor-General and the Accountant-General as well as the industrial establishment have been kept out of this centralized recruitment scheme. It should be remembered that there is a Railway Services Commission to recruit personnel for lower levels in the Railways. The Staff Services Commission holds competitive examinations to fill posts in Group C. In particular, it—

(i) conducts competitive examination for recruitment of lower division clerks in the Central Government (except, as already mentioned, in the Railways, the offices of the Comptroller and Auditor-General and of the Accountant-General);

(ii) holds competitive examination for recruitment to Grade III of the Central Secretariat Stenographers Service;

(iii) holds departmental examination for promotion from Group D to Group C (i.e., Class III) of the Central Secretariat Clerks Grade;

(iv) conducts typewriting tests in English and Hindi.

In 1911 the Staff Services Commission conducted competitive examinations for clerks stenographers, inspectors of the central excise and income-tax, senior accountants etc. and recruited nearly 18,000 candidates. Like the UPSC, it is a recommendatory body, the acceptance of its recommendations depends on the Executive. Generally speaking, its recommendations are acted upon by the ministries.

The Commission consists of a Chairman, a Member and a Secretary-cum-Comptroller of Examinations, all appointed by the Government. The Resolution setting up the Commission is silent about the tenure of its members, thus making their term of office dependent on the sweet will of the executive. The present chairman is a serving civil servant holding the rank of an additional secretary in the Government. The Commission has been given the status of an attached office of the Department of Personnel and Administrative Reforms.

RESERVATION FOR BACKWARD CLASSES, SCHEDULED CASTES AND TRIBES

Communal Representation in Services

During the British regime the pernicious principle of "communal representation" was extended to the Civil Service as well and posts were reserved in a certain proportion for minority communities like Muslims, Scheduled Castes, and Anglo-Indians. Recruitment was, thus, made partly on the basis of merit and partly on the basis of communal representation. Traditions die hard and though the new Constitution has done away with the vicious principle of communal representation, yet in the course of Constitution-making, voices were raised demanding representation in services for certain backward communities. Pleading for representation in service on the basis of population of different classes, P. S. Deshmukh said in the course of a debate in the Constituent Assembly: "There are departments after departments where 90 per cent or more of the incumbents come from a specific community. . . . In the whole of India there is 15 per cent of literacy . . . about half a dozen communities have got literacy to the extent of 90 per cent and others are literate to the extent of 98 per cent." Some members of the Constituent Assembly demanded representation in service for rural communities on the ground of their being generally backward as compared to the urban communities. Ultimately, it was decided to reserve posts only for backward classes including Scheduled Castes and Scheduled Tribes. (The term 'Scheduled Castes' is used to include, in general, castes previously called Untouchables or Depressed Castes while the term 'Scheduled Tribes' is used to mean Primitive or Aboriginal Tribes.) Thus, the Constitution, while guaranteeing "equality of opportunity" in matters of public employment (Art. 16-1), allows the State to reserve in the services under it appointments or posts in favour of any "backward class of citizens" (Art. 16-4). The term "backward," though not defined in the Constitution was interpreted by B.R. Ambedkar, the Chairman of the Constitution-making Committee, to mean Scheduled Castes and Scheduled Tribes and no other minority community. Moreover, the Constitution (Art. 335) gives a general direction to the Union and State Governments for giving special consideration to the members of these classes in the services consistent with the maintenance of efficiency of administration. This last provision means that candidates from these classes should satisfy at least the minimum educational and other qualifications prescribed for services. It must be noted that there is no fixation of a percentage of job in the Constitution for these communities; there is also no fixed period for the continuation of this preferential treatment until these communities have made substantial progress educationally and economically, and have reached a certain level of equality with the rest of the Indian society.

In the light of the above constitutional provision, the Government of India laid down its policy and framed rules according to which the share of these communities was fixed at 12 percent for all-India services on the basis of open competition, and 16 per cent for direct recruitment. Besides, the maximum age-limit prescribed for appointment was raised in their case by 3 years: in 1952, this rule was further relaxed raising their age limit to 5 years above the maximum prescribed for others. Another concession given to these classes is either complete exemption from payment of the application fee or a great reduction in such fee. The percentage of reservation was raised in 1970. In this year, the share in public services was increased to 15 percent in the case of direct recruitment made by open competition on an all-India basis but the percentage of 16-2/3 in case of recruitment otherwise than by open competition. The percentage for Scheduled Tribes is 7.5. What this means is that 22.5 per cent of government jobs are already in the reserved category—15.5 per cent for scheduled castes and 7.5 per cent for scheduled tribes. As a result of these concessions, the number of Scheduled Caste candidates who appeared at the I.A.S., etc. examinations, had gone up from 23 in 1952 to 27 In 1953, 30 in 1954, 53 in 1955,[55] 2,194 in 1975, and 2,519 in 1976.

In 1964, the representation of Scheduled Castes *vis-a-vis* total number of employees in the Central Government was 1.79 per cent in Class I, 3.01 per cent in Class II, 9.15 per cent in Class III, and 52.77 percent in Class IV. In the same year, the representation of Scheduled Tribes was .22 per cent, .21 per cent,

1.25 per cent and 2.38 per cent in Class I, Class II, Class III, and Class IV respectively.[56] In 1974 the share of the Scheduled Caste members in Class I, Class II, Class III and Class IV was 3.31 percent, 4.64 per cent, 10.28 per cent and 18.56 per cent respectively. In 1981 the shares of the scheduled castes and scheduled tribes in the various categories of the civil services were as under:

	Group A	Group B	Group C	Group D
Scheduled Castes	5.16%	7.79%	12.49%	19.19%
Scheduled Tribes	1.09%	1.30%	3.05%	5.04%

The vacancies reserved for Scheduled Castes are getting filled up. This would be clear from the following table:

I.A.S. etc. Examinations

Year	Number of Vacancies reserved	Number of Scheduled Caste Candidates appointed
1972	91	91
1973	91	93
1974	93	94
1975	99	104
1976	104	103

Anglo-Indians

The only other community, which had been given special consideration in the matter, was the Anglo-Indian community (Art. 336). Articles 331 and 333 provide for the nomination of Anglo-Indians to Parliament and to the State legislatures, Article 336 provided service reservations in the Railways, Customs, and Posts and Telegraphs Services. However, Article 336 (1) specifically mentioned that these protections envisaged in Article 336 "shall cease after a period of ten years." As a result, the special privileges for Anglo-Indians have ceased. The Backward Classes Commission (1955) had observed: "The difficulties under which they (Anglo-Indians) labour are more psychological than real. . . . We believe this to be a passing phase. Fortunately, a good majority of them are feeling one with India and with the passage of time and with goodwill on both sides, their problems will probably disappear."

Regional Representation and Linguistic Consideration

India, as a federation, is faced with problems of recruitment to services which are peculiar to all federal polities. The problem has three aspects in a federation — territorial or regional demands for representation in federal services, the desirability of federal officers administering federal affairs within a State being citizens of that State, and/or members of the linguistic group dominant in that State, and the formulation of standards for the federal service that take into account not only the linguistic diversities of the member states but also the differing standards of the State Civil Services and their educational systems.[57] "By either custom (United States), statute (Canada), or constitutional provision (Weimar), federal systems have usually provided that civil servants administering federal affairs within a State shall be citizens of the State and/or members of the linguistic group dominant within that jurisdiction."[58]

In India as well demands were made for territorial or regional representation in Union Services and for preference to local candidates for State Services. The question of preference for nationals of a State to the Services within it was raised during the debate in the Constituent Assembly on the Report of the Committee on Fundamental Rights, in respect of "equality of opportunity in matters of public employment." Mahavir Tyagi, speaking on the occasion, said: "I think, to establish self-government in the true sense of the word, it is most essential that in any part of the world, only the residents of that part should be government servants. If there are open chances for the residents of one province to serve in another, it means that the residents of that province shall not be able to enjoy self-government."[59] Later, during the course of discussion on the public service commissions, Sardar Hukum Singh raised the point in a more vigorous form: "India is a vast country and regions are not equally developed so far as education is concerned. . . . I want to draw the attention of the House particularly to the Punjab. . . . This province started in the race of education 70 years after the others had begun. . . . Naturally the Punjab . . . cannot be expected to compete with other provinces if regional considerations are ignored altogether. . . . Already the Central Secretariat is full of Menons, Swamis and Ayyangars. And in a few years we will see the provinces would be flooded with ambitious young men who would not be so familiar with the local usages or customs. Local problems would not be appreciated. The sons of the soil would be squeezed out and there would be fresh prejudices. . . . If no impetus is given to regional recruitment, the backward areas would become colonies for the educationally advanced regions of the country."[60]

Such parochial demands did have some influence on Constitution-making, and Alladi Krishnaswami, a prominent member of the Drafting Committee, had to concede "that in case of appointments under the State . . . it may be necessary to provide that residence within the State is a necessary qualification for appointment by and within the State."[61] As a result, Clause (3) was added to Article 16, authorizing Parliament to make law "in regard to a class or classes of employment or appointment to an office under any State . . . and requirement as to residence within that State prior to such employment." But so far as All-India Services and the Central Services are concerned, there is no such provision. In the case of the Indian Administrative Service there is no such rule; in fact, it is just the other way round. Under the British rule there was a definite practice that a person was never posted in his own home district. Supporting such practice, Gorwala writes: "There is a considerable body of opinion, both among the services and among non-officials, which holds that it is desirable that officers should as far as possible be allotted to provinces other than those of their birth. While it is true that this may mean less local knowledge and in some cases necessitate the learning of new languages, yet it is felt that these disadvantages are more than outweighed by the independence from localities which follows service outside one's own province. . . . In such circumstances there is as a rule no conflict, as private virtue has no sphere of operation. Moreover, such allotment would make a valuable contribution to the cause of national unity.[62] The view has prevailed with the Government and the present position is that, as a deliberate policy, at least half the recruits are sent to serve in States other than their own. So far as the recruits themselves are concerned, each candidate, while filling out the form of

Application, indicates his first and subsequent preferences for the State he would like to be posted in, and ordinarily these preferences are taken into account in making postings. However, a kind of indirect representation to the State was given in the I.A.S. when, at the time of the first emergency recruitment to this Service, in 1948-49, a number of officers of the State Executive Service were promoted to the I.A.S. rank.

So far as linguistic consideration is involved, India, with its fifteen different languages in use in different parts of the country, presents a complicated problem. The position obtaining at present is that so far as State civil servants are concerned, they have to pass a departmental examination in the official language or languages of the State concerned. Regarding the Union Government employees, they must know Hindi and pass a departmental examination in it. Hindi has been adopted as the official language of the country by Article 343 of the Constitution. As regards the All-India Services, the officers must pass a test in Hindi as well as in the official language of the state in which they are posted. There is no problem in India with regard to the difficulty caused by the different systems of education prevalent in different parts of the country. The system of education is, by and large, uniform throughout the country. However, the resident of the States with a long history of educational facilities have an obvious advantage in competitive examinations over the persons from relatively backward States where educational facilities started much later.

NOTES

1. Stahl, O.Glenn, *Public Personnel Administration*, Fourth Edition, New York, Harper & Brothers, 1956, p. 59.
2. *Better Government Personnel* (Report of the Commission of Inquiry on Public. Service Personnel, appointed by the Social Science Research Council of the U.S.A.), New York, McGraw-Hill, 1935, p. 37.
3. Pfiffner & Presthus, *op. cit.*, p. 294.
4. Stahl, O. Glenn, *op. cit.*, p. 60.
5. White, L. D., *Government Career Service*, Chicago, University of Chicago Press, 1935, p. 7.
6. *Better Government Personnel*, 1935, p. 28.
7. *Report of the Central Pay Commission*, 1950, pp. 15-16.

8. *Report of the State Reorganization Commission*, 1935, Paras 849-51, p. 230.
9. Article 16(1).
10. Kingsley, J. Donald. Quoted in Nigro, *op. cit.*, pp. 233-34.
11. Pfiffner & Presthus, *op. cit.*, p. 173.
12. Riper, Paul V., "Adapting a British Political Invention to American Needs." *Public Administration*, Winter, 1963, pp. 321-22.
13. See Maheshwari, Shriram, *The Civil Service in Great Britain*, Delhi, Concept Publishing Company, 1976.
14. Pfiffner & Presthus, *op. cit.*, p. 296.
15. *Report of the Commission of Enquiry on the Employment and Conditions of Service of Central Government Employees*, 1957-59, Ministry of Finance, Government of India, p. 111.
16. Finer, Herman, *Theory and Practice of Modern Government*, New York, Henry Holt & Co., 1949, p. 762.
17. Ibid., pp. 763-64,
18. Finer, Herman, *op. cit.*, pp. 777-80.
19. Gorwala, A. D., Report on the Public Administration, 1951, p. 64.
20. Ibid.
21. Appleby, Paul H., *Report of a Survey*, p. 11.
22. The authorized strength of the Commission is nine (including the Chairman).
23. *First Report of the Union Public Service Commission, 1950-51*, paras 18,29, 35,38,40.
24 .Second Report, 1951-52, para 33.
25. Third Report, 1952-53, para 30,
26. Fourth Report, 1953-54, para 34.
27. Fifth Report, 1954-55, para 35.
28. Sixth Report, 1955-56, para 35.
29. Seventh Report, 1956-57, para 30.
30. Eighth Report, 1957-58, para 24.
31. Ninth Report, 1958-59, para 34.
32. Tenth Report, 1959-66, para 33.
33. Eleventh Report, 1960-61, para 37.
34. Twelfth Report, 1961-62, para 32.
35. Thirteenth Report, 1962-63, para 34.
36. Fourteenth Report, 1963-64, para 35.

37. Fifteenth Report, 1964-65, para 33.
38. Sixteenth Report, 1965-66, para 33.
39. Seventeenth Report, 1966-67, para 33.
40. Eighteenth Report, 1967-68, para 32.
41. Nineteenth Report, 1968-69, para 33.
42. Twentieth Report, 1969-70, para 34.
43. Twenty-First Report, 1970-71, para 35.
44. Twenty-Second Report, 1971-72, para 40.
45. Twenty-Third Report, 1972-73, para 30.
46. Twenty-Fourth Report, 1973-74, para 41.
47. Twenty-Fifth Report, 1974-75, para 39.
48. Twenty-Sixth Report, 1975-76, para 36.
49. Twenty-Seventh Report, 1976-77, para 46.
50. Twenty Eighth Report, 1977-78, para 41.
51. Twenty-Ninth Report, 1978-79, para 35.
52. Thirtieth Report, 1979-80, park 33. .
53. Thirty-First Report, 1980-81, para 28.
54. Thirty-Second Report, 1981-82, para 29.
55. Indiagram, 6 April, 1956, p. 3.
56. Report of the Commission for Scheduled Castes and Scheduled Tribes for the Year 1963-1964, Part II, Appendices XXIV and XXV.
57. Bowei, Bobert R., & Friedrich, Carl L., Studies in Federalism,' Boston, Little, Brown & Co. 1954, p. 74.
58. Ibid., p. 75.
59. Constituent Assembly Debates, 1946-47, p. 434.
60. Ibid., August 22, 1949.
61. Ibid., p. 33.
62. Gorwala, A. D., Report on Public Administration, pp. 64-65.

7

Employer-Employee Relations

Despite its eventual failure, the last general strike of the Central Government Employees (Classes III and IV) in July 1960, has focused both public and governmental attention on the thorny problem of government's relations with its employees. The government is expected to be a model employer, and it is its duty to devise suitable machinery for resolving the grievances of its civil servants. We shall discuss this problem under the following heads:

(1) Right of association,

(2) Right to strike, and

(3) Machinery for negotiation and settlement of disputes.

Right of Association

Three problems are involved here: (1) Can public servants form their associations ? (2) Can these associations be affiliated to trade unions outside? (3) Can they join a political party? The practice differs from country to country.

United Kingdom

Civil servants in U.K. are absolutely free to form service associations and to continue to be members of such associations, whether they are recognized by the Government or not. Any such association can become part of the wider trade union movement by resolution of its Annual Meeting or by a ballot of its members. Between 1927 and 1946, however, the Trade Disputes Act forbade a permanent civil servant to belong to a union which had affiliation to an outside trade union, or any political party. The Labour Government of 1945 repealed the

1927 Act in 1946. This was followed by the re-affiliation of some Civil Service Unions to the Trade Union Congress. These included the larger Associations representing postal, clerical and similar other workers, but bodies representing professional, executive and administrative civil servants have remained aloof. As regards links with political parties, only the Union of Post Office Workers is affiliated to the Labour Party. None is affiliated to any other party. There are specific rules and conditions laid down for it. Civil Service Associations must go through a prescribed procedure before being able to join a political party. Again, unions are forbidden to use any general funds for political purposes.

United States

In the United States, the federal employees have the right to be members of any service organization or association subject to the condition that such a body does not impose upon them the duty to go on a strike against the Government, This right is based on the Lloyd La Follete Act of 1912,[1] as subsequently amended.

As a matter of practice, the civil servants' unions have voluntarily restricted their membership to certain well-defined categories of workers. Thus, there are separate unions for (1) machinists, carpenters and others of the skilled trades; (2) different occupational groups within the postal services, such as, letter-carriers, clerks and postal supervisors; and (3) the federal white-collar workers. Thus, the unions, to which white-collar civil servants belong, confine their membership to employees in that group only. Similarly, membership of the American Federation of Government Employees, or the National Association of Letter-Carriers is restricted to government servants. However, these bodies are affiliated to the American Federation of Labour (A.F.L.), which is made up of unions belonging to private sector. "This has been done by the repudiation of the strike clause in the constitution of the affiliating bodies." But, there are several unions which are unaffiliated.

India

The present position in this respect in our country is that the civil servants cannot join or continue to be members of any service association which has not either been recognized by the

Government within six months of its formation, or the recognition to which has been refused or withdrawn. Recognition of such associations is subject to the following conditions:

(1) that no person, who is not a Government servant, is connected with the affairs of the Association;

(2) that the executive of the Association is appointed from amongst members only;

(3) that the Association shall not espouse or Support the cause of individual Government servant; and

(4) that it shall not maintain any political fund or propagate the views of any political party or politician? The rules regarding non-railway industrial staffs and railway staffs (constituting 70 per cent of the total staffs under the Central Government) are more liberal. For example, their Associations are not prohibited from maintaining a political fund.

It is clear from the above description that the right of civil servants in India to form Associations is hedged in by stringent conditions. Thus, membership of an unrecognized Association is a disciplinary offence. The Constitution of India confers on all citizens the right to form Associations or unions. Why should public servants be denied this right, then? Why should disciplinary action be taken against them merely because they are members of unrecognized Associations? Again, the Government is free to grant or withhold recognition in its discretion. The Government recently used this power to withdraw recognition of such Associations as took active part in the last strike. Sometimes the Government may refuse recognition to an association on the ground that an Association of the same class of employees with a large membership already exists. The Jagannath Das (Second Pay) Commission recognized the hardships involved and recommended "that the membership of an unrecognized Association should not as such be a disciplinary offence. . . . As regards recognition of Associations, the rules framed by the Government appear to us to be rather stringent. Reasonable conditions for recognition are essential for successful working of service Associations. We, therefore consider it necessary that the rules of recognition should be conceived (*sic*), and recognition granted in a liberal spirit."[2] Despite these restrictions quite a large proportion of the Central Government employees are found organized into service Associations, which according to the Second Pay Commission, number 956 (600 unrecognized by the Government and 356 recognized ones). It is quite likely that at least half of the Central Government employees are members of these Associations and the unions.

RIGHT TO STRIKE

Of late the question of the right of civil servants to engage in or assist a strike against the Government has been under examination in our country. The July 1960 strike as well as the November 1968 (abortive) strike of the Central Government employees has focused public attention on this important problem. The position in this respect varies from one country to the other.

United Kingdom

There is no law prohibiting demonstrations or strikes by civil servants. In other words, if a civil servant goes on strike, he commits no penal offence. Striking is, howsoever, a disciplinary offence, and the Government is free to take any disciplinary action that a strike situation may demand. In practice, the civil servants do not go on strike or even threaten to do so.

United States

The civil servants are prohibited by law to engage in strikes. The Labour Management Relations (Taft-Hartley) Act 1947 makes it unlawful for any employee of the Government of the United States or any of its agencies including government corporations to resort to strike against the Government. The penalty provided for was discharge from employment, forfeiture of civil service status, and ineligibility for re-employment for three years. The ban has been made more sweeping and stringent by law enacted in 1955 (Public Law 330—84th Congress), which provides "that no person shall accept or hold office or employment in the Government in the United States or any agency thereof, including wholly-owned Government corporation, who participates in any strike, or asserts the right to strike against the Government of the United States or such agency, or is a member of an organization of Government employees that asserts the right to such strike." Violation of this provision is a felony punishable with a fine and/or imprisonment.

Other Countries

In Australia, Japan and Switzerland, it is illegal for Government employees to go on strike; and in Australia the punishment is summary dismissal. In Canada, the position is nowhere explicitly stated. The fact that Trade Union legislation excludes federal employees, may mean that the legal protection of the rights guaranteed to labour does not extend to Government servants. In the province of Quebec strikes are prohibited in all circumstances. France seems to be the only important country of the western world which permits the right to strike.

India

The position here is as in the United Kingdom. A strike by Government servants is not prohibited by law; it only constitutes a breach of discipline. Thus, the Central Civil Services (Conduct) Rules, 1955, forbid a Government servant from participating in any demonstration or resorting to any form of strike in connection with any matter pertaining to his conditions of services. The provision applies to non-industrial staffs constituting about thirty per cent of the total staffs under the Central Government. However, no such restriction is applicable to industrial staffs, except those under the Railways and Railway staffs, both industrial and non-industrial, constituting seventy per cent of the total strength.

Two issues arise here for consideration:

(1) Should Government servants be free to participate in a demonstration or to resort to a strike in connection with matters pertaining to their conditions of service ?

(2) Should a legal ban be imposed on such strikes ?

Divergent views have been expressed on this issue; and it is but to be expected. There have emerged three viewpoints on this matter. The first favours the grant of full Trade Union rights to civil servants including the right to strike. The second recommends a total ban on strikes by public servants. Between the above two opposing views comes the third school which would prohibit only certain types of strikes.

The first view has been supported by eminent writers like W. F. Mosher according to whom "the prohibition of strike by Civil Service Regulations cannot be justified either in logic or in political philosophy. . . . To deny to any group of employees the right to strike against intolerable conditions is to reduce them to a form of slavery." Secondly, there should be no distinction between the Government employees and the employees of private enterprises. The employees of Government, like other employees, should have the right to demonstrate in order to arouse public conscience about their grievances, and to secure public support for their redress, and they should have the ultimate sanction of a worker to withdraw his labour. It is, thus, argued that there is no valid reason why Government servants should not have all the rights of other employees of the Government the limitations of other employers. A distinction should be made between the State as an employer and the State as a sovereign body.

The opposite viewpoint has also been supported by substantial arguments. In the first place, it is argued that the State, being free from the profit motive, and being itself responsible for preventing exploitation of any section of the community, can be relied upon to be fair to its own employees. Secondly, as pointed out by B. Shiva Rao, "A general strike of Government employees, howsoever it might be described by its leaders, is a political weapon. Its success must mean the collapse of the administration and that no Government can permit."[3] A strike by civil servants is a pistol aimed at the very people whom they are supposed to serve. Thirdly, it should be remembered that civil servants in India, particularly those serving the Union Government, already belong to a privileged class as compared to millions of unemployed but, more or less, equally qualified persons or even the employees of State Governments, nothing to say of those serving the local governments. Even on the basis of the simple law of demand and supply there should be no incentive for a civil servant to go on strike. Government service is a package deal and must be accepted *in toto* including its privileges and disabilities. Fourthly, it is sometimes pointed out that such extreme and militant means are not meant for the civil servants. Referring to the use of this right by the civil servants in Britain, Douglas Houghton said in a lecture delivered at the

Indian Institute of Public Administration: "In the civil Service no one seriously thinks of strike action. Civil servants are inhibited by fear of the consequences (such as, loss of a safe job and of accrued pension rights); also by a spirit of self-sacrifice in a common cause. Civil servants had never chosen the path of martyrdom. . . . Civil servants liked to get results by peaceful means. We have chosen a more civilized way of communication of desires."[4] The American point of view in this matter was well brought out by President Franklin Roosevelt in the course of a letter to the President of the National Federation of Federal Emyloyees in 1937: "Particularly I want to emphasize my conviction that militant tactics have no place in the functions of any organization of government employees. Upon employees in the Federal Service rests the obligation to serve the whole people, whose interests and welfare require orderliness and continuity in the conduct of government activities. The obligation is paramount. Since their own services have to do with the functioning of the government, a strike of public employees manifests nothing less than an intent on their part to prevent or obstruct the operations of government until their demands are satisfied. Such action, looking towards the paralysis of government by those who have sworn to support it, is unthinkable and intolerable."

The third group would make a distinction between employees engaged in the public utility and strategic services and those employed on industrial operations under Government; the former, they think, should not have the right to strike, but the latter may have. The viewpoint of this school of thought was well expressed by Leonard White: "A strike that would bring direct, immediate, certain and serious danger to a primary interest of the community should be prohibited by law."

The considered opinion of the Second Pay Commission on the right to strike is as follows: "We are definitely of the view that it is wrong that public servants should resort to strike or threaten to do so; and that persons entrusted with the responsibility for operating services essential to the life of the community should seek to disorganize and interrupt those services in order to promote their interests. Apart from these moral aspects, there is little doubt that in Indian conditions, in which there is often a possibility of eruption of indiscipline in an ugly form in one section of the community or another, a strike or even demonstration by government servants cannot but be a factor making for indiscipline generally."[5]

The Administrative Reforms Commission (1966-1970), set up by the Central Government, recommended complete prohibition of strikes by civil servants. It observed: "We wish to record as our considered view that strikes are out of place in government departments. A government servant holds a special position in society in that he is a part of the machinery—the administration—on whose uninterrupted and efficient functioning depends the well-being of society, nay, its very survival. In whatever situation he may be functioning, his work and conduct have a direct effect on the people. This places him in a privileged position from which he exercises power and commands respect. Society can, therefore, rightly expect of him in return to behave as a model citizen who will not place its welfare in jeopardy by any action of his. In these days, when the effect of Government's activities is all pervasive, a stoppage thereof, be it even for a short period, will cause widespread distress to the community. So, whatever grievances a government servant may have, either as an individual or as a member of a group of government servants, redress must be sought invariably through a suitable machinery for negotiation and in no case through recourse to coercive measures that disrupt the smooth functioning of the administration. A person who enters government service should, therefore, be clear in his mind that resort to strike is not a method open to him for achieving; any objective. In order that this idea may be well-implanted in his mind, he should, at the time of his entering upon service under government, make a solemn declaration that he will not resort to strike."[6]

Thus, the weight of public opinion all over the world appears to tilt in favour of prohibition of strikes in the case of civil servants. The question that arises now is whether there should be a legal ban on strikes, or the prohibition under the Government Servants Conduct Rules would do. The Government has learnt a bitter lesson from the last strike, and there was an official move to impose a legal ban. But no such legislation has been taken in hand so far. The Second Pay Commission was of the considered opinion that no change in the present legal position was called for: "We are not suggesting amendment of the law. What we have in view is that a change should be brought about by the employees themselves abjuring the use of the strike weapon and demonstrations." On the other hand, the Administrative Reforms Commission recommended positive steps on the part of the Government. It observed: "A strike in a government department being a serious matter, it is also necessary to make it punishable under Jaw. We, therefore, welcome the Essential Services Maintenance Act 1968, authorizing the Government to prohibit strikes in essential services and providing for penalties for persons participating in prohibited strikes or instigating and financing such strikes."[7]

MACHINERY FOR NEGOTIATIONS

If civil servants are to be denied the right to demonstrate and strike on the one hand, and are not to be treated as bondsmen on the other hand, there has to be provided some machinery for negotiation and peaceful settlement of disputes between the Government and the employees. In the present "participative management" and "human relations in administration", the public officials must have some say in matters concerning the conditions of their service. We shall, now, describe in brief the position in this respect obtaining in the U.K., the U.S.A. and India.

United Kingdom

What is Whitleyism?

Since our staff committees (Councils) are based on the model of the Whitley Councils in the U.K., we should give a brief description of these bodies. Whitleyism is a method of periodical discussion at various levels between representatives of the State as employers (the official side) and representatives of civil servants as employees (the staff side). Its objects are: (i) to get full cooperation between management and staff with a view to increased efficiency of the public service combined with the well-being of those employed; (ii) to provide machinery for dealing with grievances; and (iii) to bring together . . . in the solving of problems the experience and different points of view of many kinds of civil servants. The spirit of Whitleyism is a readiness on both sides to make the machinery of joint discussion work, to aim at reaching the best possible settlements amicably and to the satisfaction of both sides. The system of Whitley Councils has been in existence in the Civil Service of the U.K. since 1919, and, in the opinion of civil service trade union leaders; senior Treasury officials and all departmental heads, the system has proved a success.

Organization

The Whitley machinery consists of a National Whitley Council for the general classes of the Civil Service, and separate Departmental Councils for staff peculiar to a Department. There is no hierarchical connection between the National and the Departmental Councils. The National Council must, however, approve all Departmental Council constitutions; and it is kept informed of departmental developments which seems to be inconsistent with national agreements or to have application or consequences beyond the department concerned. Down below, there are District or Regional Committees which deal with the purely local problems of the staff distributed throughout the country. The National Council has a total membership of 54, equally divided between the official and staff sides. The official side was originally appointed by the Cabinet, but nowadays vacancies are filled by the Treasury. Members are not appointed for any specified term of office and continue to serve until they resign or retire. The official side consists mainly of Heads of Departments, with a few Deputy Heads and Treasury Officers of lower rank. An attempt is made to secure a proper balance of departmental representation. Except for the Treasury and Ministry of Labour representatives, members are appointed in a personal capacity. Memberes are now invariably serving civil servants. From 1922-1930 the official side included three members of Parliament (of the ruling party), but this practice was dropped on the recommendation of the Royal Commission on the Civil Service (1929-1931). The staff side was originally appointed by the major groups of staff associations as existing in 1919. But staff grouping has changed since and the composition of the staff side has changed correspondingly. The staff side is responsible for filling the vacancies and for deciding from time to time the number of seats to be given to the different associations represented on it. Members are appointed annually, and usually a substantial proportion of them are full-time staff association officials and the rest civil servants. Occasionally staff association officials, who have become M.Ps, have sat on the Council; there is nothing in the constitution of the Council to prevent this. The Council has a Chairman and a Vice-Chairman. The Chairman belongs to the official side and the Vice-Chairman: to the staff side. There are four Secretaries for the Council. Each side appoints two of its members to act as Secretaries.

A Departmental Council has both sides—the official and the staff—represented on it. The official side consists normally of serving civil servants of senior rank in the department concerned, including its Establishment Officer. They are appointed by the Minister or by the Head of the Department. The Chairman is usually the Head of the Department, and the Secretary usually a member of the Establishment Division. The staff side is appointed in the first place by the associations represented in the Department which are called together for the purpose by the Head of the Department, and, like the National staff side, fills its own vacancies and decides how many seats are to be held from time to time by the different associations. Members include both the civil servants and association officials.

Proceedings

The ordinary meetings of the National Council, according to the Constitution, "shall be held as often as necessary and not less than once a quarter. A special meeting of the Council shall be called by the Chairman or the Vice-Chairman as required." In practice, however, the full National Council now rarely meets. Its business is transacted mainly by committees, and a great deal of it by personal contacts between the staff side and the leading members of the official side. An official side representative is in the chair at all council or committee meetings; in his absence another official side representative presides. The Vice-Chairman, belonging to the staff side, never presides. Questions discussed by Councils or Committees are not settled by vote; each side speaks formally as a whole. The official side is indivisible. It represents the Government, and the permanent Heads are merely the agency for the announcing of Government policy and discussing it with the staff side. The staff side is indivisible too.

So there can never be any vote on the Council. If the two sides disagree, decision cannot be reached within the Whitley mechanism. The decisions of the Council are arrived at by agreement between the two sides and have to be signed by the Chairman and the Vice-Chairman. They are, then, reported to the Cabinet, and with its consent become operative. The National staff side, however, meets regularly at least once a month, and has its own constitution and standing orders. Votes are taken at these meetings.

The position is similar in the case of Departmental Councils. Most Departments abandoned regular meetings of their full councils during the war, and although some resumed them afterwards, committees procedure is probably more usual at the present time. Most of the larger departments have branch, regional, local or office committees covering their staffs in particular towns or offices, for the discussion of purely domestic matters. They may or may not report all their proceedings to the main Department Council or to one of Its committees for ratification. Great importance is attached to these office committees, because they can do much to smooth out local difficulties and deal with the union grievances of the staff on the job. The aim of these committees is to get a basis for good team work.

Functions

The scope of National Council comprises all matters affecting the conditions of service of the staff. Its functions include the following:

(i) Provision of the best means for utilizing the ideas and experience of the staff.

(ii) Means for securing to the staff a greater share in and responsibility for the determination and observance of the conditions under which their duties are carried out.

(iii) Determination of the general principles governing conditions of service, e.g., recruitment, hours of work, promotion, discipline, tenure, remuneration and superannuation.

In the National Council, the discussion of promotion is restricted to the general! aspects of the matter and the principles upon which promotions in general should rest. In no circumstances can individual cases be taken into consideration.

It is open to the National Council to discuss the general principles underlying disciplinary action, but there can be no discussion of individual cases.

(iv) The encouragement of the further education of civil servants and their training in higher administration and organization.

(v) Improvement of office machinery and organization, and the provision of opportunities for the full consideration of suggestions by the staff on this subject,

(vi) Proposed legislation so far as it has a bearing upon the position of civil servants in relation to their employment.

There are, however, certain limitations on the scope of the functions of the Council as follows:

(i) The establishment of Whitley Councils cannot relieve the Government of any part of its responsibility to Parliament The Government cannot surrender its liberty of action in the exercise of its authority and the discharge of its responsibilities in the public interest. In the words of Douglas Houghton, "Agreements are not reached (in the National Whitley Council) and subsequently reported to Ministers. They are authorized by Ministers before they can be reached."

(ii) In practice, the staff sides do not attempt to discuss by Whitley machinery the pay or grading of the very highest posts in the Service. The Whitley Councils are concerned only with officers drawing up to $ 2,000 a year as salaries.

(iii) Whitleyism does not aim at superseding direct negotiations with the staff associations. In fact, questions of class or grade remuneration are more often dealt with by direct negotiations than by Whitley discussions. Nothing in the Whitley Council system precludes a Civil Service Association having direct negotiations with the Department or the Treasury on a matter which is exclusively of its own interest. But matters which are common to two Associations or more, or which cover the whole Service, or the whole of a Department, can only be dealt with through the Whitley Council.

(iv) The Councils have confined themselves largely to "bread-and-butter questions": they have not been agencies for authoritative staff co-operation in the great issues of administration; and they do not have an effective share in the management of the Civil Service. The Councils have not generally interested themselves in the bigger, non-economic problems of administration. Thus, matters like the policy on security measures and civil rights are Government's responsibility and beyond the jurisdiction of the Whitley Councils. What the latter can do, however, is to discuss the practical application of this policy within the framework of the Government directives.

(v) The Councils do not consider individual cases nor discuss the merits of particular cases. They can discuss only the principles underlying such cases.

The Civil Service Arbitration Tribunal

The Tribunal was set up nearly 35 years ago as the result of an agreement between the official and the staff sides. It consists of an independent Chairman, with one member drawn from a panel representing the Chancellor of the Exchequer and another member drawn from a panel representing Staff side of the National Whitley Council. The Chairman is an aged person, a distinguished lawyer. Other members are appointed by the Minister of Labour. At a hearing the Tribunal consists of the Chairman and one member drawn from each panel, with the right of the Chairman to give an umpire's award in the event of disagreement on the Tribunal. Arbitration is compulsory on three important conditions of service-pay—hours of work, and leave. All cases of disagreement on any of these three subjects may be referred to the Tribunal by either side of the National Council. The awards of the Tribunal are subject to the overriding power of Parliament to accept or reject any award, but this power of veto is not intended to be used except in the rarest cases.

Whitley Council at Work

The main feature of the working of the Whitley system is

the role of the informal. This role was well described by Douglas Houghton in his lecture at the Indian Institute of Public Administration on December 10, 1957: "To return to the day-to-day working of the Whitley Council, as I have said, most of the formalities have largely been dispensed with. There is a good deal of informal discussion and a good deal of putting cards on the table behind the scenes. The Chairman of the official side would never be in difficulties these days in sending for me or for the Secretary-General of the staff side, to say to us privately how matters stood on a particular claim. He might say—"I am just explaining to you beforehand the decision which has been reached so that you may think it over and come to our formal meeting prepared for the news I am giving you now." Sometimes we go to the official side equally informally and 'off the record' to prepare their minds or to give them information which is best given privately. During the negotiations on the Priestly Commission's Report, we had a great many informal consultations. In fact, we met every alternate day to get the job done. The official side had their own meetings; and, we too, on our side, had our own conferences. Then we had informal meetings together in the afternoon, or in the morning, so that at the formal meeting, which would be held the next day, we pretty well knew how each side stood; we did not have to waste a lot of time on 'shadow boxing'. When the official side made their statement, we had an idea what lay behind it and what room for manoeuvre there might be. The official side may say—"We cannot accept your proposals as they stand. It is not for us to suggest a compromise. If you press the matter and are able to modify your claim then we might be able to do business," The words 'to do business' are used very frequently in your informal contacts, because we all want to do business and we are trying to get the basis on which business can be done. We get no satisfaction out of discussion for discussion's sake. Sometimes things have to be put on the record because members want to know what has been said on their behalf, but the informal talk which goes on is strictly confidential and is a means of getting agreement. The record may merely recall the more formal side of the negotiations. There is nothing strange about that. Outside trade unions the employers adopt these 'off the record' methods too.

Another noteworthy feature is the anxiety of the official side to prove to the satisfaction of the staff that justice has been done. Thus, though the Councils are precluded from discussing individual cases, in practice, official side is prepared to go into the merits of individual cases solely out of a desire to satisfy staff representatives of the fair-mindedness of the decisions taken. Lastly, the staff side too has behaved with great responsibility and in a constructive and cooperative spirit. In the words of Houghton, "It is really a study in human relations in which each side has something to give, each side something to gain."

United States

In the United States, there is no machinery analogous to the Whitley Councils in England. No special institutional device has been created for the purpose of conducting negotiations between the Government and the employees. However, efforts have been made to strengthen employer-employee co-operation through other methods. For this purpose, representatives of organized employees' unions are requested to put forward their views regarding personal policies which are of general interest to employees for further consideration by officials. These policies and procedures are invariably published and made available to all employees and organized employee unions.

In practice, employee unions[8] are allowed to make recommendations and proposals regarding any policy regulation, administrative instruction, or practice affecting employment in the various concerns. Such recommendations are not easily overlooked by the employing agencies. Careful consideration is given to such proposals, and such action as necessary is taken after a full and fair consideration of the matter.

Regulations regarding employer-employee co-operation also state that consultation with employee groups should be conducted informally, and at a mutually convenient time, during regular working hours. The nature of the subject to be discussed has also to be stated beforehand.

The general practice is to consider only those proposals that have bearing on the group[9] of employees as a whole. This does not, however, rule out completely proposals involving an element of individual grievances. Even the existence of a grievance machinery is not to be considered an excuse for prohibiting issues in which individual interests are involved.

The members chosen to represent the interests of different categories of employees are chosen from organized employee groups in each category. It is also not known, however, for the department concerned, to require security clearance of any representative of an organized employee group. It is felt that for security reasons, such a clearance is necessary in cases dealing with information regarding records or details of agency operation, where it is against law to disclose such information to persons who are not so cleared.

Regarding appropriate unit for employee representation, it is generally stated that the ungraded employees shall be represented by class, craft, administrative division, subdivision or other appropriate employment unit of any bureau. Administration, agency, corporation, establishment or undertaking of the Department has the right to designate the organization which will represent all such employees for the purposes of this policy. Organization so designated is regarded as the representative for all of the employees concerned so long as written agreements establishing procedures for determining rates of pay, regulations of hours, working rules and the adjustment of differences of methods for promoting such joint activities as employee training, accident prevention and labour management co-operation, or schedules stipulating pay rates, working rules and regulations governing hours of employment, may be promulgated, without first granting individual employees affected a hearing, if requested to present their views concerning terms of such agreements.

It will be seen from the preceding paragraphs that the existing practice with regard to union-management relations in the Federal Service differs from those in the private industry. While the federal employees are prohibited by law from resorting to strikes against Government and are restricted in their right of association, to the extent that they cannot be members of an union, which advocates the right to strike, no such laws curb the freedom of the private sector employees. As regards union-management relations, it is left to each .agency to decide the type of relations that best suit their specific activities. For instance, the Tennessee Valley Authority and the Broneville Power Administration regularly consult and deal with employee unions on such matters as wages, lay-off, seniority grievances and working conditions. This formal procedure has not been adopted by all employers. It may be of interest to note here that in the United States of America, the House of Representatives also takes a keen interest in the matters. It takes pains to obtain the views of the unions concerning proposed personnel legislation. The same practice has been adopted by the Civil Service Commission also in the formulation of personnel programmes and policies.

The objectives of Government employee unions are to improve the pay and working conditions of federal employees and to further other employee interests (such as, retirement, overtime and leave laws). They are unlike the industrial union in one very important aspect, that is, they do not have the right to strike against the Government. This prohibition, as embodied in the Public Law 330, 84th Congress, states:

> "No person shall accept or hold office or employment in the Government of the United States or any agency thereof, including wholly-owned government corporations who:
>
> (1) advocates the overthrow of our constitutional form of government in the United States;
>
> (2) is a member of an organization that advocates the overthrow of our constitutional form of government in the United States knowing that such organization so advocates;
>
> (3) participates in any strike or asserts the right to strike against the Government of the United States or such agency; or
>
> (4) is a member of an organization of government employees that asserts the right to strike against the Government of the United States or such agency knowing that such organization asserts such rights."

The employee unions have devised various means for achieving their objectives. Some of these methods may be mentioned here:

(1) they may affect changes by petitioning Congress for the passage of new laws;

(2) they may appeal directly to the President or the heads of executive agencies; or

(3) they may publicize their views by means of union journals and by operating union schools.

There are several government unions for employees. The workers may join these unions. The Civil Service Commission has no official connection with these unions, but, as such organizations provide the only existing means of joint employee expression, they are very often consulted in connection with personnel proposals and problems.

India

It was the First Pay Commission (Varadachariar Commission), 1946, which was specifically asked to report on the machinery for negotiating and settling questions relating to conditions of service which may arise out of differences between Government and its employees. In its Report, submitted in 1947, the Commission indicated its general approach to the problem in these words: "Government must recognize the importance of convincing its employees that representation and grievance of the latter will receive due and immediate considerations. We lay particular emphasis on the point, because the evidence before us disclosed absolute distrust, not to say despair, on the part of most grades of public servants as to their ever receiving a fair response from Government to their representation." The Commission came to the conclusion that some machinery should be kept in operation to "secure co-operation, consultation, discussion and negotiation between the staff and the Government," and further that it was wrong to think that any thing in the nature of the Whitley system could not be usefully introduced in India. They, accordingly, recommended establishment of joint councils for Government employees, excluding those in Class I, on the lines of Whitley Councils. The Commission went further and enunciated four main principles based on what is called practical as well as authoritative opinion: (i) in the adjustment of differences between the State and its employees, the best source is to prevent such differences developing into a dispute; (ii) even when a question has developed into a dispute, it is desirable to secure its settlement by negotiation between the two sides; (iii) if, however, it becomes necessary to secure outside help it must rather be for the purpose of mediation and consultation than for adjudication; and finally, (iv) if all attempts at consultation fail, adjudication should be sought by voluntary settlement rather than by compulsory reference.[10]

A powerful plea was made by the Second Pay Commission (Jagannath Das Commission), too, for the setting up of an adequate negotiating machinery in the following words:

> "We, however, recognize that there is another and equally important aspect to the relationship between Government and its employees. The Government is, no doubt, free from the profit motive in the usual sense; and even in Government's industrial and commercial undertakings the profit motive is subordinated to wider considerations of the public interest. But the community's pressure to keep down taxes and the desire for economy in governmental expenditure may sometimes have the same effect as considerations of profit among private employers. Though divergently inspired, the ultimate result in both cases may be identical—resistance to reasonable demands for increased remuneration, or for improvement in conditions of service. The Central Government are increasingly undertaking business and industrial functions, which is another factor tending to blur, in the eyes of a considerable proportion of their employees, the distinction between the Government as an employer, and other employers. In the circumstances if a proposal that Government servants should give up the strike weapon is to have a just basis and is to secure reasoned acceptance by them, there should be set up an adequate machinery for negotiation, redress of grievances and settlement of disputes: and there should, further, be provision for arbitration to which recourse can be had, should a difference on question of remuneration or some other particularly important condition of service, such as, leave and hours of work, remain unresolved. It is only thus the government would be discharging the obligation towards their employees which they would be assuming by requiring them to give up the right to withhold their labour. If it is in the public interest that Government servants should not use a weapon which, in the hands of other employees, is an effective instrument

for securing fair remuneration and satisfactory conditions of employment, it is only just and right that the Government servants should have an alternate arrangement for securing equitable treatment. If strikes and demonstrations can be eliminated from the public service, and a fair treatment can be ensured to public servants through orderly processes, introduction of an adequate machinery for removal of grievances, including compulsory arbitration would not be an unreasonable price to pay."[11]

Staff Committees (Councils)

Despite the underlying note of urgency displayed in the Report of the First Pay Commission no action was taken for several full years in the direction of implementing its recommendation regarding the setting-up of joint councils, and the reason given was that in view of the impending changes in the structure of the Central Secretariat Services, it was premature to introduce such Councils. It was in 1954 that the matter was taken in hand by the Ministry of Home Affairs which sent round a circular In July 1954, urging all the Ministries to establish Staff Committees. Model instructions, approved by the Cabinet, indicating the constitution and nature of the Staff Committees, were also circulated along with the office memorandum. The Ministries were left free to make minor modifications which may be necessitated by special circumstances obtaining in their particular cases. Next step was taken in 1957 when the Home Ministry altered the name of Staff Committees to Staff Councils. In addition, welfare officers were attached to each ministry modelled on the British system. Their comprehensive functions were to include the organization of social activities, clubs, recreation centres, provision of facilities for indoor and outdoor sports, provision of canteens in offices, improvement in working conditions, including hygienic conditions, assistance to Government servants in regard to the contributory health scheme, assistance in relation to transport, housing, education of children, pensions, gratuity etc.

Each Ministry has now got two Staff Councils—a Senior Staff Council for Classes II and III employees and a Junior Staff Council for Class IV employees. Class I employees are excluded from this arrangement. This Senior Staff Council is composed of

Government nominees and the representatives of Section Officers, Assistants, Stenographers, Clerks, etc. The Ministry concerned nominates a few officers not below the rank of Under Secretary, and heads of attached offices or their nominees to represent the Administration. The number of persons to represent the official side is not fixed. In practice, 7 to 10 persons are represented on the official side. The staff representatives are elected directly by the staff, and are not nominated, as in England, by the staff associations. The representation on the staff side is on the basis of one for every twenty from different grades, i.e., Section Officers, Assistants, Stenographers and Clerks. These representatives were originally elected for a year, but since 1957, the term has been extended to two years. One difficulty that has been experienced in this respect is the possibility of imbalanced nature of the staff representation. Thus, it is quite possible for some Sections being over-represented and others being under-represented or even unrepresented. The Secretary or a Joint-Secretary of the Ministry is the Chairman of the Council. The Secretary of the Council is nominated by the Chairman in consultation with the staff representatives. The composition of the Junior Staff Council does not differ fundamentally from that of the Senior Staff Council. The Government is represented by officers of a rank not lower than that of Assistant, and the Chairman is a Deputy Secretary of the Ministry concerned. The staff representatives are directly elected from two groups of Class IV employees. The first group consists of *Daftaris* and Record Sorters, and the second group comprises Peons, *Jamadars, Farashes,* Sweepers, etc. Each group is permitted to elect an additional representative who must be a Government servant belonging to a higher class, but not holding a post above the rank of Section Officer. The provision is there to enable the staff to have a representative fit enough to put forth its points of view on the Council. Here again, the Chairman nominates the Secretary in consultation with the staff representatives.

Proceedings

The Council is required to meet at least once in three months; but, on a requisition by one-fifth of the staff representatives, the Chairman has to call a special meeting. The agenda for the meetings is prepared by the Secretary and is approved by the

Chairman. It is circulated to the members at least three days in advance of the meeting. Members, who wish to have any particular item included in the agenda, are required to inform the Secretary well in advance of the meeting. One-third of the members on the staff side forms a quorum. The Council can make a recommendation only if it is agreed to, by a majority of members, each side; and the Ministry concerned decides as to what action, if any, should be taken on a recommendation. The proceedings of the Council are submitted to the Minister, and his attention is particularly drawn to points of disagreement.

Functions

The model Constitution, setting up the Staff Committees (Councils), gives an impressive list of objects of these bodies, as follows:

(1) to consider suggestions for improving the standard of work;

(2) to provide to the members of the staff a machinery for making their point of view known to Government on matters affecting their conditions of service; and

(3) to provide means of personal contact between officers and staff with a view to developing cordial relations between them, and encouraging the staff to take keener interest in their work. As regards their functions, the model Constitution describes them as 'advisory bodies,' but they can discuss any matters relating to (i) the conditions under which the members of staff are required to work: (ii) general principles regulating the conditions of service; (iii) welfare of the staff; and (iv) improvement of efficiency and standard of work. The discussion on individual cases is completely excluded from the purview of these bodies.

Co-ordination Committee

A Co-ordination Committee consisting of three senior officers of the Ministries of Home Affairs, Finance and Works, Housing and Supply has been constituted recently to deal with matters which remain unresolved at meetings of the Staff Councils. It is for the Ministry, administratively concerned with a Staff

Council to decide what matters should be placed before this Committee. The criterion suggested by the Home Ministry is that any matters which cannot be disposed of by the Ministry itself without consulting other Ministries should be referred to the Co-ordination Committee.

Staff Councils at Work

In response to the persistent and repeated questioning by B. Shiva Rao, the Government placed on the table of the Rajya Sabha in December 1959, a tabular statement mentioning the number of meetings held, the recommendations made, both those accepted and those implemented, separately, by Staff Councils from the period of their establishment to the end of 1958, as follows:

Senior Staff Councils	
Number of meetings	205
Number of recommendations made	763
Number of recommendations accepted	604
Number of recommendations implemented	558
Junior Staff Councils	
Number of meetings	141
Number of recommendations made	447
Number of recommendations accepted	393
Number of recommendations implemented	372

As regards the individual Ministries, "in the Home Ministry, the sponsor of the whole scheme, there were 26 meetings, 103 recommendations were made, 63 were accepted and all of them were implemented. In the Health Ministry, 73 recommendations were made, of which 62 were accepted and all were implemented. That was the tabular statement placed on the table of the Rajya Sebha. The practice, judging from this statement, varied as between different Ministries. Taking all the branches of the Finance Ministry, there were 22 meetings of the Senior Staff Councils: 85 recommendations were made, 74 were accepted and 71 implemented. Food and Agriculture Ministry also did well. It had 22 meetings which made 154 recommendations, 115 were accepted and 106 implemented. At the bottom of the table comes the Defence Ministry. The Senior Staff Council held 15 meetings, made only three recommendations, but none was accepted or implemented."[12]

The above record looks quite impressive. Thus, out of 763 recommendations made by the Senior Staff Councils only 54 recommendations were not accepted and of these only 21 were not implemented. The Government, too, was satisfied with the working of these bodies. Replying to a question of B. Shiva Rao, the Home Minister stated in the Rajya Sabha in December, 1959: "The experience of the last 13 years has shown that the non-acceptance of the First Pay Commission's recommendation in regard to the negotiating machinery has done no harm to anyone." However, the Staff Committees (1954-1957) had failed to make any impact so much so that even their existence was known to only a few outsiders in 1957 at the time of the threatened strike of the Posts and Telegraphs Department. The Second Pay Commission reviewed the working of these Councils and found it unsatisfactory:

> "The evidence before us indicates that there is a great deal of dissatisfaction with the present position; the criticism of the existing machinery made on behalf of employees' organizations ranged generally on the fallowing lines: that the will was lacking on the part of the Government to accept 'the principles of joint consultation as an effective instrument for the prevention of disputes'; that even where the machinery was well conceived it was not being worked efficiently; that meetings were not being held regularly; that some of the officers did not have the right attitude towards the machinery which they were supposed to work. Some of the employees' associations referred with regret to the effect that the Varadachariar Commission's recommendations in this matter had not been accepted by the Government and in proposing that the present situation required the establishment of machinery which fully in spirit and largely in form followed the Whitley machinery in the U. K., they appeared to us to represent the general feeling amongst employees' organizations. Some of the staff associations in fact wanted a great deal more participation of the staff in management and administrative processes, including a voice in promotions and disciplinary cases. A great deal of support for permanent machinery for consultation, negotiation and settlement of disputes has some witnesses also and there are in fact few dissentients."

A study of the working of the Staff Councils reveals the following limitations in their working:

(1) Though the recommendations of the Council have been accepted in a large number of cases, these cases have been comparatively of minor interest. Thus, the Councils have been successful in improving the conditions of work within the office. For example, arrangements have been made, at their instance, to provide cold drinking water in summer; canteen facilities have been improved, facilities for medical help have been bettered by way of more dispensaries and providing first-aid boxes in Ministries, etc. Other recommendations implemented dealt with matters like transport facilities, grant of leave, office uniforms, etc. However, the Councils have failed to make any impact on matters like classification of posts, preparation of seniority list and promotions. Most of the questions regarding promotion, recruitment, hours of work, tenure and remuneration are still to be determined at the Government level; the employees are merely permitted to discuss them.

(2) The attitude of the officers has not been conducive to the development of the Whitley spirit. A psychological hiatus still separates the two sides. The officers are prone to adopt a condescending attitude and the staff side, not unoften, lacks a capacity to participate in discussions freely.

(3) Staff Council meetings are not held regularly.

(4) The recommendations of the Councils are not attended to promptly.

In brief, though modelled on the British Whitley system, the Staff Councils lack the form and the spirit of Whitleyism. Thus, at present Staff Councils are just individual entities in different Ministries lacking a national organization like that of the National Whitley Council in Britain, The Co-ordinating Committee is only a clearing house of conflicting views of several Ministries. Again, the Staff Associations are not represented on the Councils; while in Britain much of the success of Whitleyism is due to the close link existing between the Councils and the Staff Associations.

As regards the spirit animating the official side, the Second Pay Commission has pointedly referred to the lack of the will on the part of the Government to accept the principle of joint consultation as an effective instrument for prevention of disputes.

The Commission has made the following suggestions to improve the working of the Councils:

(1) The establishment of a Central Joint Council to cover both the industrial and non-industrial civil service.

(2) The setting-up of compulsory arbitration tribunals to deal with matters, like pay, hours of work, leave, etc.

(3) The Ministry of Labour should be closely associated with important matters concerning staff relations.

JOINT CONSULTATIVE MACHINERY

On October 10, 1960, the Government of India published a scheme to bring the Staff Councils in line with the Whitley Councils. The main features of the scheme are as follows: A three-tier machinery is proposed to be set up consisting of Local or Regional Councils, Departmental Councils, and the National Council. The Local or Regional Councils shall deal with matters pertaining to all Government offices in the particular region, The Development Councils shall deal with matters concerning a particular department, and each Ministry shall have a council. The National Council shall consider the matters relating to the working conditions of the employees with special reference to schemes for their general welfare. There will be an Arbitration Committee consisting of one representative each of the Government and the employees. The members are to be chosen from a panel of five names submitted by the two parties. Any dispute, which the National Council is not able to settle, will be referred to the Committee. In September 1963, the Government announced its decision to establish these bodies on a non-statutory basis on the condition that the employees' organizations abjure strike. The scheme covers all regular civil employees of the Central Government, non-industrial and industrial, except Class I Services, Class II Services other than the Central Secretariat Services, and other comparable Services whose duties are mainly ministerial, and the managerial, administrative and supervisory staff in the industrial establishments. The police and railway protection force have also been excluded. The scheme for Joint Consultative Machinery and Compulsory Arbitration for Central Government employees was inaugurated in October 1966. Its objectives are: (i) To promote harmonious relations between the Government and its employees, (ii) to secure co-operation between the Government and the general body of its employees in matters of common concern, and (iii) to increase the efficiency of the public service.

The Joint Consultative Machinery (J.C.M.) discusses matters relating to conditions of service and work, welfare of the employees and improvement of efficiency and standards of work and general principles in regard to recruitment, promotion and discipline. It is strictly precluded from discussing individual cases. It consists of the National Council, the Departmental Councils, and the Regional and/or Office Councils. The Joint Consultative Machinery is a three-tiered one, but each tier is completely independent of others in its composition as well as in functioning.

The Joint Consultative Machinery includes all civil servants except, (i) Class I (now called Grade A) Services, (ii) Class II (i.e., Grade B) Services other than the Central Secretariat Service, (iii) persons in industrial establishments employed mainly in managerial or administrative capacity and those employed in supervisory capacity, (iv) employees of Union Territories, and (v) police personnel.

The National Council

The National Council is the apex level body consisting of the official side and the staff side. The Cabinet Secretary is the Chairman of the National Council. The official side consists of 25 Members who are appointed by the Central Government. The staff side has a maximum membership of 60 who are nominated by the recognized Staff Associations, the distribution of seats being fixed by the Chairman of the Council in consultation with them. The staff side elects a Leader from among its members.

The National Council deals with matters generally affecting the government employees, such as, minimum remuneration, dearness allowance and pay to certain common categories, for instance, office clerks, peons and the lower grades of workshop staff and matters relating to categories of staff common to two or more departments and not grouped together in a single Departmental Council. The National Council does not deal with matters of interest to employees of a single department.

The Council holds meetings atleast once in 4 months. A matter once disposed of by it cannot be taken up for discussion during the following 12 months.

The Departmental Council

The Joint Consultative Machinery Scheme provides for a Departmental Council for each department, but there can be a single Council also for 2 or more small departments under a Ministry. The Department of Personnel and Administrative Reforms has a Council to deal with the matters affecting the personnel of the Central Secretariat Services. The Departmental Councils are concerned with the problems of employees who are working in a Ministry/Department and the subordinate and attached offices of the Department. The Secretary of the Ministry concerned represents the official side and is the Chairman of the Departmental Council. The official side is nominated by the Government and may not have more than 10 members. The staff side has membership ranging between 20 and 30, the exact number depending upon the total strength of the staff and the number of grades and services in the department. The staff side is elected by the staff associations for a term of 3 years. A Departmental Council may meet not less than once in 3 or 4 months.

Regional and/or Office Councils

Such Councils deal with only regional or local matters relating to condition of work, welfare, improvement of efficiency and standards of work, and are set up only where the structure of a department permits such a course. The Office Council consists of not more than 5 members on the official side and 8 members on the staff side.

It should be pointed out that these various tiers are distinct and separate ones with no formally designed links between them. They are in no way hierarchically integrated bodies and thus, do not impinge on the concept of ministerial responsibility, which is a hallmark of the parliamentary system of government.

The Joint Consultative Machinery Scheme provides for compulsory arbitration in the event of a disagreement between the two sides. But the compulsory arbitration is limited to, (i) pay and allowances, (ii) weekly hours of work, and (iii) leave of a class or grade of employees.

Conclusion

The Joint Consultative Machinery has not been very effective in India. The essence of Whitleyism lies in an enduring spirit of give and take, and it is this spirit which is lacking in the machinery of joint consultation in India. The Government has not always taken the staff side into confidence with the result that unimportant matters are seen to crowd the agenda of the Councils whereas momentous subjects get excluded from discussion. Nor is the staff side serious and responsible enough in making its demands. The Councils meet irregularly and the agenda for discussions is compiled in a somewhat casual way. The Joint Consultative Machinery scheme has not been fully implemented; so far only 14 Departmental Councils have been set up whereas the Government had promised to establish 21 such bodies. Moreover, the present machinery does not seek to redress the grievances of what are called 'officers"—the incumbents of Grade A and Grade B. The Machinery for Joint Consultation suffered the greatest set-back during the internal emergency (June 25, 1975 to March 23, 1977); it merely existed as a show-piece. Its low effectiveness may be gauged from the fact that since the JCM's inception in 1966 the National Council has met only 27 times. Its last meeting was held in 1980.[13]

NOTES

1. Section 6 (c) of the Act states: "An employee has the right, without interference, coercion, restraint and fear of discrimination or reprisal, to be member of or refrain from being member of, any lawful group, organization, union, or association; and no employee, and no one seeking employment, shall be required, as a condition of employment, transfer, promotion, or retention in the service, to be a member of, or to refrain from being a member of, any lawful employee group, organization, union or association, except that agencies, whose functional programmes are concerned with labour relations, may refuse to recognize unions, which are affiliated with

organizations involved in controversies with which any such agencies deal."

2. *Second Pay Commission*, p. 540.
3. Staff Councils and Associations in the U.K. and India, New Delhi, Indian Institute of Public Administration, 1960, p. 36.
4. "Whitley Councils in the British Civil Service", a lecture delivered by Douglas Houghton, M.P., Chairman, Staff Side, National Whitley Council, Great Britain, on 10th December, 1957.
5. *Second Pay Commission*, p. 541, para 15.
6. Vide, Maheshwari, S.R., *The Administrative Reforms Commission*, Agra, Lakshmi Narain Agrawal, 1972, pp. 119-20.
7. Quoted in Maheshwari, S. R., *op. cit.*, p. 120.
8. It is an organization which provides representation for members who are employed within the service, in consultation with management, on matters pertinent to their employment.
9. Group proposals include recommendations, or complaints made by organized employee groups involving policy, practice or procedure affecting employees on such subjects as working conditions, safety in service, training, employee management, co-operation, methods of appeals, methods of adjustments of grievances, terms of duty, rates of pay, granting of leave, promotion, demotion, removal and reduction in force.
10. Shiva Rao, B., *op. cit.*, pp. 22-23.
11. *Second Pay Commission*, pp. 541-42.
12. Shiva Rao, *op. cit.*, pp. 27-28.
13. *Annual Report of the Department of Personnel and Administrative Reforms, 1981-82*, pp. 53-54.

8

Minister-Secretary Relationship in India

The system of Government prevalent in India postulates a Minister, who is a part of the legislature, at the top of, and holding command over, a body of permanent professional civil servants whose administrative head is the Secretary. It is based on a combination of the lay politician and a politically neutral, permanent civil service. This system is different from that obtaining in the United States. In U.S.A. the political head of a department does not hold a seat in the Congress but is a nominee of the President, staying in his office at the pleasure of the latter; and there is no civil servant corresponding to the Secretary in India.

The relationship between the Minister and the Secretary is of critical importance to the effective functioning of the machinery of Government. There has not yet fully developed a body of well-crystallized conventions to inform this relationship. The Minister is a professional politician who comes to his office with a knowledge of what people expect from the Government and what they 'would not stand'. He comes and goes, depending on the fluctuations of party fortunes. He has to his credit legislative experience and, may be, some governmental experience. The Secretary, on the other hand, is a permanent civil servant possessing wide administrative experience. Each lacks what is best in the other and, therefore, supplements the other. When, however, one over-steps, or does not interpret his role properly, friction, misunderstanding and disharmony are in store, obstructing the speed of administration.

Policy and Administration

The Minister lays down the policy and it is the duty of the Secretary to implement it in all earnestness. Even when he gives the decision orally, the Secretary must record it briefly but concisely to remove any room for ambiguity or confusion. A policy can be formulated only on the basis of relevant information and data. This is made available by the Secretary. The Secretary is the principal adviser to his Minister and this advice he must tender without fear or favour. The Secretary should keep his Minister fully informed of all important developments in the sphere of his responsibility and should show sensitiveness to Minister's political and parliamentary responsibilities which are no less onerous.

It is, however, not possible to separate policy from administration. Both are in practice intermingled. A close and intimate relationship must, therefore, exist between the Minister and his Secretary for the optimal efficiency of the Ministry. The Minister must have complete trust and confidence in his Secretary and the latter must fully cooperate with his Minister and should respect his views and share his anxieties. As the Minister is accountable to Parliament, the Secretary must always bear in mind that he is only his adviser, the ultimate authority to take decision on policies must necessarily be the Minister's.

As the Minister is a professional politician, he carries, necessarily, a combination of popular, political and parliamentary responsibilities which he can afford to neglect only at the risk of eclipsing his political career. Among the multitudinous duties of the Secretary lies that of seeing that his Minister retains a favourable public image outside.

As the Minister has to decide on policies, he must be clear in his own mind about what he wants to achieve during the period at his disposal and what is his scheme of priority. He must know or soon make up his mind on all important issues, concerning his Ministry. As Herbert Morrison has aptly said:

> "Indeed, it is my general experience that if the Minister in charge knows what he wants and is intelligent in going about it, he can command the understanding co-operation and support of his civil servants. The kind of Minister who is most tiring to the officers of a department is the Minister who

does not know his own mind and cannot make it up. If the policy of a department is hazy, vacillating and ineffective, it is, after all, the responsibility of the Minister; it is quite as likely to be his fault as that of his civil servants".[1]

Also, a weak Minister who easily gives way to his officers' views and wishes is no good prospect. Herbert Morrison remarks:

> "A great many points of policy will be initiated by civil servants, who should not be discouraged from expressing their views frankly. But in addition to being the man who decides questions put before him, the Minister should be an initiator of policy and action; for example, by addressing minutes to the permanent Secretary or the parliamentary Secretary calling for factual information, by requiring consideration of and reports on particular questions, or by giving directions. Clearly, it is desirable that he should be intelligent, responsible and selective and not throw paper about merely for the fun of the thing or out of a mere sense of self-importance; but also it is desirable that the department should be conscious of the presence of a live personality at the head of its affairs, and that he is the active master of the department and not a sleeping partner. In my experience our civil service generally prefers a Minister with a mind of his own to a mere rubber stamp."[2]

Earl Attlee, the ex-Prime Minister of Britain, holds a similar view. "In my opinion, they (the civil servants) prefer a 'difficult' Minister to one who is of no account. They like to have someone who will put up a fight, someone in whom they can have some pride."[3]

Qualities of a Minister

A Minister must be a good learner; he must acquire a deep, if not complete, understanding and knowledge of the subject under his charge. He needs constantly remind himself that there are no substitutes or short cuts to industry and application. Indeed, he should be made up of a strong moral, mental and physical stuff, and be farsighted without becoming a mere visionary, firm without looking obstinate, temperate without being devoid of moral sensitivity. These qualities he should adroitly employ as P.M. Morarji Desai observed, 'to warn, to comfort and to command'. "Obviously, the warning has to be again the consequences of failure of duty. The comfort has to be in terms of the hard lot of administrative existence, namely lack of appreciation on the part of those for whose welfare administration exists. The word of command has to be as befits the head of a vast organization through words and policies which will carry instinctive or instant or deliberate obedience, as the case may be."[4]

Nor should the Minister try to look omniscient or appear arrogant and uncommunicative. He should cultivate the habit of meeting the senior civil servants regularly and encourage frankness in discussions. He should be a profound listener. He is likely to obtain the best out of the civil service if the latter has a feeling that it gets a fair deal at the hands of the Minister and has a participatory role in policy-making. Of course, the Minister should not allow the discussions to continue interminably; he must, after listening to all concerned, arrive at a decision. Sardar Patel followed this practice which paid back so fabulously. N.V. Gadgil who himself was a Minister in the first cabinet of Free India recalls:

> "Vallabhbhai (i.e., Sardar Patel) was watchful regarding the State of affairs in the Government. He used to invite the secertaries of the various departments to tea or dinner almost every week by turns, listen to their problems and difficulties, and advise and guide them. The civil servants were greatly encouraged by this and worked with greater self-confidence. The Cabinet had introduced the innovation of referring difficult problems to committees of the secretaries of the Ministries. This too has encouraged the civil servants who considered the problems with enthusiasm and offered their suggestions. This innovation was entirely Vallabhbhai's."[5]

It is appropriate to quote Sir Warren Fisher, who, with enviable conciseness and lucidity, defined the Minister Secretary relationship in his evidence before the Tomlin Commission on the Civil Service (1929-31) in Britain:

> Determination of policy is the function of Minister and once a policy is determined it is the unquestioned and unquestionable business of the civil servant to strive to carry out that policy with precisely the same energy and precisely

the same goodwill whether he agrees with it or not. That is axiomatic and will never be in dispute. At the same time it is the traditional duty of civil servants, while decisions are being formulated, to make available to their political chief all the information and experience at their disposal, and to do this without fear or favour, irrespective of whether the advice thus tendered may accord or not with the Minister's initial view. The presentation to the Minister of relevant facts, the ascertainment and marshalling of which may often call into play the whole organisation of a department, demands of the civil servant the greatest care. The presentation of inferences from the facts equally demands from him all the wisdom and all the detachment he can command.

The preservation of integrity, fearlessness, and independence of thought and utterance in their private communion with Ministers of the experienced officials selected to fill the top posts in the service is an essential principle in enlightened Government; as whether or not Ministers accept the advice thus frankly placed at their disposal, and acceptance or rejection of such advice is exclusively a matter for their judgment—it enables them to be assured that their decisions are reached only after the relevant facts and the various considerations have, so far as the machinery of Government can secure, been definitely brought before their minds.[6]

Intangible Elements

It would be appreciated that the relationship between the Minister and his Secretary depends essentially on such intangible elements as trust, confidence, understanding etc. By its very nature it cannot be completely reduced to writing. In a very real sense it is like the relationship subsisting between husband and wife—close, intimate, personal, even psychic.

This is easier said than practised. The advice given to the Minister today is not that which is in the best interest of the country but very often one which the Minister may like. The Secretary quite often anticipates his minister's wishes and trims his sails to every wind that blows and treads on the primrose path of convenience. This has occurred notwithstanding the fact that the Secretary is regarded as the Secretary to the Government as a whole, not to his Minister alone. Slowly but steadily, the objectivity has been giving place to palatability at the hands of a civil service which enjoys the unparalleled distinction of protection by the Constitution itself. The game was started by a top few—perhaps, at Delhi—but soon all levels seem to have mastered it. This happens when careerism becomes an obsession with the civil service. As the Administrative Reforms Commission observes:

> "There is a disinclination among quite a number of Ministers to welcome frank and impartial advice from the Secretary or his aids and an inclination to judge him by his willingness to do what they wish him to do. Instances are not wanting of Ministers preferring a 'convenient subordinate to a strong one and thereby making the latter not only ineffective but a sulky and unwilling worker. This has also bred a tendency on the part of an increasing number of civil servants to attempt to anticipate the minister's wishes and proffer their advice accordingly. A further development of this unhealthy trend is the emergence of personal affiliations leading to an element of 'politicalisation' among the civil servants. All these cut at the root of the healthy relationship. . . . The Prime Minister should take special interest to curb this tendency with the assistance of the Cabinet Secretary and the central personnel agency,"[7]

The Minister often oversteps his legitimate function of laying down policies and starts interesting himself in tasks of day-today administration, thus undermining the sense of initiative and independence of the civil service. A Minister should confine himself to his role of a policy-maker and leave implementation of policy and day-to-day administration to his civil servants. But a popularly elected Minister who has necessarily an eye on the-net election is under pressure from several quarters and may desire a particular course of action on a certain issue—often, without being aware of its full repercussions. It is the duty of the civil servant to apprise him of the consequences that would flow from his contemplated action. The Minister is, after all, a reasonable human being and may be convinced about the harmful results of his proposal. If he remains adamant and the civil servant thinks the contemplated course of action to be detrimental to public interest, he must put down his views in writing and wait for and abide by the Minister's decision. The civil service must appreciate that it is not for nothing that the nation has, through its Constitution, conferred on its bureaucracy a charter of privileges. This has been done to reinforce the sense of independence and fairness of the civil service and such are the occasions when these qualities are tested and the founding fathers hopes vindicated. Although privately the civil servants dub such ministerial moves as 'interferences' many of them, today, vie with each other in gladly acquiescing in such demands; this is considered to be the royal road to promotions and other recognitions.

Such a deep-seated reluctance to offer advice without fear to favour has gradually sunk down to all levels in the administration. Those who prize frank advice from their subordinates are not many, and those who have the courage and frankness to proffer advice are still fewer. This is a new, discouraging phenomenon, not known to the pre-Independence administration. A.D. Gorwala reveals, in his own characteristic style, a glimpse of the earlier period when advice was frankly given as well as sought:

> "It was a great merit of Government in this period and of Government under the same Constitution even later that it neither punished frank expression of opinion from its officers nor even resented it. When for instance a commissioner had, after expressing his views in writing about the transfer of a particular officer seconded for a time to another department, discussed the matter with the Governor and obtained his consent and the file had been passed down through the Secretary to the other Secretary concerned, it did not arouse resentment when the other Secretary resubmitted the file asking for further consideration and in noting said that it seemed to him that in not allowing this transfer which he had originally mooted, every interest had been considered except the public interest. Again it was quite possible for a Governor to say smilingly to a Secretary who had elaborated greatly on the immorality of a course of conduct proposed to the Governor by even higher authorities than himself. "I have read with interest your convocation address. I will pass it on. It should have its effect." So too an adviser who had set his

mind firmly upon a particular course of action would still ask for his subordinates,' view, or if he did not ask, would be prepared to consider views put to him. One, a very strong, decisive and able individual, whose grasp of principles was exceeded only by his knowledge of, and ability to go into, details, on a certain occasion outlined to his principal officer what he obviously considered a really brilliant plan to meet a dangerous and emergent situation. Having listened to it at length, the officer said: "It can't be done". "What do you mean?" said the adviser, quite annoyed. "I've worked it out in detail. Of course it can be done", said the officer looking at him gravely: "Physically, of course, Sir, it can be done. What I mean when I say it can't be done is that it would be wrong to do it". He then proceeded to explain briefly why it would be wrong. Though still red in the face, the adviser listened attentively. He then dropped off into a brown study and for several minutes so complete a silence engulfed the room that one could clearly hear the ticking of the small clock on the table. Suddenly he said: "Yes, you are right. It would be wrong. I have very nearly set my heart on it but we won't do it". This then was the measure of some of the men who held power. Is it any wonder that they were well-served."[8]

After the Fourth General Election

The advent of the coalition governments in several States as an aftermath of the fourth general election (1967) has imparted a new twist to the relationship between the Minister and his Secretary. A Minister in a coalition government remains seized with insecurity; he is only too anxious to strengthen his power and position *vis-a-vis* other Ministers, to make secure the position of his political party *vis-a-vis* other parties represents in the coalition government as well as of the coalition government itself. With the triple aim in mind, he is inclined to take recourse to measures which may bring cheap, short-term popularity but which may be fraught with dangerous consequences. Confronted with the prospect of changing loyalties of legislators and parties, the coalition government, instead of discouraging the individual Ministers in such ultimately harmful exercises, encourages and even initiates such moves. In such a situation, a Minister who is politically strong and secure stands, in the matter of his relationship with the Secretary, on a different footing from one who is politically more vulnerable and may be mere fleeting phantom. The latter's experience of his Secretary (as well as of the bureaucracy) is likely to be one of occasional indifference and obstruction on the part of his Secretary. A politically strong Minister may face no such problems. But the very fact that the coalition government lacks stability does render the bureaucracy unusually powerful in the parliamentary system of government.

Since the Minister is accountable to Parliament, should he enjoy the freedom of choosing his Secretary. A Minister inherits his Secretary: he does not appoint him, although departures from this practice have been too frequent. N.V. Gadgil, while narrating his reminiscences as a Minister, observed: "I found, that, like the singer asking for a particular *tabalchi,* some Ministers insisted on having a particular Secretary."[9] A Secretary is assumed to serve any Minister with equal competence, zeal and loyalty. There are, however, a few instances when a certain Minister does not find his Secretary co-operative enough and asks for his replacement. A decision on change of the secretary is taken by the Prime Minister who is head of the Council of Ministers. The question was forced to the surface in 1966 when Gulzari Lal Nanda, the Home Minister, had twice asked the Prime Minister for the Removal of the Home Secretary and was vetoed on both the occasions. It may be appropriate here to quote from the letter that he later wrote to the Prime Minister:

> Throughout these eight or nine months I have pleaded time and again that I may be allowed to strengthen the political wing of the Ministry. On a number of occasions I brought to your notice that I was not getting adequate secretarial assistance. I wanted the setup to be suitably strengthened. All these appeals were ignored. . . I had asked my secretary to let me have the papers regarding the instructions about processions not being permitted within a two-mile radius immediately after the informal meeting of the Cabinet had discussed the subject. Would you believe that the paper actually came to me only today? He has taken one full month to discover that no instructions as stated by Mr. Patil do in fact exist. Is it going to be suggested that the omissions of a Secretary, whom I had desired to change, should be foisted

upon my head?"[10]

The Prime Minister did not concede to the right of a Minister to have his Secretary changed. "It was not always possible to accommodate Ministers in this matter", she said.[11] On another occasion, she observed: "As far as the appointment of the Secretary is concerned that is a departmental affair. There is a special Appointments Committee of the Cabinet which goes into the matter."[12]

Such an attitude is neither helpful nor constructive. As Parliament holds the Minister accountabie, he may be given the freedom of relieving himself of a Secretary with whom he finds it difficult to work. This does not imply that the Minister should have an unfettered freedom of getting a Secretary of his choice. There should be prepared a panel of names eligible for secretaryship in Government and a minister's choice must, as a rule, be limited only to this panel. It is very likely that a Minister himself may not have to change his secretary frequently for the fear of inviting public criticism.

History of Minister-Secretary relationship

Historically, the politician-minister made his advent in the machinery of Government for the first time in 1921, when the Montagu Chelmsford Reforms of 1919 throwing upon a limited sphere of provincial administration to the popularly elected minister were inaugurated, For the first time in 1921 (when the Government of India Act of 1919 was enforced) in the administrative history of this country, the Secretary was called upon to work under a lay Minister. The experiment in Minister-Secretary relationship did not go off entirely without friction and conflict. Many of the Ministers later complained before the Reforms Enquiry Committee (1924) about lack of co-operation on the part of the Secretary. Even L.W. Rushbrook Williams had to admit that "despite the general harmony which seems to have characterized the relation between the Ministers and the permanent officials of the departments under their control, the position has not been free from difficulty: and there is reason to believe that some Ministers have considered themselves unduly fettered."[13] It is to be noted that C.Y. Chintamani, who was holding the portfolio of education in the United Provinces resigned on the issue of having been bypassed in a certain matter which, instead, was communicated directly to the Governor.

Consequent upon the passing of the Government of India Act, 1935, which envisaged, in the provinces, a nearly complete, and at the Centre, a measure of, responsible government, the question of the Minister-Secretary relationship again came to the fore—and more prominently. The introduction of the responsible government under this Act directly affected the functions and status of the Secretary in three ways. The Minister, who was to be from the public life of the country, might not possess governmental experience and besides, would certainly be called upon to devote a sizeable part of his time to political, parliamentary and public duties. Secondly, the Minister was liable to change from time to time and, certainly, more frequently than the members of the Governor-General's Council. Thirdly, the machinery of public administration which was the instrument for execution of the government's policy was to have a separate and continuous existence of its own. The minister's accountability to the legislature implied, as its essential counterpart, the undivided responsibility of the Secretary of the Ministry to the Minister. This was vital both for departmental efficiency and discipline. The Committee on Organization and Procedure set up, in 1937, under the chairmanship of R.M. Maxwell, examined, *inter alia,* the question of proper relationship between the Minister and the Secretary. It pointed out that the Minister had a right to expect advice based on the widest administrative experience available in the department, and, further more, the Secretary was the only officer in the department qualified by experience to give such advice. The Minister, who was naturally not in a position to attend to the day-to-day business of administration, expected administration to be efficiently carried on. This was impossible to ensure if the control of the department under the Minister was divided. The Secretary was the sole administrative head of the department under the Minister, responsible to him for the implementation of the ministerial policy, and the final adviser of the Minister on all administrative questions within the department's purview. The Committee held that the Minister had the freedom to consult experts or other departmental officers on technical or even administrative questions but, all the same, the Secretary was to be invariably associated with such consultations, and, what is more, the final decision on matters thus discussed should not be taken without giving the Secretary an opportunity of expressing his views. The Committee wrote:

> "Apart from the general considerations which we have already urged in favour of this practice, we feel that its adoption is essential if the Secretary is to discharge his statutory responsibility of bringing to the notice of the Minister concerned and of the Governor-General any matter appertaining to his department which involves or appears likely to involve any special responsibility of the Governor-General."[14]

In view of the political, parliamentary and public preoccupations of the Minister the Committee recommended that matters of only major importance should be referred to the Minister for his decisions. With this in mind, it suggested the following classes of business to be submitted to the Minister:

1. Cabinet business, that is, business which, under the rules, must be brought before the Cabinet or about which the Minister may wish to consult the Cabinet.
2. Business which is likely to have political repercussions.
3. Parliamentary business.
4. Patronage.
5. Any other class of business which, in the opinion of the Secretary, is of sufficient importance to be submitted to the Minister.

The Maxwell Committee laid particular stress on the need for giving the Secretary enough discretion and freedom in transacting day-to-day business of administration:

> "Unless Ministers wish *all* business to be put up to them for orders in which case they will either be overwhelmed or the disposal of business will be liable to be very much delayed, they must leave to someone else the responsibility for determining what business out side the specified categories should come up to them and that responsibility can obviously be entrusted only to the Secretary as administrative head of his department. As we contemplate the Secretary should be in close personal touch with the Minister and should keep

him informed orally of everything of importance that may be going on in the department, there is no reason why the arrangement proposed by us should not function satisfactorily and without detriment either to the responsibility of the Minister to his colleagues or to the collective responsibility of the Cabinet."[15]

It concluded:

"We are emphatically of the opinion that the machinery of administration will not function smoothly unless the relations between a Minister, who will be the political head of his department and the Secretary, who will be the chief of his staff for administrative purposes, are relations of mutual confidence and trust."[16]

The intransigence of some of the civil servants has been occasionally forced to the surface in the course of the onward march of representative Government in India. It must be stated that, at least during the early days of independence, some of these officers had entertained somewhat strange views about their own position in the emergent administrative set-up and found it rather difficult to act in complete harmony and cooperation with the political element in the Government *viz* Ministers. Sri Prakasa, the former Indian High Commissioner in Pakistan, recalls the difficulties he had encountered in getting his instructions implemented by an Indian Civil Service officer who was his deputy in the High Commission. He finding consolation in a similar discomfiture experienced by even Jawaharlal Nehru, writes:

"It would be interesting to recall that even the Prime Minister had his own sad experience. He told me, when comparing notes about the time, that high ranking Indian Civil Service officers thought that Government should be run according to their own directions, and that he himself had difficult times keeping them in check and getting his policies implemented. When he had to encounter such opposition, the position of small folks like myself can well be appreciated."[17]

After Independence

In independent India, an open rift between the Minister—T.T. Krishnamachari—and the principal finance secretary— H.M.

Patel—occurred for the first time in 1957. The subject under issue was the purchase of shares of certain private companies by the nationalized Life Insurance Corporation. According to the Minister, the principal Finance Secretary only 'casually' mentioned to him about the purchase of these shares whereas the Secretary maintained that he had been acting all along with the knowledge and approval of the Minister.[18] About the mode of consultation with the Minister, the Vivian Bose Board of Inquiry, which was appointed by the Government to examine the propriety of this deal, observed, "And about that, all we can say is that if that is Mr. Patel's way of briefing his Minister on a grave issue that requires a high level decision of policy, he is very much to blame; and from the Minister's point of view, we cannot blame him if he thought, as he says, he did that this was just casual information about the Life Insurance Corporation which did not require any decision from him". The upshot of this episode was that the Minister, on grounds of constitutional responsibility of the Minister for any actions of the civil servants, resigned from his office, and the Secretary, too, preferred retirement from government service, although he had been eventually exonerated of all charges.

In 1966 the Minister-Secretary relationship again attracted widespread publicity when Gulzari Lal Nanda, the Home Minister, complained of non-cooperation by the Home Secretary L.P. Singh and sought his replacement. ". . . Denied the kind of assistance and cooperation I needed from a civil service not setup in tune with my ideas, I was made to feel that I had no say in the making of decisions at policy-making level Have you (i.e. the Prime Minister) ever thought to yourself how I was expected to function with the kind of tools you gave me to work with"? he complained to the unobliging Prime Minister.[19] The controversy ended with the Minister resigning from his office the Secretary remaining in position.

A significant dimension to the Minister-Secretary relation ship was added in 1969 when a Deputy Minister of the Central Government felt 'hurt' by certain remarks made by the Secretary of the Ministry. Although this quarrel did not remain an entirely internal affair of the Ministry, when the Deputy Minister threatened to resign, it was hushed up with the characteristic

Indian habit of not directly and courageously facing an unpleasant problem and of devising a solution in accord with the supreme commitments. When this incident was discussed in the Lok Sabha, the Deputy Minister said that the Secretary addressed him 'in a hard tone' and in a 'very objectionable manner.[20] Later clarifying the matter, the Cabinet Minister in charge of the concerned Ministry, told Rajya Sabha, "On 16 April, I had before me a file of the Defense Ministry which had been sent for legal advice. I commented adversely on the procedure adopted by the Deputy Minister with respect to that case. I recorded a note to that effect on the file in the presence of the Deputy Minister. The Law Secretary agreed with my view. In the discussion that took place the Law Secretary raised his voice perhaps to emphasise his point. . . . This appeared to have hurt the feelings of the Deputy Minister . . . I asked the Law Secretary to make amends by expressing regret. He did so in my presence and the Deputy Minister said that he was satisfied with his expression of regret. He told the Law Secretary and me that the matter may be taken as closed!"[21] The curtain finally fell on this incident without anyone—the Deputy Minister or the Secretary—losing his head and without the genera] public emerging any wiser with regard to the larger issue of proper relationship.

The special position of the Secretary had already stood clearly recognised in the Gulzari Lal Nanda case. The Secretary losing his post because of an incident with a Deputy Minister was, therefore, quite out of the question[22] this time. This incident highlighted the unenviable position of a Deputy Minister in the administrative set-up. Even at the best of times, a Deputy Minister is a bird beating its not so luminous wings in the void, as it were. He has little by way of formal authority and status which may assert his distinctive position in the Ministry. He has to remain content with whatever use the Minister makes of him, basking, in the remaining time, in the reflected glory of his political master. The Secretary of the department generally condescends to suffer his existence, often forgetting his important obligation of 'tutoring' and building up the Deputy Ministers. The Deputy Ministership is essentially a training post meant for young but promising parliamentarians and it is the duty of both the Minister and the Secretary to assist in the building up of the incumbent. A Deputy Minister too, ought to bear in mind that he has to learn a lot from both—political wisdom from the Minister and the craft of general administration from the Secretary.

The latest in the series of strained relationships between the Minister and his Secretary but absolutely unique in its own style was the rather extremely unsavoury case involving K. Hanumanthaiya, the Railway Minister, and Bankim Chandra Ganguli, the Chairman of the Railway Board. This occurred in October 1971. The Chairman of the Railway Board, it may be recalled, enjoys the rank of a Principal Secretary to the Government of India, and, thus, is senior in status to the other Secretaries. K. Hanumanthaiya had differences with his senior civil servants in the Ministry; he did not see eye to eye on a number of issues with B.C. Ganguli. The Minister passed several orders which had the effect of changing the assignments of the Chairman of the Railway Board and all this was done by him without the knowledge, much less consent, of Ganguli. The relations between the two steadily worsened; once Ganguli asked for half day's casual leave (to extract his teeth) but the Minister insisted on his taking full day's leave! This ugliest exhibition of the ministerial temper was, however, witnessed on 8 October 1971 when Hanumanthaiya summarily cancelled a tour of B.C. Ganguli by ordering that the carriage which Ganguli had already boarded be detached from the train minutes before it was to move along with B.C. Ganguli. B.C. Ganguli made a somewhat pathetic observation: "See what can happen to the Chairman of the Railway Board, who controls 52% of Indian government employees, who, I believe, is next only to the President and the Cabinet in the warrant of precedence, and who has three months and six days to go before he retires".[23]

Although the carriage was detached from the train, B.C. Ganguli decided not to come out of it in protest. On 12 October 1971, the Government terminated his services, thus bringing the glorious career of one who had the rare distinction of building the bridge over the hitherto untamed Brahmaputra to an apparently inglorious end. Ganguli asserted that he sought to improve the finances of the railways; to improve the finances "I had to dislodge certain vested interests and this meant shifting some people in the officers' category so that I could proceed with the main purpose of improving the finances of the railways. I issued some orders but there was reaction from the vested interests. There was press criticism to vilify me. Certain orders were not carried out. Some of the orders were altered by Mr. Hanumanthaiya. . . . If I made the railways profitable . . . the loss of the railways (so far) must have been going into some pockets. This did not suit some body."[24] Although the Chairman of the Railway Board was made to go under rather humiliating circumstances, the whole episode stunned and shocked the nation in general and the bureaucracy in particular. *The Hindustan Times* observed in its leading article: "Mr. Ganguli has asserted that he was sought to be removed because his drive against corruption and efficiency had begun to hurt vested interests. This is a major serious charge which the Prime Minister cannot allow to go unanswered. A quick, independent inquiry is urgently necessary and even as Mr. Ganguli is retired Mr. Hanumanthaiya should be relieved of his portfolios for the singular inaptitude that he has shown as the political head of the Ministry and the seeming inability even now to recognize his ministerial responsibility whatever the lapse on the part of the Chairman. The silly cleverness that the Minister has displaced is an example of low intrigue that brings the entire Cabinet into disrepute. Far from disciplining what he might have thought was a wayward or arbitrary subordinate, Mr. Hanumanthaiya has encouraged boorishness and indiscipline at the highest level which must tell on the morale of the railway administration as whole. The spectacle of the Chairman being literally shunted out to a railway siding where he continues his extraordinary sit-in is both comic and shabby in the extreme."[25]

NOTES

1. Morrison, Herbert: *Government and Parliament,* London, Oxford University Press, 1964, p. 320.
2. Morrison, Herbert, *op.cit.,* pp. 325-26.
3. Attlee, Earl, 'Civil Servants, Ministers, Parliament and the Public', in Robson, William A. (Ed.): *The Civil Service in Britain and France,* London, Hogarth Press, 1956, p. 17
4. Morarji Desai's Jawaharlal Nehru Memorial Lecture on 'A Minister and His Responsibilities', delivered at the Institute of Constitution and Parliamentary Studies on November 12, 1968. Desai, Morarji: *A Minister and His Responsibilities,* New Delhi.

National Publishing House, 1970, p. 13,

5. Gadgil, N.V.: *Government from Inside*, Meerut, Meenakshi Prakashan, 1968, pp. 181-82.
6. Royal Commission on the Civil Service: *Minutes of Evidence*, London, H.M.S.O. 1931, p. 1268.
7. *Report on the Machinery of the Government of India and its Procedure of Work*, New Delhi, Administrative Reforms Commission 1968, para 56.
8. Gorwala, A.D.: *The Role of the Administrator: Past, Present and Future*, Poona, Gokhale Institute of Politics and Economics, 1952, p. 12.
9. Gadgil, N.V., *op. cit.*, p. 158.
10. *The Indian Express*, November 10, 1966, p, 2.
11. Indira Gandhi's speech in the Congress Parliamentary Party Executive, November 9, 1966, *The Indian Express*, November 11, 1966.
12. *Lok Sabha Debates*, Vol. LX, No. 8, November 10, 1966, c. 2510.
13. Williams, L.W. Rushbrook: *India in 1923-24*, Calcutta, Central publication branch, 1924, p. 52.
14. *Report of the Committee on Organization and Procedure*, Delhi, Government of India, 1937, para 5.
15. *Ibid.*, para 7,
16. *Ibid.*, para 9.
17. Sri Prakasa, 'Early Days in Pakistan—II: Public Men and Permanent Officials', *The Hindustan Times*, March 17, 1963, Sunday Magazine, p. 1.
18. Such contradictory statements constrained the Vivian Bose Board of Inquiry to observe:

    "We find some of the highest officials in the land shirking responsibility and hiding the truth. We find each trying to wash his hands of a matter that has evoked much public criticism and each trying to throw the blame on the other. A Minister blames his principal Finance Secretary; the Secretary blames the Minister and a colleague who holds a high office; the colleague shifts the onus to a co-worker, the managing director of a large national institution in which both hold high and responsible office; and the managing director, in turn, blames each of the other. All these gentlemen, and a Governor of the Reserve Bank as well as the Chairman of the State Bank of India give differing and mutuallv contradictory versions of the same incident. Men of standing in the business world give us childish explanations to cover up something of which they are either frightened or ashamed. We have not been told the whole truth and some, at least, of what we have heard must be false." (*The Vivian Bose Board of Inquiry Report*, p. 36).

19. Quoted in *The Indian Express,* November 10, 1969, p. 2.
20. *Lok Sabha Debates,* April 28, 1969, c. 267.
21. *Rajya Sabha Debates,* May 1, 1969.
22. N.G. Ranga, Member of Parliament, commented "If the former Home Minister, Mr. G.L. Nanda, could not get his Secretary changed, what could a poor Law Minister or Deputy Minister do?" *Lok Sabha Debates,* April 28, 1969, c. 275.
23. Vide *The Statesman,* 11 October 1971, p. 9.
24. *The Statesman,* 9 October 1971, p. 7.
25. *The Hindustan,* 13 October 1971, p. 9.

9

Department of Personnel and Administrative Reforms

The need for a central personnel agency entrusted with personnel functions in the Central Government has been felt for quite sometime, particularly in the context of rapid expansion in the number of the civil service since Independence. The Estimates Committee of the Third Lok Sabha recommended that "the ever-expanding role of the Government, in a welfare state with its natural concomitant of a large civil service, calls for effective personnel control through a single agency. In the opinion of the Estimates Committee, the present position regarding the administration of public services involving dual control by the Ministry of Home Affairs from the point of view of 'effects on the efficient functioning of the services in general' and by the Ministry of Finance from the point of view of 'financial implications' is not conducive to their efficient management."[1] The Administrative Reforms Commission, too, urged upon the Government to set up a separate Department of Personnel to be placed directly under the Prime Minister to serve as a nodal agency for the personnel functions of the Government. It emphasized "It is necessary, to set up a central personnel agency. . . . A central agency with overall responsibility in all important matters and manned largely by specialists will obviously be able to devote concerted attention to formulation of new policies, set new standards and raise the quality of administration."[2] The Central Government accepted this recommendation and as a consequence the Department of Personnel was set up in August 1970 and placed within the Cabinet Secretariat.

The Department of Personnel took over the functions performed hitherto by the Services Wing of the Ministry of Home Affairs. The Ministry of Home Affairs was responsible for determining the method of recruitment arid conditions of service of general application to the entire civil service and for the interpretation of existing orders of general application relating to such recruitment or conditions of service. It dealt with general questions (other than those which have a financial bearing) including conduct rules relating to all-India services and central civil services (excluding civil services under the control of the Ministry of Railways and the Department of Atomic Energy).

Thus, the responsibility of, the Ministry of Home Affairs pertained to the determination of general conditions of service other than those which had a financial bearing while for laying down conditions of service involving any financial implications the ultimate responsibility rested with the Ministry of Finance. However, the Ministry of Home Affairs was the administering and the controlling authority for a number of services like the Indian Administrative Service, Indian Police Service, the Central Secretariat Service, Indian Economic Service, Indian Stàtistical Service, and for laying down all service conditions with or without financial bearing in regard to these services. But in regard to service conditions of other services, such as pay scales, fixation of pay, grant of increments, special pay, deputation allowance, compensatory and other allowance it was not incumbent that the Home Ministry be consulted. Nevertheless, since the Home Ministry possessed expertise in service matters and directly controlled a number of key services, when general questions as distinct from individual cases, connected with service conditions in relation to these matters were under consideration, this Ministry was also consulted. This was with a view to ensuring that similar guiding principles were followed for all the services in respect of general matters and service conditions. Thus, while the ultimate responsibility in these matters rested with the Finance Ministry, the Home Ministry took into account the general repercussions of these service conditions on the general functioning of the services. The line of demarcation therefore could at best be roughly defined in the following: The function of the Ministry of Finance was to consider the financial implications of these matters and that of the Ministry of Home

Affairs to take into account their effects on the efficient functioning of the services in general.

As said earlier, the Department of Personal was set up as part of the Cabinet Secretariat and thus functions directly under the Prime Minister. Its day-to-day administration, however, was entrusted to a Minister of State in the Ministry of Home Affairs. In February 1973 the Department of Administrative Affairs, hitherto located in the Ministry of Home Affairs, was transferred to the Department of Personnel and the latter's name was changed to the Department of Personnel and Administrative Reforms. This did not prove to be a very satisfactory arrangement. The way the Department functioned indicated that it was a move towards centralization, and an ambitious Prime Minister could use the new powers to promote his own personal position to the detriment of over all efficiency, and it is exactly this what happened. When matters relating to civil service were handled in the Ministry of Home Affairs, there were certain checks and balances ensuring fairness. All these became inoperative when the Department was put directly under the Prime Minister. We all know the misuse made under, the internal emergency. The Janata Government, therefore, transferred the Department of Personnel and Administrative Reforms to the Ministry of Home Affairs in 1977. The Department of Personnel and Administrative Reforms has one Secretary, one Additional Secretary, six Joint Secretaries, one Chief Welfare Officer, four Directors, ten Deputy Secretaries, one Officer on Special Duty and twenty-two Under Secretaries. The Additional Secretary looks after matters which were the charge of the Department of Administrative Reforms. In addition, it has the following six divisions—each division being under a Joint Secretary:

(i) Policy and Planning Division
(ii) Training Division
(iii) All-India Services Division
(iv) Establishment Division
(iv) Vigilance Division
(vi) Establishment Officer's Division.

The Policy and Planning Division formulates and gives shapes to the policy and planning activities in the field of personnel administration in the Central Government. The Training Division functions as a clearing house for all training activities of the Central Government and undertakes both 'leadership' and 'service' functions in this field. The All India Services Division attends to all matters relating to the IAS and the ICS including creation of new all-India services. The Establishment Division deals with matters relating to recruitment, promotion and morale of the central civil services. Subjects relating to the conditions of service of the central government employees, the Union Public Service Commission, joint consultative machinery, machinery for the redress of stall grievances and service associations are also attended by this Division. The Vigilance Division, as the name indicates deals with cases of corruption against civil servants. The Central Bureau of Investigation functions under this division. The Establishment Officer's Division looks after staffing arrangement for the posts of Under Secretary and above at the Centre, borrowing of officers from the state cadres of IAS and central civil services for holding posts at the Centre, cases requiring approval of the Appointment Committee of the Cabinet including appointments in the public sector undertakings, career management and development of personnel, etc.

The Department of Personnel and Administrative Reforms deals with all functions central to modern personnel administration and administrative reforms. The key functions entrusted to it are listed below:

(i) Survey of the contingent needs of public services in the context of total developmental goals of the administration.

(ii) Manpower planning.

(iii) Cadre management.

(iv) Job evaluation and position classification system.

(v) Recruitment.

Positive recruitment.

Talent-hunting.

Selection techniques.

Psychological tests.

New modes/methods of induction from outside and inside (lateral recruitment).

(vi) Training and development programmes.

(vii) Career systems planning.

(viii) Compensation and remuneration administration.

(ix) Motivation and productivity, participative management principles, other welfare programmes.

(x) Conduct, discipline and public service ethics,

(xi) Separation and terminal benefits systems.

(xii) Developing personnel organization.

(xiii) Personnel research and other developmental aspects as establishing broad policies, and standardised procedures, developing guides and information, and stimulating best personnel practices through a constructive public reporting and public relations system.

(xiii) Administrative reforms.

(xv) O & M.

It may be necessary to enumerate all the functions allotted to the Department of Personnel and Administrative Reforms in view of its key role in the central public administration. This is given below:

I. Recruitment, Promotion and Morale of the Services

1. Reservation of posts in civil services for certain classes of citizens.
2. General question relating to recruitment, promotion and seniority pertaining to central services except Railway Services and services under the control of the Department of Atomic Energy.
3. General policy regarding age limits, medical standards, educational qualifications and recognition of non-technical degrees/diplomas for appointment to Government service.
4. General policy matters regarding classification of posts and grant of gazetted status in relation to Services other than Railway Services.
5. Recruitment of ministerial staff for the Government of India Secretariat and its Attached Offices except that for

the Ministry of Railways and the Department of Atomic Energy.

6. Appointment of Non-Indians to Civil posts under the Government of India except posts under the Ministry of Rail ways and the Department of Atomic Energy.
7. General policy regarding employment assistance to persons of Indian origin coming from various countries.
8. Concessions to war service candidates in respect of appointments to civil posts and services.
9. General policy regarding resettlement of displaced Government servants from areas now in Pakistan, and retrenched temporary employees.
10. Concessions to political sufferers in the matters of first appointment or re-appointment to the public services.
11. General policy regarding grant of extension to or re-employment of superannuated officers.
12. Issue of certificates of eligibility for appointment to Civil Services and the posts under Union in respect of persons other than Indian citizens.
13. (a) Deputation of Indian experts abroad under the Indian Technical and Economic Cooperation Programme of the Ministry of External Affairs on bilateral basis to the developing countries of Asia, Africa and Latin America.

    (b) Deputation of officers for placements with the United Nations and its allied agencies, as also with other international agencies, like ILO, FAO, etc.
14. General policy regarding verification of character and antecedents-suitability of candidates for appointment to Government service.
15. Policy matters relating to issue of 'no objection' certificates to serving personnel for registration with the Employment Exchange, for higher posts.
16. Matters relating to personal staff of Ministers.
17. Re-deployment of staff rendered surplus in Central Government offices as result of:

    (i) administrative reforms;

(ii) studies made by the Staff Inspection Unit (S.I.U.);

(iii) winding up of long-term but temporary organizations.

II. Training

18. Advising Ministries on proper management of various cadres under their control.

19. (a) Formulation and coordination of training policies for the all-India and central services.

(b) Lal Bahadur Shastri Academy of Administration and Institute of Secretariat Training and Management.

(c) Training programmes for the Indian Administrative Service, Central Secretariat Service, Indian Economic Service and Indian Statistical Service,

(d) Preparation and publication of training material and of information of training techniques, facilities and programmes.

(e) Liaison with training institutions within the states and abroad.

(f) Refresher and special courses for Middle and Senior Management levels.

III. Vigilance and Discipline

20. (a) The Prevention of Corruption Act, 1947, enforcement, viz., investigation adjudication and prosecution of cases arising out of breaches, under the Foreign Exchange Regulation Act, 1947; the Central Bureau of Investigation (the Delhi Special Police Establishment including the Legal Division, the Technical Division, the Policy Division and the Administration Division); the Food Offences Wing: the Economic Offences Wing and the Directorate General of Revenue Intelligence-cum-Directorate of Enforcement.

(b) Accord of sanction for the prosecution of any person for any offence investigated into by the Delhi Special Police Establishment where such sanction is required to be accorded by the Central Government.

(c) Central Vigilance Commission.

(d) All policy matters pertaining to vigilance and discipline among public servants.

(e) Relationship between Members of Parliament and the administration; matters relating to the code of conduct for legislators.

IV. Service Conditions

21. General questions (other than those which have a financial bearing) including conduct rules relating to all-India and Union Public Services except in regard to services under the control of the Ministry of Railways and the Department of Atomic Energy.

22. Conditions of service of Central Government employees (excluding those under the control of the Ministry of Railways and the Department of Atomic Energy) other than those having a financial bearing and in so far as they raise points of general service interests.

23. Leave travel concessions for civil employees other than Railway employees.

24. The Central Services (Temporary Service) Rules, 1949.

25. General Policy regarding retrenchment 'and reversion of temporary government servants except those under the Ministry of Railways.

26. Administration of the Central Services (Safeguarding of National Security) Rules.

27. Uniforms for Class IV and other Government servants in the Central Secretariat and its attached offices.

28. Working hours and holidays for Government of India offices.

29. Administration of service rules with financial content under specific delegation made by the Ministry of Finance.

30. Advice on proposals in respect of the Ministry of Finance relating to the number of grade of posts or to the strength of Service or to the pay and allowances of government servants or any other conditions of their service having financial implications.

31. General policy regarding reimbursement of legal expenses incurred by government servants.
32. Proposals for grant of ex-officio secretariat status.
33. Government servants having families in Pakistan, cases regarding grant of permission to government servants to visit Pakistan.
34. Honorary appointments of persons in civil posts.
35. Oath of allegiance to the Constitution.

V. Senior and Middle Managements

36. All aspects of Senior Management (i.e. Joint Secretaries and above and their equivalents) including development of personnel for it.
37. (a) Establishment Officer to the Government of India.
    (b) Appointments Committee of the Cabinet.
    (c) Central Establishment Board.
    (d) Career Development for Middle Management (i.e. Directors, Deputy and Under Secretaries and their equivalents).

VI. Grievances and Staff Welfare

38. (a) Service associations of the employees of the Government of India.
    (b) Joint consultative machinery; departmental council for the Department of Personnel.
    (c) Machinery for the redress of staff grievances.
    (d) Staff welfare including sports, cultural activities, griha kalyan Kendras, canteen, cooperative Stores, etc.

VII. Union Public Service Commission

39. Union Public Service Commission.

VIII. Centralised aspects of managing IAS, inter-Ministry cadres including Career Planning for the Members thereof

40. (a) Creation of new all-India Services.
    (b) Rules and regulations under the All India Service Act,

(c) All matters relating to the Indian Administrative Services including the Indian Civil Service,

(d) All India Civil List and History of Services.

(e) Central Secretariat Service (Reorganization re-enforcement) Scheme, Central Secretariat Stenographers' Service Scheme and Central Secretariat Clerical Service Scheme.

(f) Indian Statistical Service and Indian Economic Service.

IX. Career Planning

41. (a) General policy questions regarding career planning for the all-India and Central Government Services.

(b) All matters pertaining to the career planning for the IAS, Central Secretariat Services, Indian Statistical Service and Indian Economic Service.

X. Personnel Management Agencies

42. Coordination of the work of personnel management agencies within various Ministries.

XI. Research in Personnel Administration, etc.

43. Research in Personnel Administration, liaison with State Governments, professional institutions etc., in personnel matters.

XII. Allocation of personnel and integration of Services as a result of States Reorganization

44. (a) Allocation of services personnel affected by reorganization of States.

(b) Division and integration of services affected by the reorganization of States other than in the Union Territories.

(c) Protection of service conditions of personnel affected by reorganization of States.

(d) Other matters relating to State services affected by the reorganization of States,

XIII. Administrative Reforms

45. Administrative reforms
46. O & M

The present discussion would remain incomplete without a mention of the Advisory Council on Personnel Administration established in September 1972 to (a) to advise the Central Government on broad policy matters in personnel administration specially with a view to acting as a feeder line of new ideas and thinking in the field; (b) to consider and recommend broad lines of policy in the field of personnel administration: and (c) to advise on matters in the field specifically placed before the Council for consideration. The minister of State in charge of the Department of Personnel and Administrative Reforms is the chairman of this body and the Secretary of the Department is its vice-chairman. It consists of senior civil servants drawn from both the generalist and specialist areas of central administration and citizens who are experts in different aspects of personnel administration. The Advisory Council on Personnel Administration, the setting up of which was recommended by the Administrative Reforms Commission, is expected to act as a 'thinking group' for the Department.

NOTES

1. *Ninety-third Report of the Estimates Committee* (Third Lok Sabha), New Delhi, Lok Sabha Secretariat, 1966, pp, 18-19.
2. Administrative Reforms Commission: *Report on the Machinery of the Government of India and its Procedures of Work*. Delhi, Manager of Publications, 1968, p. 71.

10

District Administration

The basic territorial unit of administration in India is the district, and the 'district administration' is "the total management of public affairs within this unit."[1] It is at this level that the common man comes into direct contact with the administration. The difference between good and bad administration is, consequently, made—and felt—at this level. A district has been placed under the charge of a district officer—called either Deputy Commissioner or District Collector—who virtually acts as the eyes, ears and arms of the State Government, A district has also been the unit of administration for various other departments of the State Government, Thus, many state functionaries like the Superintendent of Police, Assistant Registrar of Cooperative Societies, District Agricultural Officer, District Medical Officer, etc. are located at the district headquarters and the jurisdiction extends to the district. The district is, thus, a multiple one, having a galaxy of officers for administering the affairs of Government. There are, to be sure, some notable exceptions to this general arrangement. The unit of administration of the department of irrigation, for instance, is not co-terminous with the district; the unit follows channels of irrigation quite often transcending district boundaries, agencies operating in the district come under the coordinating discipline of the District Collector.

The District Collector succeeded the *Karori-Faujdar* of the Moghul Government. With the decline of the Moghul Empire, however, this institution, too, suffered decay and eventual disappearance. The present office is the creation of the British rule in India. It dates back to the year 1772 when the East India Company had made the historic decision to (in the words of the

Board of Directors of the Company) "stand forth as *diwan* and to take upon themselves, by the agency of their own servants, the entire care and administration of the revenues," and appointed Collectors 'to superintend the revenue collections and to preside in the courts.'[2] Steadily, the District Collector's authority and power increased, and before long he emerged as the pivot of district administration, representing the State Government in its totality. The duty of assessing and collecting the land revenue, which originally imparted to this office its title, was by no means his only duty; which has always remained more undefined than defined. Other public functionaries posted in the district look to him for help, advice, sometimes even orders, and even the citizens almost instinctively flock to him whenever they have grievance to be redressed or have any problem the solution of which they do not seem to know or agree with. Not incorrectly did *The Imperial Gazetteer of India* observe:

> "A Collector of strong and sympathetic character and with the gift of insight may gain the strongest hold over the affections and imagination of the peasantry, and talks of his sagapity and good deeds, will be told in remote villages many years after his name has ceased to be borne on the civil list of his province."[3]

Such an unparalleled role of the District Collector has been the theme of numerous writings on Indian administration, many of them becoming classic ones with the passage of time.

Sir George Campbell, the then Lieutenant-Governor of Bengal, wrote in 1872: "It is the Lieutenant Governor's wish to render the head of district no longer the drudges of many departments and masters of none, but in fact the general controlling authority over all departments in each district. . . . he has, therefore, striven to make the Magistrate Collector of a great Bengal district . . . the real executive chief and administrator of the tract of country committed to him and supreme over everyone and everything except the proceedings of the Court of Justice." The District Collector was verily the 'British rule incarnate'. 'The father and mother of district', 'Respected, feared, trusted to his 800,000 he is Omnipotence'.[4] A fairly vivid description of his position has been given by Sir William Wilson Hunter writing as far back as 1892:

"The district officer, whether known as Collector-Magistrate or as Deputy Commissioner, is the responsible head of his jurisdiction. Upon his energy" and personal character depends ultimately the efficiency of our Indian Government. His own special duties are so numerous and so various as to bewilder the outsider and the work of his subordinates, European and native; largely friends upon the stimulus of his personal example. His position has been compared to that of the French prefect, but such a comparison is unjust in many ways to the Indian district officer. He is not a mere subordinate of a central bureau, who takes' his colour from his chief and represents the political parties or the permanent officialism of the capital. The Indian Collector is a strongly individualised worker in every Department of rural well-being, with a large measure of local independence and of individual initiative. As the name of Collector-Magistrate implies, his main functions are two-fold. He is a fiscal officer, charged with the collection of the revenue from the land and other sources. He is also a revenue and criminal judge, both of first instance and in appeal. But his title by no means, exhausts his multifarious duties. He does in a smaller local sphere all that the Home Secretary superintends in England, and a great deal more; for he is the representative of a paternal and not a constitutional Government. Police, jails, education, municipalities, roads, sanitation, dispensaries, the local taxation, and the Imperial revenues of his District are to him matters of daily concern. He is expected to make himself acquainted with every phase of the social life of the .country. He should be a lawyer, an accountant, a surveyor, and a ready writer of State papers. He ought also to possess no mean knowledge of agriculture, political economic and engineering."[5]

Even in 1930 when dyarchy had begun to have its impact on this institution, the Indian Statutory Commission made the assertion that the District Collector "is in the eyes of most of its inhabitants the Government." Ramsay MacDonald went a step further and compared this functionary with that tortoise on whose back stood the elephant of the Government of India.

The office of Deputy Commissioner has, however, changed fundamentally in terms of its prestige and powers since independence. This has come about as a result of almost simultaneous operation of at least three factors. First, the adoption of parliamentary form of Government has transformed this institution from being an agent of a paternalistic alien rule into a sensitive instrument of a popularly elected democracy. The constitutional position of the executive being held continually accountable to the legislature has caused an unmistaken concentration of power and authority in the hands of the Minister and his office namely the Secretariat with the consequence that the District Collector is no longer the final decision maker in many matters as he used to be during the days of the alien rule. Secondly, the environment in which he necessarily functions today has altered in a basic way. The people ruled by him are no longer so subject, servile, uncomplaining and subordinate as they were during the British period. The District Collector is today increasingly called upon to explain, to convince and to persuade the people, not to coerce them. Also, the political network in the district is much more active virile and vigilant, thanks to the existence of various political parties in the district. More importantly the *panchayati raj* has led to the emergence of a new class of district level politicians who have come to command not inconsiderable patronage and power, even influence over the State Government, thus obscuring even to an extent eclipsing, the position and place of the District Collector in the state administrative system. Once called the eyes and ears of the State Government, today the latter counts on many who act as such, he being only one. Even otherwise, democratic polity suffers no bureaucratic institution to exist and function on what may be called colonial terms. Thirdly, the District Collector of today is also less adequately equipped for his job the complexity of which has, if any, increased manifold since 1947 than his counterpart of the British era. A member of the Indian Administrative Service is appointed to this post in the fourth or fifth year of his joining the service whereas member of the Indian Civil Service could expect to get charge of a district much later in his career. Besides, as E.N. Mangat Rai has observed, "the work of the Deputy Commissioner has less importance in the entire career of an officer than it did. A member of the Indian Civil Service in the British period . . . could expect to spend 12 to 18 of his 35 years work in the district whereas a member of the Indian Administrative Service today may spend an average of 4 to 6 years in this way".[6]

Despite these momentous changes overtaking this institution the fact is, as K.K. Dass appropriately remarks, "There is not, and never has been, an official quite like the Collector any where else".[7]

The District Collector belongs to the General Administration Department of the State Government while the officials over whom he exercises control and supervision belong to a variety of departments, in the district hierarchy of which he may or may not have a formal assignment. His position is illustrated in the following chart.[8]

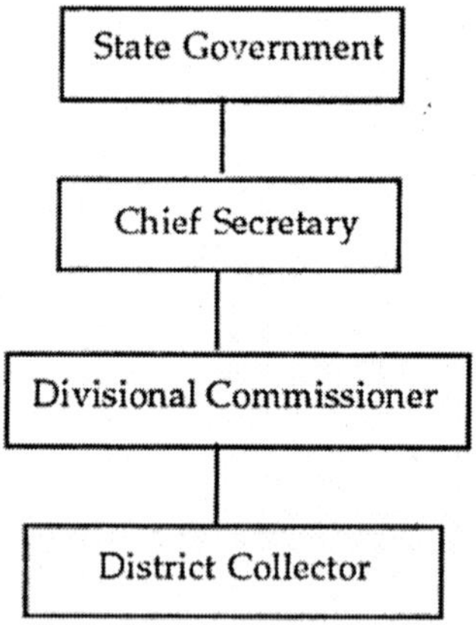

As head of the district, the District Collector is involved in a network of inter-relationships with other district level functionaries. With the latter his relationship may fall in one of the following four categories:

(i) Officers whose head at the district level is the Collector in all matters and who represent departments having no district heads of their own, for example, the Tahsildar;

(ii) Officers whose head at the district level is the Collector for only administrative and certain disciplinary matters but who in technical matters are under the control of their own district level officers; for example, district agricultural officer, district excise officer;

(iii) Officers who are themselves heads, at the district level, of their field staff but are made subordinate to the Collector only in certain specified matters. Apart from these, they are under the control of their own respective regional officers. The Superintendent of Police, the Civil Surgeon, the Assistant Registrar of Cooperative Societies, the Executive Engineer of the Public Works Department etc. come under this category;

(iv) Officers, the control over whom does not at all vest in the Collector—Labour Officer, Sales Tax Officer, etc.

The District Collector is normally a member of the Indian Administrative Service. As the IAS consists of (i) direct recruits and (2) promotees from State Civil Services, these two sub-groups constitute the two natural sources from which the District Collectors are drawn. The District Collector who was recruited to the IAS directly (that is, through competitive examination) is a young man, usually in his thirties. The post of District Collector is also occupied by officers who were originally recruited to the State Civil Service and who have since been promoted to the IAS. This category belongs to a higher age group. There may also be some District Collectors who are not members of the Indian Administrative Service. Such officers still belong to the State Civil Service but are likely to be soon promoted to the IAS; or are on verge of retirement, and, therefore, afforded the satisfaction of functioning—and, then, retiring—as District Collector.

It appears that a large number of District Collectors at present belong to the last two categories taken together. This, at least, is the emerging picture in some of the States. In U.P., for example, out of a total of 54 Collectors, only 18 (33%) were according to a study completed in 1966, those directly recruited to the IAS whereas 16 (about 30%) were promotee IAS officers and the remaining 20 were still borne on the State Civil Service. The directly recruited officers thus appear to be in short demand as District Collectors. The reasons underlying this seem to be the following:

1. A direct recruit is generally not believed to be very effective as a District Collector because of his lack of sufficient administrative experience.
2. As other district level functionaries are normally middle-aged officials they are reluctant to submit to the superior authority of the 'young' Collector.

3. The political considerations, too, seem to dictate the posting of the promotee I.A.S. officer as a District Collector. According to some the direct recruit, because of his youthful idealism, may not be easily amenable to the pressures of district and higher level politicians. The promotees do not generally have traditions of independence nor have they such unsullied idealism and, therefore, are preferred by politicians.
4. It is also said that the direct recruits have a natural preference for the kind of sheltered life which is promised in the Secretariat.

Duties of the Collector

The District Collector continues to remain to this date the pivot of district administration, shouldering direct responsibilities in both traditional and emerging fields. His principal duty today is as it has always been to maintain law and order in his district, which is the basis of orderly, civilized life. A Collector who fails in this respect is unworthy to hold office, and would, indeed, soon be replaced. Prompt and fair collection of land revenue and other taxes is his second important duty. Historically, this has been his first charge as the title 'Collector' signifies. The third one is the direction and fulfilment of developmental plans with which the country's destiny is inter-linked. His fourth important duty is to act as some kind of a buffer between citizens and administration, protecting one against the possible harassment by another. Towards these ends, the District Collector undertakes regular tours in his district, visiting even far-flung villages, meeting people and understanding, even solving their problems and, above all seeing that the programmes of the Government are being efficiently carried out The aphorism that "in Indian public administration the tent is mightier than the pen" was coined consciously and vividly to impress on the Collector the necessity of field visits to meet the people in their normal surroundings and to see the things for himself. Among other duties which a good Collector would never neglect are to develop friendly relations with governmental personnel operating in his district so as to maximize goal achievement, to train junior officers, and to keep his office efficient. While his responsibilities have markedly increased, he, today, operates with distinctly reduced status and prestige, thanks, among others, to the emergence of a network of district level functionaries who no longer regard him as an unquestionably superior authority, and of the *panchayati raj*. Notwithstanding these momentous changes, it is to him that the Government instinctively turns in times of emergency. And, he has been responding to these challenges in a manner so as to confirm the resilience and vitality of this institution. Truly, the Collector's functions are more undefined than defined. A word may be said here regarding his role as the district magistrate. The Constitution of India is committed to the separation of the judiciary from the executive and this process is already under way. Under separation, the head of the magistracy is the District and Sessions Judge who works directly under the High Court of the State. The Collector nevertheless continues to be responsible for law and order and related matters,

An attempt is made here to list functions and responsibilities generally entrusted to him.

I. As District Officer

1. Postings, transfer and leave of the gazetted officers within the district.
2. Postings, transfer and leave to the *naib tahsildars* and *tahsildars*.
3. Appointing the punishing authority in respect of ministerial and inferior servants of collectorate and tahsil staff and other allied officers.
4. To deal with pension cases of district staff.
5. Controlling, drawing and disbursing officer of the district staff.
6. To submit annual budget estimates.
7. Preparation of estimates of works in respect of revenue buildings and responsibility for maintenance of all Government buildings under the charge of Revenue Department.
8. In-charge of the Treasury and District Stamp Officer and responsible for verification of the security of Government treasurer.

9. Chairman/President of various local institutions. Some are members of Regional Transport Authority, Roadways Advisory Committees, etc.
10. To issue tentative tour programme of Ministers and V.I.Ps,
11. Acts as chief protocol officer in the district.
12. To arrange for stay of VIPs at circuit house or other inspection houses.
13. To compile and submit annual administration report of the district.
14. To attend to the work of enquiries relating to character verifications.
15. To supervise the proper conducting of the civil suits in which States are a party.
16. To appoint in the district Government counsels and panel of lawyers.
17. To countersign fee bills of district Government counsel,
18. To make enquiries relating to the issue of certificates to homoeopaths and correspondence regarding registration and enrolment.
19. To countersign the grant-in-aid bills of various educational institutions.
20. Sale of excise shops.
21. Recovery of pauper suits dues and deficit court fees under Stamp Act.
22. Interview with members of public and officials.
23. To make enquiries regarding grant of financial aid to the cadets as well as to the scholars applying for scholarship/ technical education loans, etc.
24. The principal agency of Government in the matters of general administration in district, looks after the interest of the Government in general.
25. Responsible for proper implementation of Government orders.
26. To train junior officers in official procedures, administrative work as well as in personal conduct and behaviour.

27. To ensure that public grievances against the administration in the district are properly and effectively dealt with.
28. To effect coordination in the work of all the district level officers and to preside over the District Plan Implementation Committee.

II. As Collector

1. Collection of land revenue.
2. Collection of canal dues.
3. Collection of other Government dues.
4. Distribution of *taccavi* loans.
5. Recovery of *taccavi* dues.
6. National calamities—assessment of losses to crop and recommendations for relief.
7. Distribution of distress *taccavi.*
8. Relief of fire sufferers.
9. All matters relating to land records.
10. Control over land records establishment.
11. To collect and furnish multifarious agrarian statistics regarding rainfall, crops, etc.
12. Land acquisition work.
13. Supervision of treasury and sub-treasuries.
14. To sanction land revenue assignment.
15. Payment of Zamindari Abolition Compensation and Rehabilitation Grant.
16. Assessment and realization of agriculture income-tax.
17. As Ex-Officio Deputy Director of Consolidation of Holdings hears appeal from the orders of the lower authorities.
18. Taking relief measures in case of scarcity conditions caused by natural calamities like fire, drought, flood, waterlogging and excessive rains, etc.
19. Enforcement of Stamp Act.
20. Management of Government estates.

III. As District Magistrate

1. To control and supervise the subordinate magistracy, to order magisterial postings during festivals.
2. To promulgate orders whenever there is any danger of breach of public peace and tranquillity,
3. To dispose of all the petitions and miscellaneous general complaints received from Government and others.
4. To make jail inspections and expeditious disposal of cases of under-trial prisoners.
5. Grant of superior classes to prisoners.
6. Premature release of prisoners.
7. Release of prisoners on parole.
8. To deal with mercy petitions from prisoners.
9. As head of criminal administration of the district to control and direct the action of police.
10. To submit an annual criminal report to Government.
11. Appointment and punishment of village *chowkidar*.
12. Inspections of police stations once a year.
13. To sanction expunction of a crime from the Crime Register.
14. Recovery of repatriation charges.
15. Accidents.
16. Payment of compensation under the Workmen's Compensation Act.
17. Labour problems, strikes, etc.
18. Recovery of canecess
19. Prosecution under Sugar Factories Control Act.
20. Infringement of Trade Mark Act.
21. Sanction of temporary electric connections including enquiries regarding breach.
22. Grant and cancellation of many kinds of licences.
23. Supervision over supply office and rent control and eviction officer under Rent Control Act and in supply matters

24. Supervision and control over local bodies, municipal boards, notified areas and town areas and channel for correspondence.
25. Enforcement of the Cinema and Entertainment and Betting Tax Act.
26. Recommendations for the issue of passports and visas,
27. Supervision of the work of probation officer.
28. Making of reception orders for lunatics.
29. Enforcement of the Press Act and disposal of declaration in respect of press and newspapers.
30. Administration of *nazul* lands.
31. Recommendations of schemes for the development of forests.
32. Issue of permits for the cutting of trees.
33. Control and supervision of the work of elections in the district.
34. Issue of certificates for domicile, scheduled and backward classes, guardianship of a political sufferer, etc.
35. To provide for affixation of poles, etc. on a private land or building for conveyance of the electric current.

IV. Returning Officer

The Collector is the Returning Officer for elections to Parliamentary and Vidhan Sabha Constituencies, and has the responsibility for coordination of the election work at the district level.

V. As District Census Officer

As the District Census Officer, the Collector is responsible for conduct of census operations once in ten years. This work entails a more elaborate arrangement than the election. He appoints enumerators, provides for their training and arranges timely supply of forms, etc.

Even the above list, formidable looking as it is, leaves many things unsaid. In fact, functions not specifically allotted to any officer by any department but which nonetheless are required to be performed at the district level, devolve naturally on the

Collector. He has to collect information in regard to matters including parliamentary questions concerning his district. To the above list may be added the following functions:

1. Work relating to civil defence,
2. Responsibilities in the field of agricultural production.
3. Collection of loans, donations and subscriptions.
4. Role as the public relations officer of the Government.
5. Responsibilities in the field of municipal administration.
6. A natural leader in an emergency such as floods, famine, earthquake, internal and external aggressions, etc.
7. Liaison with military authorities and welfare of members of the armed forces—both serving and retired.

All this obviously entails an enormous amount of work for the District Collector. An effort was made in 1959 by the Bombay Committee on Reorganization of District Revenue Offices to analyse the collector's workload and the analysis is interesting:

"An average district seems to provide him (Collector) with the following amount of annual work:

Correspondent	1600	hrs.
Meetings	200	"
Case hearings	100	"
Jamabandi and inspections	80	"
Village inspections	200	"
Field inspections	250	"
Journeys	240	"
VIPs	180	"
Daily visitors	125	"
Total	2975	hrs

If we were to allow for Saturdays, half Saturdays, and other holidays, the whole daily workload comes to about 11.4 hours and if he were only, to allow for Sundays, it comes to 9.9 hours. The pressure no doubt is heavy. This has made the general control so tenuous as to become almost ineffective. This position leaves the head of the district in a most dissatisfied state of mind and makes a cynic out of him".[7]

Similarly, the Madras District Revenue Administration Enquiry Committee (1955) analysed the work-load of the

Collector and concluded: "Speaking generally, a Collector at the present day, for fulfilling his role adequately, has to be prepared to accept as his daily routine hours of work far beyond those usually recognized as official hours. Almost every Collector has more than a fair day's work and he finds no difference between a working day and a holiday. Frequently a Collector has to work from early morning till late at night, even to cope with his normal work. When the routine is upset (as it often is) by something special—the visit of an important personage or an emergency like floods or bad seasonal conditions or something on the law and order side—arrears accumulate and call for an extra spurt for return to normal".[10]

The strains he is subjected to at present are almost infinite. Paul H. Appleby has thus portrayed the District Collector of the pre-*Panchayati Raj* period: *Panchayati Raj* has put additional strains on him.

> "... no Ministry knows how much of his time it is entitled to and none has any capacity for insuring that it receives that portion of his time and energy.
>
> ... overburdening, understaffing, and lack of stringent administrative evaluation of performance are generally characteristic of the Collector's situations. The Collector is so broadly responsible and overburdened that one of his two primary functions has suffered seriously. One sits in his office only to hear him receive along with streams of citizen visitors, telephone calls from all of the State Ministries who lay their most pressing problems at the door; he is responsible to everybody for everything, though with varying degrees of clarity. No one can hold him responsible for anything in particular and few facilities for checking his performance exist. He struggles valiantly in an outmoded structural situation.
>
> ... no single programme can be given sustained emphasis, although the matter of special emphasis is the essence of the attainment of special objectives.
>
> ... the dimensions and urgency of the development programme, and to some extent novelty, throw into high relief all of the crankiness and cumbersomeness of an administrative system designed to serve the relatively simple interest of an occupying power".[11]

The Collector is thus an overworked official. Inevitably some of the work remains neglected and some only superficially attended to. It is, therefore, in the interest of the efficiency of this office that he be provided relief by:

1. reducing the size of the district;
2. relieving him of some of his work and giving him adequate staff facilities;
3. reducing the number of committees over which he has at present to preside;
4. doing away with the time-wasting protocol duties which he has at present to perform.

Altering the boundary of the district is replete with profound administrative and, what is more, political implications, and, therefore, does not appear to be a very feasible proposition. These apart, there is no unanimity about the optimum size of the district. As the Bengal Administration Enquiry Committee (1945) commented: "There is clearly a limit, although there is no clear limit, to the size of a District. . . . Apart from the fact that it is 'impracticable to redraw the boundaries of all the Districts in the Province, it is not possible to find a formula which enables one to fix with precision the ideal size of a District, So much depends on the density of the population, the topography of the area and the nature and state of its communication."[12] The balance of advantages lies, indeed, in favour of *status quo* in this matter. Arrangements, therefore, must be devised to afford him relief within the framework of the existing size of the district. The States seem to have taken home this point and have adopted measures without disturbing the boundaries of district. . . . In the .first place, the gradual implementation by States of the constitutional provision urging separation of judiciary from the executive has been relieving the Collector of what is essentially judicial case work. Secondly, consequent upon the emergence of *Panchayati Raj*, developmental work in the district has been transferred to the popularly elected three tiered system, which has, to this extent, reduced the Collector's direct involvement. Maharashtra and Gujarat have each separated the Collector from developmental work by putting the latter under the charge of a chief executive officer/ district development officer who is a full-time functionary drawn from the Indian Administrative

Service. And lastly, States have adopted definite measures to provide him relief although the precise arrangement has varied from State to State.

Some States like U.P. have arranged assistance by appointing an officer to share with him the burden of work. In U.P. the Collector is assisted by an additional district magistrate (executive), who is normally a senior officer of the State Civil Service. In Maharashtra the Collector has been provided with a resident deputy Collector with the rank of the Additional District Magistrate.

The real point is that if a new officer is to afford adequate relief to the Collector, he should be in a position to deal directly with the State Government and other higher authorities in matters entrusted to his charge. Equally important is the unity of district administration, which must be maintained by a precise demarcation of functions.

Tamil Nadu on the one hand and Maharashtra and Gujarat on the other have each responded differently to the emergent functions of development. Maharashtra and Gujarat have relieved the Collector of his responsibility in developmental field by appointing a chief executive officer/district development officer in each district to look after developmental functions. Tamil Nadu, on the other hand, has concentrated developmental administration in the Collector's hand, and has appointed a new authority, called District Revenue Officer, to deal with land revenue and general administration. The Tamil Nadu scheme makes fullest utilization of the time-honoured office of the District Collector and the unique halo surrounding it in the new but pressing tasks of development.

The Collector is the appropriate person to look after developmental activities in the district and in support of this, the following arguments may be cited:

(i) The development work requires personal direction to a much greater extent than the ordinary duties of land revenue and general administration;

(ii) This work is of a novel character, and hence, should be entrusted to the time-tested institution of the Collector;

(iii) This work calls for effective coordination of the work of district officers of all the different development departments. The District Collector can achieve this more effectively;

(iv) Since the developmental activities involve personal dealings with legislator and members of the *panchayati raj* institutions, the District Collector is likely to prove more effective.

The District Collector is head of the administration in the district and for performance of his function he has a well-knit hierarchy in the district which may be illustrated by the following chart:

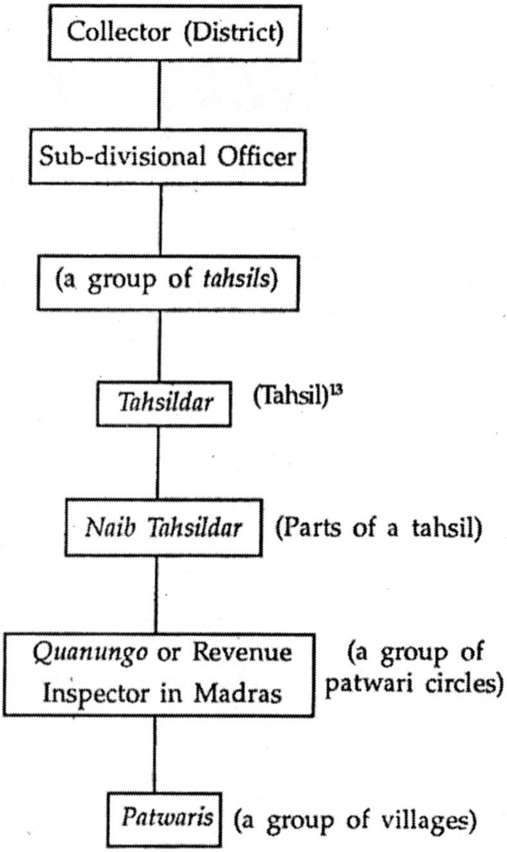

Revenue Division /Sub-division

The district is geographically divided into a number of units known as Sub-divisions in Uttar Pradesh and Madhya Pradesh, Revenue Divisions in Tamil Nadu and Prants in Maharashtra. The official-in-charge of this unit bears a variety of names; he is called Sub-Divisional Officer (SDO) or Sub-Divisional Magistrate (SDM) in U.P., Revenue Divisional Officer or Sub-Collector in Tamil Nadu, Prant Officer (Deputy Collector or Assistant Collector) in Maharashtra. This unit serves to further decentralization of authority as well as to provide field training to recruits to the Indian Administrative Service. The S.D.O. is either newly recruited member of the IAS (and, therefore, quite young in age) or a member of the State Civil Service. The former, it has been observed, generally does not take any marked interest in the administration of the subdivision as he regards this as a mere training post, and a stopgap arrangement. Like the District Collector, the S.D.O. is a generalist area administrator. Again, like him he speaks with the voice of the Government in his own sub-division. He is a link between the District Collector and the *tahsildar* in revenue matters and the district magistrate and the station officer (police) in matters relating to law and order.

The sub-divisions, may be classified into two broad types—'office' type sub-division, and 'touring' type sub-division. In the former the S.D.O. maintains the Office just as a Collector or a *tahsildar* does. Here, the headquarters of the sub-division is usually located within the sub-division itself. This type came into existence during the earliest phase of the British rule in India and has since continued. Bengal, Bihar, Orissa, Tamil Nadu, Maharashtra, Gujarat, Andhra Pradesh, Karnataka, Assam, and Rajasthan represent this type. There is also a touring type sub-division in which the SDO does not maintain an office. He is a touring officer gathering information, transmitting it to his district chief, contacting people, supervising subordinate officials and, finally, looking after the execution of the governmental activities in his sub-division. His 'core' role in both the types is the same. He is "primarily . . . an inspecting, testing, and supervising officer, hearing appeals and trying cases. He moves about the villages and ascertains the villagers' grievances and wants and gains experience."[14]

The S.D.O. is thus a valuable field aide to the District Collector and is an integral part of the district administration.

The S.D.O in many States (U.P., for example) do not live within their sub-divisions. They reside at the district headquarters. Naturally, they cannot be quite effective in their work, and the public, too, is put to considerable inconvenience by having to come to the district headquarters for even small items of work. As a matter of policy, the S.D.O. and other sub-divisional level officers must reside at the sub-divisional headquarters.

Tahsil

The sub-division comprises one or two *tahsils*. A tahsil called *taluk* in Tamil Nadu and *taluka* in Maharashtra, is the basic unit for purposes of general administration, treasury, land revenue, land records and other items of work. It has the closest and widest contact with the rural population. The officer in charge of the *tahsil* is the *Tahsildar*, who belongs to the State Civil Service. He is the principal official in the district administration responsible for actual revenue collection. His performance, also, is judged by his efficiency as a Collector of the revenues. He is the sub-treasury officer, thus accepting the payment of the revenue. "But a *tahsildar* who merely sits in a Tahsil waiting for the land revenue to come in would not get very far,"[13] He recommends remissions or other concessions to the District Collector in times of distress. He is assisted by *naib* or deputy *tahsildar*, *kanungos* and *patwaris*. The administration at the tahsil level is the farthest unit of administration for revenue and land questions. It is not necessary that all departments are represented at this level, for the distribution of the staff below district level follows departmental needs.

Pargana

The next lower unit in revenue administration is known as *pargana* in U.P., *circle* in Maharashtra and *firka* in Tamil Nadu. The head of this unit is called supervisor *quanungo* in U.P., circle inspector in Maharashtra and the revenue inspector in Tamil Nadu. He is in, charge of revenue administration and land records of every village within his area. He is the first line supervisor in the chain of revenue administration in the States.

Village

The lowest unit for all administrative and fiscal purposes in all the States in India is the village which is administered by a village establishment, comprising *lekhpal* and *chowkidar* in *U.P.*, *patel* and *talati* in Maharashtra and village headman and *karnam* in Tamil Nadu. The village headman in Tamil Nadu is the most powerful governmental functionary at the village level combining as he does the police and revenue functions. He is the head of the village police. Also, he collects revenue and deposits it in the treasury. He is the custodian of all governmental property in the village. In fact, he is the representative of the Government in the village. The functionary equal to him is the *patel* in Maharashtra, who performs police, revenue and administrative functions. U.P. has no functionary corresponding to the village headman in Tamil Nadu and the *patel* in Maharashtra. The bottom level functionary is lekhpal in U.P., *talati* in Maharashtra and *karnam* in Tamil Nadu. The patwari is responsible for all the work connected with land problems. He is the busy-body of the Government for performance of a multitude of functions including collection of village statistics. S.S. Khera calls him "the king pin of the revenue administration in the district." "Anyone who either comes from a village or has lived in a village, or has had anything to do with a village especially concerning the land or agriculture, will appreciate what is meant when we say that a patwari is the king pin of the revenue administration in the district."[16]

Coordination at the District Level

Most state departments are represented at the district level by their own officers. As a result, the district headquarters, today, hum with the music of activities, functioning as if these were the subsidiary capitals of the State. Both the number and nomenclatures of the departments represented at this level vary from State to State but the following may be considered to be a representative list (see page 232):

The District Collector is a generalist, normally an officer of the Indian Administrative Service, while other district officers are technical personnel, and, what is more, are borne on specialized state services, created on department lines. They thus, represent two different administrative cultures displaying different norms of behavior. The relationship between the generalist Collector and these technical functionaries has always been a thorny problem of district administration. The technical personnel are responsible to their respective heads of department.

Representative List

	Department	District Head of the Department
1.	Revenue and General Administration	Collector
2.	Police	Superintendent of Police
3.	Excise	Superintendent of Excise
4.	Medical	Civil Surgeon
5.	Public Health	Health Officer
6.	Forest	Forest Officer
7.	Education	District Inspector of Schools
8.	Agriculture	District Agricultural Officer
9.	Cooperation	Assistant Registrar of Cooperative Societies
10.	Veterinary	District Veterinary Officer
11.	Industry	District Industries Officer
12.	Information	District Information Officer
13.	Planning	District Planning Officer
14.	Judicial	District Judge
15.	Backward Classes	Backward Classes Welfare Officer

As the technical officer is borne on the cadre of a specialized state service, he is obviously assertive of departmental independence, preferring to hoe his roe. Democracy, too is to be accounted for this amount of exclusiveness and departmental independence. Because each technical department, today, functions under a popularly elected Minister accountable to the legislature, there is a deep-seated reverence for chain of command with consequent resistance to accepting of instructions from other lateral or diagonal authorities such as the District Collector.

The foregoing does not imply that the district officers function in complete independence of the District collector or in isolation from each other. The District Collector is involved in varying ways and to varying degrees in the administration of most subjects, although the manner and extent of his involvement is generally believed to be not commensurate with the requirements of the situation. "The present position", wrote the Bengal Administration Enquiry Committee (1944-45), "is, in our judgement, thoroughly unsatisfactory, both from the point of view of efficiency of the Government machine and the welfare of the people in the district. The lot of the district officer, like that of the comic opera policeman, is not a happy one. He is expected to see that nothing goes wrong in his district but he has little power outside the Magistrate and Collector field to see that go right. He is supposed to "compose differences between other officers" but he has no power to impose his will upon the recalcitrant. He can cajole and persuade: He cannot compel. He is regarded as responsible for stimulating the activities of the officers of other departments, but he has no real control over them, and, although they are under an obligation to keep him informed of their activities, the extent to which this obligation is discharged depends in most cases on the personal factor. Even if they keep him informed of what they are doing, they are under no compulsion to discuss their plans with him in advance."[17]

Of crucial importance, consequently, is the need for coordination and integration of activities of these different functionaries. Increase in the tempo of development activities has caused an increase in the number of district officers and, also, their former commitments in terms of departmental programmes.

How to weld and coordinate these sectoral programmes has been both baffling and intriguing. Who should be charged with this responsibility of coordinating the activities of technical functionaries operating in the developmental field? Should, in other words, a new authority be created for discharging this responsibility? Or the District Collector be utilised for the work? Maharashtra and Gujarat have each created a new parallel district authority, called chief executive officer in Maharashtra and district development officer in Gujarat, who is in charge of development activities in the district, and who functions independently of the District Collector. The Bengal Administration Enquiry Committee (1945) was emphatic in its view that the District Collector, combining in himself as he does the final authority in regard to all district affairs, is expected to more effectively execute development plans than any other parallel authority to be set up in the district. It, indeed, recommended that all technical heads of district administration should be made directly responsible to the District Collector in every respect save that of the technical aspect of their work. The Balvantray Mehta Team for the Study of Community Projects and National Extension Services recommended: "At the district level, the Collector or the Deputy Commissioner should be the captain of the team of officers of all development departments and should be made fully responsible for securing the necessary coordination and cooperation in the preparation and execution of the district plans for community development."[18]

The District Collector, however, has not been able to emerge as an effective coordinator. As a commentator said: 'The position of the Collector in the most States of the Union is not an enviable one."[19] Lal Bahadur Shastri drove, home this lacuna in the following words:

> "In regard to developmental activities, the difficulty at the present moment is that there is no proper coordination. Formerly, the District Collector used to be the coordinating authority. He was in overall charge of every activity in the district. The District Collector is there but there are also, at the district level, officers of different departments, like P.W.D., agriculture, cooperation, education, etc. There is also some one in charge of the community development work. These different units function in a district but they are not under the District Collector or supervision of the District Collector. They have their direct connections with the respective heads of department sitting in the State Secretariat, or in some cases with the departmental officers at the divisional level. The result is that there is no proper coordination."[20]

This crucially important role of the District Collector is being gradually realized. This role is all the more important in terms of our commitment to achieve agricultural self-sufficiency. The Ministry of Food and Agriculture had set up, in 1963, a Working Group on Inter-departmental and Institutional Coordination for Agricultural Production under the chairmanship of Ram Subhag Singh to report on how to ensure speedy execution of the agricultural production programmes and to bring about effective coordination between the activities of agriculture, cooperation and other allied departments in the States and of the community development and *Panchayati Raj* institutions. This Group assigned a crucial role to the Collector. Significant in this respect are the following recommendations made by it:

1. The District Collector should be the Chairman of the Agricultural Production Committee of the *zila parishad*. If there is no *zila parishad* such a committee should be formed with the district officers of the departments concerned with agricultural production and representatives of non-official organizations, as members, and the Collector as Chairman. This Committee should be responsible for coordination of the activities of all departments concerned with agricultural production. In particular, the committee should consider and approve a coordinated agricultural production plan for the district, assign specific tasks and responsibilities to the officers and institutions concerned, receive and review progress reports from them and remove any bottlenecks or difficulties. The Member-Secretary of this Committee should be a senior class I officer of the status of a Deputy Director of one of the departments concerned with agricultural production, and he should be designated district agricultural production officer.

2. The district agricultural production officer should assist the Collector in coordinating the efforts of all the departments concerned with agricultural production at that level and should function under the overall direction of the Agricultural Committee. State heads of departments will continue to deal directly with their district officers as at present, but in matters relating to the work of the Agricultural Production Committee, they should communicate through the District Collector.

3. The District Collector should be effectively involved in assessing the work of district level functionaries. The Deputy Directors at the regional level should initiate the annual entries in the character roll of all district officers under their control and route them through the District Collector to the Heads of Departments concerned. The District Collector should add his own remarks on the works and conduct of the district officers involved in agricultural production before forwarding the Deputy Director's remarks to the heads of Department. The District Collector should write the character roll of the district agricultural production officer.

District Collector and separation of Judiciary

The Constitution enjoins on the State to separate the judiciary from the; executive, and many States have already done this. This separation however has created its unique problems. Under the pre-separation dispensation, the executive officers including the District Collector were enabled to acquire a detached and objective outlook to men and matters as well as an experience of judicial work also; while engaged in judicial work, the District Collector, for instance, obtained an intimate insight into the lives, problems, anxieties, aspirations etc. of the people in his charge. This, to be sure, was among the most valuable experiences of a District Collector, and it is precisely this which stands completely disrupted now. This inevitably creates a wide gap in the intellectual make-up and growth of this functionary. No less serious gap is observed in the post-separation judiciary in the district. The separation has caused an emergence of a new class of exclusive judicial officers who interpret the laws without having had any opportunity of acquiring first-hand experience of how the executive officers function under various circumstances, and what their problems and difficulties are. As a consequence, they are prone to interpret the laws in a rather abstract way. A complete absence of knowledge and experience of the functioning of the executive branch of Government has thus created an imbalance in the experience-alignment of the judicial officers. Both the problems underlined here need attention and appropriate remedial action.

NOTES

1. Khera, S.S., *District Administration in India,* Bombay, Asia Publishing House, 1964, p. 21.
2. Hunter, Sir William Wilson: *The Indian Empire: its People, History and Products,* London, Smith, Elder & Co., 1892, p. 456.
3. *The Imperial Gazetteer of India,* vol. IV, Oxford, Clarendon Press, 1909, p. 52.
4. Steevens, G.W.: *In India,* Edinburgh, William Blackwood & Sons, 1901, pp. 51-61.
5. *Report of the Indian Statutory Commission,* cmd 3568, London, H.M.S.O., 1930, p. 281.
6. Mangat Rai, E.N.: *Civil Administration in the Punjab,* Massachusetts, Harvard University, 1963, pp. 42-43.

7. *Report on Reorganization of Collectorates*, Lucknow, Government of Uttar Pradesh, 1956, p. 4.
8. In Tamil Nadu and Andhra Pradesh where the institution of Divisional Commissioners does not exist, the Board of Revenue comes in direct contact with the District Collector.
9. *Report on the Reorganization of District Revenue Offices*, Bombay, Government of Bombay, 1959, p. 24.
10. *Report of the (Madras) District Revenue Administration Enquiry* Committee, Madras, Government of Madras, 1955, p. 64.
11. Appleby, Paul H.: *Public Administration in India: Report of a Survey*, pp. 21-22.
12. Report of the Bengal Administration Enquiry Committee (Chairman: Sir Archibald Rowlands) 1945, para 104.
13. Bihar has no *tahsils*.
14. *Report of the (Bombay) District Revenue Offices*, Bombay, 1949 p 18.
15. Khera, S.S.: District Administration in India, *op. cit.*, p. 181.
16. Op. dt.t p. 38.
17. *Report of the Bengal Administration.Enquiry Committee*, 1944-45, (Chairman; Sir Archibald Rowlands), para 65.
18. *Report of the Team for the Study of Community Projects and National Extension Service*, vol. 1, Committee on Plan Projects, New Delhi, 1957, pp. 39-40.
19. Fletcher, A.L.:. 'The Collector in the Nineteen Sixties", in The *Indian Journal of Public Administration*, vol. XI.
20. *The Indian Journal of Public Administration*, vol. X, no. 4, October-December, 1964, pp. 595-6.

11

The Indian Administration Service

At present there are three all-India services in existence. Of these three the most important, both from the point of social prestige and of promotional prospects right up to the administrative top, is the Indian Administrative Service, popularly known by its abbreviated name I.A.S. On it has fallen the mantle of the old Indian Civil Service (I.C.S.). There are, how-ever, some major differences between I.C.S, and I.A.S. First, I.C.S. was the generalist, omnibus service. Its members used to man superior positions in all the branches of the Government including the judiciary (but excluding police), The I. A.S. has been provided with a more limited area to operate. Secondly, in the Central Secretariat there was a reservation of posts for members of I.C.S. No such reservation exists for I.A.S. And, thirdly, there has been a certain amount of qualitative decline also in I.A.S. As the annual intake in it did not exceed a dozen or so, and, as also the Government was, then, the only significant employer in the country, the I.C.S. was, as a rule, able to draw only the exceptionally bright persons to its fold. The I.C.S. examination was quite a tough one, confirmed by an account given by a contemporary aspirant and published in *The Statesman* in the year 1898. "A correspondent who, has just been facing the trying ordeal of the Indian Civil Service exami-nation, writes to the *London Daily Telegraph:* "It would be well that all candidates should know what they are letting themselves in for before they enter. On most subjects two papers are set, on others even three, in all of which it is practically compulsory to answer six questions. Thus, a man takes up the minimum number of nine subjects, he has at least ten days' or sixty hours' writing before him. Few can stand this without regular training. No man should face the examination without (a) first-hand advice from one who has been through the mill; (b) being first medically examined, since the medical test is a very stiff one. If he neglects (a) he will read either far too much, or else write off the point; while if he neglects (b) he may find to his sorrow that, though he has been mentally successful, he is pronounced physically deficient".[1] The I.A.S. cannot probably claim to be the only repository of talent, and talent only. As the annual intake, today, is many times that number there is room, in I.A.S., for mediocrity also. Besides, the private sector, too, has started offering suitable employment opportunities to young and capable graduates. As a consequence, there has been a decline in the number of first classes in the I.A.S.

As an all-India service the I.A.S. is under the joint control of the Centre and the States. The members of the I.A.S. are divided into state cadres. The ultimate control rests with the Central Government but immediate control is exercised by the State Government, to which a member has been allotted. The strength of each state cadre is fixed in such a way as to Include a reserve of officers who can be deputed to the Central Govern-ment under the tenure system. In 1972 the authorized strength of the I.A.S. was 3,650 but only 2,883 members were in position. This number was 800 in 1948. The strength of State cadre is fixed by an enumeration of all superior administrative posts above that of the district collectors (The Divisional Com-missioners, Members of Board of Revenue and Secretaries in administrative departments), all posts of District Collectors, and those of heads of offices and providing for a reserve of officers for deputation to the Central Government. The strength and composition of each of the cadres is determined by the Central Government in consultation with the State Governments.

Recruitment to the I.A.S. is made by the following three methods:

(1) By open com;petitive examination, administered to young persons in the age group 21-28 possessing at least the bachelor's degree.

(2) By promotion of members of State Civil Services.

(3) By selection in special cases from among persons who hold gazetted posts under the State Governments but are not members of the State Administrative Services.

The annual recruitment, which is at present nearly 140, is so fixed as to provide for:

(1) The maintenance element for meeting death, retirements, and other casualties in the direct recruitment quota.

(2) A growth element to meet the anticipated extension of the quota.

(3) An element to reduce the present gap.

The examination is administered by the Union Public Service Commission, which prepares a list of successful candidates and submits this list to the Department of Personnel. The actual appointment letters are issued by the Government, the Union Public Service Commission's role being advisory. In practice, however, the list sent by the Union Public Service Commission is generally accepted by the Government.

The intending candidate to I.A.S. took examination in (i) three compulsory subjects—Essay, General English and General Knowledge (ii) three optional subjects out of over 20 subjects being taught in the Indian universities and (iii) two additional subjects out of a list of over 15 subjects being taught at the post graduate level in the Indian universities.

As already discussed in the chapter on 'Public Services', the scheme of competitive examination for the Indian Administrative Service (and other higher civil services) has undergone a change since 1979 as a result of the acceptance by the Government of the .Kothari Committee recommendations. As a result since 1979 there is a combined, common competitive examination for the Indian Administrative Service, Indian Police Service and higher central services. It consists of two parts: a qualifying Preliminary Examination (objective type) and the Main Examination (comprising written test and interview). The Preliminary Examination consists of two papers: one in General Studies and the second in an optional subject out of the list mentioned on page 243.

The Main Examination consists of two parts; the written

examination and the interview the details about which are given on pages 244-45.

The candidates are given the choice to write their papers, other than English and the Language papers, in any language mentioned in the eighth schedule to the Constitution or in English. However, the question papers, for the Preliminary as well as the Main Examination, would be in English and Hindi only. Those who qualify in the written part of the Main Examination alone are called for interview. The marks for interview are 250. The upper age limit for civil service examination has been raised by 2 years from 26 to 28, with the usual relaxation for candidates belonging to scheduled castes and scheduled tribes. The candidates are allowed 3 chances for the civil service examination. The scheduled caste and scheduled tribe candidates are however, allowed to take the examination without any restriction on the number of chances, subject of course, to the prescribed age limits. The minimum educational qualification for appearing at the Main Examination continues to be a University Degree. The allocation of the candidates to different services is made on the basis of the Main Examination and interview taking into consideration their rank in the final examination and preferences.

Most of the subjects taught at the university level are included in the syllabus. One, however, finds one serious omission. Public Administration does not figure at the stage of the Preliminary Examination. This omission appears to be a hang-over of the past when there was no provision for its teaching in the Indian universities. Now, a number of universities have introduced Public Administration at the post-graduate level while many others have included it as a paper or group of papers in Political Science at the university level. The importance of this subject is obvious in the system of a competitive examination which has the avowed objective of recruiting future generalist administrators.

Then the rank-order list is prepared for the successful candidates. The top few are posted to the States of their choice. The rest are normally posted to States other than their own.

After selection the candidates are called probationers. All the probationers nave compulsorily to undergo training—more correct term would be an educational course—at the Lal Bahadur

Shastri National Academy of Administration, Mussoorie (a training school operating under the Department of Personnel). The training programme for the I.A.S. has under-gone a change since 1969. In 1969 the Central Government introduced what is called the sandwich course of training fo. the newly recruited members of the I.A.S. The I.A.S. probationers are required to undergo two spells of training with an interval of one year. The first spell consists of a foundational course and professional training. Its duration is six months. In the foundational course the I.A.S. probationers are joined by probationers of other central services (except those of the Central Secretariat Services who are trained at the government-owned Institute of Secretariat Training and Management, New Delhi). In addition to the foundational course, probationers undergo a measure of professional training also. The idea underlining the 'foundational' course is that officers of the higher services should acquire an understanding of the constitutional, economic and social framework within which they have to function, as these largely determine the policies and programmes towards promoting and execution of which they will have to make their contribution. They should also acquaint themselves with the machinery of government and broad principles of public administration, The foundational course is also intended to cover such matters as rights and obligations of the civil services, and the ethics of the profession—objectivity, integrity, morality etc.[2]

After the completion of the foundational course and the first phase of training at the National Academy of Adminis-tration, the I.A.S. probationers are sent for district training in the State to which they have been allotted. Broadly speaking the district training, which continues for full one year, is divided into three parts in most States. The probationer is sent to the State of his allotment. He begins his stay by calling on the Chief Secretary and, other Secretaries in the State Secretariat. Where there is a training school, the probationer is attached to it for institutional training for a certain period. He then goes to a district and works as an understudy in various administrative capacities. It is here that he obtains, for the first time, a good grasp of all facets of district administration and develops a capacity to study institutions, policies and programmes. The district selected for his posting is normally such as gives him a fairly good cross-section of district level problems. Equal care is taken to see that the District Collector is one who is passionately interested in the training of the young probationer. The probationer works under the tutelage of the District Collector and effectiveness of the on-the-job training depends upon the interest and enthusiasm shown by the District Collector. The choice of the District Collector is therefore very important. The probationer then comes to the Secretariat and moves from desk to desk to learn about the functioning of the headquarters of the Government. There is a counsellor at the Academy with whom the probationer remains in contact when he is on district training. The probationer regularly writes to his counsellor giving an account of what he is studying, his impressions and problems. The probationer is required to prepare reports on various subjects which are allotted to him at the Academy itself before the district training begins. These subjects primarily relate to district administration. These reports are evaluated at the Academy and thus taken into account in his final evaluation.

It is thus obvious that choice of the District Collector (as well as of the district) is of crucial importance in the effectiveness of the district training. The Academy sends broad guidelines to the Chief Secretary but the final decision regarding choice of the district rests with him. These guidelines expect that the district selected should be such as would give a good cross section of the problems to the probationer. In other words, the district should neither be a sleepy one where there are not many problems nor a highly industrialized or urban one which, again, is an out-of-the mill district. Also, the District Collector should be one who takes personal interest in the training of the young probationer. This is really a difficult problem. Sometimes even when the District Collector is chosen with considerable care, he gets transferred and the probationer certainly would not follow him to his next posting. Does the degree of interest depend upon whether the District Collector is himself a direct recruit or a 'promotee'? One cannot safely generalize in this regard. The general belief that the promotee-I.A.S. officer does not take much interest in the probationer (who is a direct recruit) does not seem to be very correct. Of course, the probationer would like to be placed under a Collector who is direct recruit—like himself; he is not very enthusiastic about his placement under a promotee

District Collector.

The reports prepared by the probationers form the basis of discussion and exercises during the second phase of training at the Academy, which continues for seven months. At the end of the training the probationer appears at an examination conducted by the Union Public Service Commission.

The probationer now becomes an officer and sent to the State of his posting. He is, then, given the charge of a sub-division. In order to enrich and diversify his experience he is, as a matter of deliberate policy, transferred from district to district after every two years' stay, and is even sent to the Secretariat for nearly eighteen months, as an Under Secretary. All this is prelude to eventually making him a District Collector, and is, thus, in a way, 'training' of the officer concerned. The object is to give a young officer a variety of experiences before he becomes ripe for a senior post in the sixth or seventh year of service. The I.A.S. cadre is meant primarily to provide officers for senior posts, the appointment of officers to junior posts is intended mainly to train them for the superior posts.[3] It is normally in the sixth or seventh year of service that the member of the I.A.S. is expected to be able to hold the posts of District Collector, cr any other posts of equivalent responsibility, although there are instances of officers possessing even three years' experience 'doing the district'.

NOTES

1. *The Statesman*, 7 September 1898.
2. *Report on Indian and State Administrative Services and Problems of District Administration* (Chairman: V.T. Krishnamachari) New Delhi, Planning Commission,, 1962, p, 14.
3. Ibid., p. 18.

12

All-India Services

HISTORICAL DEVELOPMENT

A remarkable feature of the administrative system in federally governed India is the deliberate retention of the all-India services, the personnel of which are interchangeable between the Central and the State Governments.[1] The all-India services constitute an administrative device peculiar to India and to Pakistan which was a part of the subcontinent prior to partition. Independent India had two all-India services in 1947—the Indian Administrative Service and the Indian Police Service.[2] In 1963 three more were set up—the Indian Service of Engineers, the Indian Forest Service and the Indian Medical and Health Service. The Indian Service of Engineers and the Indian Medical and Health Service, however, proved to be stillborn owing to the states' refusal to participate in them.

Historically the all-India services, then known as the Secretary of State's services, were formed when India had a unitary, centralized system of Government. They were ideally suited to the requirements of that time as their members acquired experience in both the Central Government and with local and provincial levels. Recruitment by the Secretary of State for India and his control over conditions of service of the personnel who could be deployed in any part of the country were the essential attributes of the all-India services. Such a power was thought to hold the key to the exercise of British control over the country, because it guaranteed control over the whole administration. As the British Government wanted only British officers in key positions in India, and as these officers were not willing, nor was it expedient to compel them, to serve under Indian control, recruitment to, and control over the top services by the Secretary of State was considered to be essential. The all-India services as an institution had strategic control of the framework of law and order, which the imperial rule considered necessary for its survival. The dependence of the imperial government on them became steadily more obvious as the popular desire for fully responsible government became more vocal and assertive.

The all-India services were not all created at the same time. The oldest was the famous Indian Civil Service (ICS) which owes its origin to the Macaulay Report submitted in 1854. The last to be added to the list was the Indian Agricultural Service, constituted in 1906. On the eve of the Government of India, Act 1919, there were the following nine all-India services.[3]

(1) The Indian Civil Service

(2) The Indian Police Service

(3) The Indian Forest Service

(4) The Indian Educational Service

(5) The Indian Agricultural Service

(6) The Indian Civil Veterinary Service

(7) The Indian Forest Engineering Service

(8) The Indian Medical Service (Civil)

(9) The Indian Service of Engineers

When the Government of India Act 1919 introduced for the first time in 1921 responsible government in a limited sphere at the provincial level through the device of 'transferred' subjects under popular; control, described in political parlance as 'dyarchy', the Central Government ceased to be the sole Government of the country, although not departing, constitutionally speaking, from the existing unitary set up. From then onwards the division of responsibility between the Centre and the provinces became vertical, the latter acquiring, free from central control, a sphere of functions defined by the Act itself. The propriety of the all-India services under such an arrangement was questioned for the first time. The Royal Commission on the Superior Services in India, set up in 1923 under the chair-manship of Viscount Lee of Fareham, recommended[4] that no further recruitment be made to four of the nine all-India services then in existence: the Indian Educational Service, the Indian Agricultural Service, the Indian Veterinary Service and the Indian Forest Service[5] (only in Bombay and Burma) "The personnel required for these branches of administration should in future be recruited and appointed by local governments".[6]

The principle that generally guided the Commission was that responsibility had to be matched with authority, and this meant control over the recruitment and conditions of service of the personnel charged with responsibility. The Lee Commission itself did not carry this reasoning to its logical conclusion. The Indian Medical Service and the Indian Service of Engineers which were recommended for continuance were clearly in violation of the principle. A section of Indian public opinion was however, averse to the retention of the institution of all-India services. R.K. Shanmukham Chetty, a member of the Central legislative assembly, for instance, observed:

> "The Honourable Leader of the House very rightly remarked that the (civil) services must be responsible to the authority whose policy it (*sic.*) is meant to carry out. The position is no doubt realized by the [Lee] Commission, But in what way have they tried to give effect to it? No doubt, in so far as they recommended that all the services under the departments that have been transferred to the provinces must be provincialized, they recognize this principle. But in so far as they are perpetuating, with regard to the other administrative branches in the provinces, the same system that is continuing at the present day . . . I contend that it is perpetuating the present system which, when the other subjects are transferred in the course of time, will present serious obstacles in the way of administration by Ministers. As was observed in the able memorandum presented by the Madras Officers' Association to the Royal Commission, the all-India hallmark exists only for the purpose of enabling these officers to claim to be appointed, confirmed and dismissed by an extra-provincial authority and to escape effective control either by provincial executive or by the provincial legislature. An all-India service with these extraordinary privileges is an anachronism in any system of provincial responsible

government and, we would add, is a violation in the spirit of the Government of India Act of 1919. Therefore, Sir, in so far as no serious and deliberate attempt is made by the Commission to do away with this invidious distinction, I must say that this House cannot find its way to accept its recommendations."[7]

Such opinions proved of little avail and His Majesty's Government to whom the Report was submitted accepted the recommendations made by the Lee Commission including its recommendations regarding the all-India services.

The same year the Reforms Enquiry Committee, set up by the Central Government, found itself sharply divided on the question of all-India services. The nationalist members of the committee 'ventured' to think that "under the present system, the entire Constitution, the methods of recruitment and control of the services are incompatible with the situation created by the Reforms (of 1919) and the possibility of their further developments."[8]

In 1928 the all-parties conference set up a committee under the chairmanship of Motilal Nehru to determine the principles of the Constitution for India. It is significant that this committee did not recommend the continuance of the all-India services in independent India. It recommended, instead, separate civil services for the 'commonwealth' and the provinces.

In 1929 the nationalist members of the Indian Central Committee (1928-29) constituted by the Central Government to liaise with the Indian Statutory Commission pressed for provincialization of the services. They observed in their dissenting note: "...no self Government is possible unless the services are provincialized and all officers are placed under the Ministers. If any European officers are required, there is little doubt that the new governments will be able to obtain their services from the Government of India; or would, even after full provincial responsibility is conferred on them, continue, to recruit them."[9] Similarly, the Committee appointed in 1929 by the United Provinces Legislative Council to cooperate with the Indian Statutory Commission showed awareness of the implications of provincial autonomy and of the anomalous position of the all-India services in the emergent political set-up. It remarked: "...we hold that the retention of these (i.e., all-India) services in a system of full provincial autonomy would unnecessarily complicate matters".[10] It also called for an immediate provincialization of the all-India services.

This institution again became the subject of investigation at the hands of a sub-committee which the first Indian Round Table Conference (12 November 1930 — 19 January 1931) had constituted. The thirty-four member Sub-Committee on Services, set up under the chairmanship of Sir William Jowitt, lacked, as was not unusual with the committees of this era, unanimity in its recommendation on the future of the all-India services. There was an undercurrent of opposition to the continuance of the all-India services under the new political set-up contemplated for the country.[11]

Two out of twenty-six Indian members who sat on the sub-committee, B. Shiva Rao and Sreepad Balwant Tambe, demanded immediate and total discontinuance of the all-India services, while three others—Bhimrarao Ambedkar, Zafrullah Khan and Sampuran Singh—were averse to further recruitment on the all-India basis for the Indian Civil Service and the Indian Police Service. The majority of the members, however, recommended the retention of the Indian Civil Service and the Indian Police Service as all-India services except that recruitment for judicial offices from the Indian Civil Service, as was the prevalent practice, was to be discontinued.

A few years later, the British Indian Delegation in its memorandum[12] to the Joint Committee on Indian Constitutional Reform (1933-34), constituted as its name implies to frame the Constitution for India, urged that the officers serving under the provinces should be recruited on a provincial basis, and that the all-India services were incompatible with provincial autonomy. The Joint Committee, while appreciating 'the force of this line of argument', did not accept it. It regarded the need for a regular supply of officers: both Indian and British, of the highest quality as vital to the stability of the proposed constitution itself, and the all-India services, recruited and controlled by the Secretary of State, assured this. Secondly, it wanted to play safe by not introducing any change in the civil service, 'simultaneously with the introduction of fundamental changes in the system of

Government'. "It is of the first importance that in the early days of the new order, and indeed until the course of events in the future can be more clearly foreseen, the new constitution should not be exposed to risk and hazard by radical change in the system which has for so many generations produced men of the right, calibre."[13] In addition to the Indian Civil Service and the Indian Police Service, the two 'security' services, the Joint Committee Recommended the continuance of the Indian Medical Service (Civil); in deference to the British officers in that service, though it had been recommended for abolition by the services sub-committee of the First Round Table Conference. The Joint Committee, remarked: "We are . . . convinced on the information supplied to us that the continuance of the civil branch of the Indian Medical Service will provide the only satisfactory method of meeting the requirements of the war reserve and of European members of the civil services, and that it will be necessary for the Secretary of State to retain the power which he at present possesses (although medical matters have since 1920 been under the control of Ministers) to require the provinces to employ a specified number of Indian Medical Service officers. In making these recommendations we have not been unmindful of the natural desire ' of the provinces to develop medical services entirely under their own control. But the requirements of the army and of the civil service have an overriding claim"[14] (italics supplied.)

These recommendations found expression in section 244 of the Government of India Act 1935, which listed three services, the Indian Civil Service, the Indian Police Service, and the Indian Medical Service (Civil) as all-India services.[15]

Political India had thus set its face resolutely against the institution of all-India services. The same, however, may not be said so firmly about the attitude of the largest minority in India, namely the Muslims, although Sir Shafaat Ahmed Khan, a prominent member of the All-India Muslim League, argued for the provincialization of all-India services in his book *The Indian Federation*, published in 1937.[16] The Muslims appeared to be equivocal in their views on the all-India services. They were a majority community in some provinces and a minority in others, which put them in a dilemma. To the Muslims of the provinces where they were in a minority, the existence of all-India services with a British element in them offered protection against domination by the Hindus. So they wanted the retention of all-India services with a suitable provision for the employment of British officers in them. Sir Shafaat, who has been quoted above in favour of provincialization, took in 1929 the opposite view and pleaded for the continuance, 'for some time to come', of the Indian Civil Service and the Indian Police Service.[17] However, Muslims could, at the same time, see dangers in all-India services. As the Central Government would be controlled by the Hindus, these services might be a useful instrument for the Centre to contain and even thwart the autonomy of the Muslim majority provinces. It was this apprehension which in 1946 impelled the Muslim majority provinces of Sind, Bengal and Punjab to opt out of the scheme of all-India services prepared by the interim Central Government in 1946.

Indian reaction at the time of Independence

History has the uncanny habit of often thrusting on people and institutions roles of which they were at one time outspoken critics. When in 1946 the independence of India appeared to be in sight, the nationalist stance on the all-India services underwent a sudden and fundamental change. The national leadership took a leaf out of the Secretary of State's book and assumed a role which the latter had consistently played in regard to the all-India services. This is reflected in the interim Central Government's quick initiative in convening a provincial premiers' conference in October 1946 to consider the question of replacement of the Indian Civil Service and the Indian Police. This conference met on 21 and 22 October 1946 under the chairmanship of Vallabhbhai Patel, the Home member in the interim Government. He referred to the situation created by the decision of the Secretary of State to stop further recruitment to the above mentioned two services in view of the impending constitutional changes and also the likely vacancies resulting from the retirement of the existing members of these two service, after the expected announcement of the terms on which their services would be terminated. In view of the imminent disappearance of the Indian Civil Service, he made a plea for an 'all-India administrative service'. The arguments advanced for this were the obvious importance of maintaining the highest possible standard of efficiency, of giving the civil service 'experience .... at the Centre leading to efficiency, and administrative experience of the district', of serving as 'a liaison between the provinces and the (Central) Government', and of introducing, both in the provinces and m the Centre, 'a progressive and wide outlook and freshness and vigour of administration'.

Gaining provincial acceptance for the proposed 'all-India administrative service' was not an entirely smooth affair, despite the indomitable personality of the Home member and the political composition of the conference. The provinces where the Indian National Congress was the ruling party were represented by the premiers who were expected[18] to fall in line with the Centre's wishes, although at least one of them, Govind Ballabh Pant, was reported to have opposed the proposal with unusual force. Punjab, where the Unionist Party was in power, was represented by its Home Minister. Sind and Bengal, where the Muslim League was at the helm of affairs, sent the Chief Secretary and the Additional Secretary respectively to this conference. The provinces generally made a distinction between recruitment and control; while a majority of them were in favour of recruitment of personnel on an all-India basis, there was a general inclination to favour retention of provincial control over such personnel, A 'consensus', however, appeared in favour of an all-India administrative service with the pay scale of Rs. 350-400-450-450-500[19] for the first five years. Having discovered that the provinces were pliable enough, the second day of the conference was utilized to secure agreement to another service, namely 'an all-India police service'.

All this was a magnificent victory for the Centre and, more truly, a personal triumph for Vallabhbhai Patel. Indeed Patel may rightly be acknowledged as the father of all-India services. His task was probably rendered less arduous by the Muslim League's initial abstention from the interim Central Government. The Muslim League joined the Central Government after the provincial premiers' conference had finished its deliberations.

Nevertheless it must be stated that the provinces evinced little enthusiasm for the all-India services; the latter were pushed down their reluctant throats by Vallabhbhai Patel. The Unionist Party under the leadership of Sir Khizar Hayat Khan, premier of Punjab, lost no time in publicly repudiating such an administrative arrangement, declaring 'Punjab is one of those provinces which would prefer to have a superior service of their own instead of an all-India administrative service under contemplation for this purpose'.[20] Punjab was soon joined by Sind and Bengal in its opposition to an all-India administrative service.

A week after this conference, there was an interpellation in the central legislative assembly. Patel's terse reply was: "A conference of provincial premiers was convened on the 21st October 1946 by me to discuss arrangements to replace these (the Secretary of State's) services. The consensus of opinion at the conference was in favour of the formation of new ail-India services for this purpose. Details are being worked out in consultation with the provinces and when arrangements are finalized a public announcement will be made."[21] When one member (Sri Prakasa) further asked: "Have the Government assured themselves that such services are at all necessary in future?", Patel merely said, 'That is the consensus of opinion of the provinces".[22] The partition of the country in 1947 cleared the way for the acceptance by all of the all-India services.

All-India, services and the Indian Constitution

The drafting committee of the Indian constituent assembly did not originally provide a constitutional base to the all-India services. Explaining its views, the committee observed: "The committee has refrained from inserting in the Constitution any detailed .provisions relating to the services; the committee considers that they should be regulated by Acts of the appropriate legislature rather than by constitutional provisions, as the committee feels that the future legislatures in this country, as in other countries, may be trusted to deal fairly .with the services."[23] The draft constitution accordingly makes no mention of the all-India services. Yet the Constitution which finally emerged from the constituent assembly not only embodies reference to it, but also includes provision for the creation of new all-India services.[24] The constituent assembly accepted these without demur.[25]

Such sudden solicitude for the all-India services was due to the Home Ministry's special insistence on its inclusion in the supreme constitutional document of the land. A constitutional base was deliberately preferred with a view to making it more lasting and less vulnerable. Vallabhbhai Patel, who was by then the Home Minister, was the principal advocate of this institution. The 'steel-frame of the whole structure', a sobriquet for the all-India service, endeared itself to the Iron Man of India[26]. The dominance of a unified political party like the Indian National Congress rendered its acceptance easily. Besides, the time was such that there was firm support for whatever appeared as an agent and symbol of centralism and national unity. As the nation was at this time passing through a critical period in her history in the wake of partition, communal riots and other disturbances, the constituent assembly itself, which originally contemplated a rather weak centre, ultimately plumed for an extraordinarily powerful Central Government. The constitutional provision for the all-India services was but one manifestation of the prevalent national mood.

ARGUMENTS FOR AND AGAINST ALL-INDIA SERVICES

The plea for an all-India service is ostensibly based on three grounds.[27] The all-India service is considered to be a bulwark of national integration as its members possess an all-India outlook. Secondly, being recruited on an all-India basis it tends to attract the best talent in the country so vital for the accomplishment of national tasks. Thirdly, it reinforces the sense of independence and impartiality of its members by affording protection against local pressures and influences.

These arguments will be examined one by one.

All-India Outlook

The plea of all-India outlook assumed in an all-India service is neither supported by logic nor borne out by actual experience. Competence of a person as judged through written examination and brief interview, which form the initial basis of his recruitment, and an essentially cultural trait like all-India outlook are not directly connected factors. No correlation need exist between the recruitment to a particular service and an individual's outlook. To say that merely by being recruited to an all-India service a person comes to possess an all-India outlook is highly conjectural. If this were not so, the personnel of a State civil service could be thought to have a provincial outlook; a university teacher but a university-wide outlook. A cure to all these would apparently lie in creating an all-India service for every aspect of administration.

Membership of particular services does make individuals absorb certain traditions and habits of thought, which in turn tend to influence their behaviour and perception of roles. The members of all-India services, especially of the Indian Administrative Service, have become, if anything, too conscious of their membership of particular service *vis-a-vis* the other services, too conscious of their status and privileges, too resistant to sharing their privileged position with members of other services. A consequence is that even the members of all-India services remain dominated by feelings of 'exclusiveness and do not, generally speaking, visualize their role against the totality of operations. Internally also, a particular all-India service hardly shows much emotional cohesion. This is true of even the IAS, the direct successor to the Indian Civil Service. Unlike the ICS, the IAS is not homogeneous in character. It is composed of persons who hail from different geographic regions, belong to different social groups and economic classes, come from different universities and, what is more, through different avenues, and remain subject to regional, linguistic and other pressures and rivalries. As it is recruited by many methods there is even a tendency among its members to form groups round the mode of recruitment itself. The cumulative result is that the IAS, as any other all-India service, is made up of clusters in terms of region, caste, language, mode of appointments, etc. with sharply identifiable loyalties to them.[28]

Nor is an all-India outlook necessarily demanded from civil servants. The all-India services have been divided into State cadres and members are initially posted to a State. The local influences—political and social—operate upon them during this period; they tend to project themselves during the officer's service under the Central Government and must militate against an all-India outlook. In a federation disputes between the Centre and the constituent States are not uncommon. An all-India outlook of the members of all-India services is of little avail when their members are required under ministerial pressure to join in Centre-State or inter-State conflicts, and find themselves preparing briefs and memoranda claiming for their state something under dispute—a town or a steel mill or an oil refinery.

Bureaucracy as an instrument of government and for the fulfilment of the objectives of the Constitution must, indeed, foster national integration through administrative policy and action, but its impact will necessarily be restricted: it can at best do little more than counteract fissiparous manifestations and disruptive forces. But the building-up of cohesion is a positive process which depends more upon extra-governmental organizations like the national parliament, political parties, the press, academic institutions, voluntary organizations, and the myriad professional and interest groups. The contribution of the all-India services in this direction is bound to be peripheral. What is more, it may even be dangerous to single out one range of services for the performance of the difficult task of nation-building. Imperceptibly, but perhaps with more enduring benefits, trade, commerce, industry and the academic world have already begun to release forces and set in motion reactions which inevitably result in greater intermingling of people of different regions, thus working towards national unity.

Closely related to the above is the aspect of leadership in administration. The members of the all-India services number about 4,000 out of some 7.8 million persons who are presently in all the three levels of Government in India. Of this a considerable number is employed at junior and middle level positions never coming into direct contact with the top men of the all-India services. Where, indeed, leadership is desperately needed is at the middle operational and supervisory levels. Members of the all-India services man these positions rather early in their career and for comparatively short periods. It is the state civil services which remain at this level for long periods and the members of these somewhat neglected services that have to be utilized, if at all, for leadership purposes in administration. It is too much to expect the limited personnel of the all-India services to provide leadership and cohesion in an administration which employs no less than 7.8 million persons at all the three levels. When it is further considered that each service is today bedevilled by inter-service and intra-service cleavages, the weakness of the claim that the all-India services, including the IAS, can act as a leaven in administration becomes obvious.

All-India services: repository of talent

The second argument behind the all-India service is that it attracts talent. That a service should be enabled to recruit the ablest is unexceptionable. But India is so vast and local diversities are so numerous and basic that a deep insight into them should be considered as an essential rather than a merely desirable qualification for a successful public servant. A person who may have distinguished himself academically, but who cannot with ease converse in the regional language and has no deep understanding of local customs, culture and mores cannot make a 'good' civil servant. He will have no heart in the place and will, always be on the look-out for an opening in the Central Government. Though formally he continues to be borne on that State Government's cadre, most of his official life may be spent in the service of the Central Government. The State Government remains practically deprived of his services. This is precisely what is happening in the IAS today. Among the officers allotted to a particular state cadre of the IAS are those who have not been the regular residents of that State: these, officers are usually the keenest to come to the Central Government and are the most reluctant to go back to the State to which they were allotted. Many of them do not feel at home in the State to which they are posted, and both psychologically and emotionally feel closer to the Central Government. Although half of the vacancies in the state cadre of each of the all-India services to be filled by competitive examination are since 1957 set aside for persons who are inhabitants of another State, the 'national integration', which it is hoped to promote in this way, is more apparent than real. Generally a person opts for a neighboring State. It is, for instance, not common for a northerner to seek a posting in a State in the south, and vice versa.

Taken even on its face value the 'merit' criterion appears to be over-emphasized. A majority of candidates joining the all-India services in a particular year are but of average abilities, having graduated in the second division.[29] This has happened because of bulk recruitment of candidates[30] and also because of the prevalent practice of reservation of posts for scheduled castes and scheduled tribes.[31] All this is in addition to two other features marking recruitment to the all-India services. These are a relatively large intake from sources other than competitive examination and, second, provision of a sizeable quota (25 per cent of the intake) for the state service personnel. Given the present condition of the country, the disappearance of the all-India services may not cause any significant damage to the totality of the civil service. If there were no all-India services, the persons preferring government service to other forms of employment would surely be pulled into the state services, though admittedly some might be lost to well-paid business positions. Even today, a person simultaneously appears in several competitive examinations, including the state service examination. If the all-India services are abolished, the talent, would get diverted to and absorbed into the state services, for the nation's pool of talent does not expand with the setting-up of an all-India service nor does it shrink with its closure.

Indeed, the state civil services which today suffer from a degree of inferiority would be likely to acquire a better image if the corresponding all-India services were abolished. As all senior positions in a State are as a rule held by members of the all-India services, particularly the IAS, the state civil service personnel always function in subordination to the latter. They are, indeed, perpetual vice-presidents in the state administrative hierarchy, meant for lesser roles and receiving lower scales of pay. The senior positions in the State would become available to the members of the state services if the all-India services disappeared and this would automatically improve the career prospects of State civil servants. Such an incentive would help sustain the morale of these services and in the long run prove more conducive to all-round efficiency.

Bulwark of the Independence and impartiality of the Civil Service

There is also the centre's apprehension of a general politicalization of the state bureaucracy if its recruitment and control were vested in the individual States, This, indeed, was the central argument advanced by Vallabhbhai Patel in his letter to the Prime Minister in which he argued in favour of the all-India service and its enshrinement in the Constitution itself. He wrote: "I need hardly emphasize that an efficient, disciplined and contented (civil) service assured of its prospects as a result of diligent and honest work is a *sine qua non* of sound administration under a democratic regime even more than under an authoritarian rule. The (civil) service must be above party and we should ensure that political considerations either in its recruitment or in its discipline and control are reduced to the minimum, if not eliminated altogether. In an all-India service, it is obvious, recruitment, discipline and control, etc., have to be tackled on a basis of uniformity and under the direction of the Central Government which is the recruiting agency."[32] At this argument suspecting the States' capability to develop 'an efficient, disciplined and contented' civil service is bound to offend their susceptibilities, it is not now much voiced publicly. On merits too the argument is hardly tenable as the Central Government may be equally subject to political pulls and pressures. After all, recruitment to the political cadres of the Central and State Governments takes place from the same source and it would be incorrect to ascribe political foibles to the state level only. Indeed if a country has not generally developed attitudes favourable towards the political neutrality of the civil services, it is unreasonable to assume that some services will remain immune to political influence and others will not.

Taken all together it is an error to exaggerate the benefits of the all-India service. It can activate itself only in the event of the President taking over the administration of a State under the emergency provisions of the Constitution, for the Central Government can justifiably count more on the loyalty of officers of the all-India service who, in the last analysis, are its employees than on the members of the state service.

The obverse is also clear. The State Government may induce itself to repose more trust in the state service personnel than in the officers who remain subject to the remote control of the Central Government and whose loyalty is thus questioned. This is not unlikely thinking on the part of the units. When, however, the units come to be founded in a federal Constitution, the resistance to a centrally recruited and controlled civil service undergoes a qualitative change. The two governmental systems, operating independently of each other, more so in a competitive polity, also postulate two separate civil services.[33] The all-India service is incompatible with the federal character of the Indian Constitution, although it does find a mention m it. In the never-ceasing see-saw game of adjustment and bargaining between the Centre and the States in a federal cum competitive polity, neither its all-India outlook, nor its talent, nor even its supposedly steadfast loyalty to the Centre conies into active play. On the contrary, a lingering suspicion about its fidelity is likely to make it look like the proverbial mote in the States' eyes as the latter gain a larger measure of self-confidence and self-assertion. Operating as it does under the ultimate control of the Central Government, it presupposes the superior excellence and wisdom of the latter *vis-a-vis* the states. While this was, or may have been, historically true, its validity as a concept in federalism is questionable. Also the resultant relativity, established through the interchange of personnel with a, prospect of their eventual retention by the Centre, may not affect the latter adversely, but tends to have a constraining effect on a more forward-looking State.[34]

Indeed, the all-India services arc already becoming suspect in the eyes of the States ruled by political parties adopting a leftist or regional stance. Some at least of the constituent states are intensifying their opposition to the all-India services and their number is increasing. E.M.S. Namboodiripad, the former Chief Minister of Kerala and a member of the Communist Party, openly questioned while' in office the validity of the all-India services, the members of which are recruited and trained by the Congress Government at the Centre and posted to States in many of which there are non-Congress government," adding "suddenly one morning I find a few young boys and one or two girls before me saying they have been posted to Kerala. What shall I do with them? What do I know of them?"[35] One item in the thirty-two-point programme on which the political parties in West Bengal constituting the united front fought the mid-term election in 1969 related to the State Government acquiring 'complete' control over all civil servants occupying posts under the State. M. Karunanidhi, the former Chief Minister of Tamil Nadu belonging to DMK, a regional party confined to one State, sought control overall civil servants working in the State Government. Even

Ajoy Kumar Mukherji, leader of Bangla Congress and former Chief Minister of West Bengal, pointed out: "The ICS and the IAS are too costly for the States, not commensurate with the supposed benefits from them. The present all-India service should be gradually liquidated."[36] It is significant that although the upper chambers of the Indian Parliament passed a resolution in 1963 in favour of the creation of two more all-India services—the Indian Education Service and the Indian Agricultural Service—this proposal has been finally dropped in view of the States' 'revised . . . stand on the need for these services'.[37]

Broadly, the arguments against the all-India services are as follows. Firstly, the States ought to enjoy the right to recruit and control the civil service for the performance of tasks which have been allotted to them under the Constitution. An all-India service restricts the degree and sphere of their autonomy—and patronage. Secondly, in order to attract people from all over the country, and also to enable them to serve efficiently even in remote parts of the country, the pay scale of the all-India services is kept more favourable than that of the state civil services. This imposes heavier financial burden on the States, leaving them with correspondingly less resources for development tasks. Thirdly, the all-India services keep the members of the state services alienated and thus have a demoralizing effect on the totality of the civil service.

Besides, the all-India services have to encounter from now onward practical difficulties which may render them increasingly unworkable. The recruitment to these services through the medium of regional languages makes maintenance of a common standard in the candidates highly improbable.[38] Also, the States where the majority of the personnel of the all-India services are to work are increasingly switching over to the regional languages. Indeed, they have already started transacting an increasing volume of business in their own languages, A person selected to an all-India service may not know the language of the State to which he has been posted. He may, to be sure, acquire working familiarity with the regional language of the adopted State but may not become fully proficient in it. Besides, a member of the all-India service also comes to the Central Government from time to time for a tour of duty. As the language in vogue in the

Central Government is English, he may not prove to be effective in it. Indeed, a member of the all-India service is likely to be effective only at one level because of the language itself The adoption of the regional language as the medium of instruction in the universities is already producing a regular supply of young educated persons largely bereft of a knowledge of English. The Government too has, in part, responded to this situation by agreeing to hold the competitive examination through the regional languages, besides English and Hindi. As a result there is the risk of a person's remaining 'frozen' into ineffectiveness if he does not know the language of the Central Government as well as that of the State to which he has been posted.

Future prospects

The foregoing analysis suggests that the all-India service as an institution is unlikely to remain unscathed in the foreseeable future. Statesmanship lies in starting a meaningful dialogue with the States on this question. A suggestion has been made that, apropos the wording of Article 312 of the Constitution, an all-India service need be constituted only after its specific endorsement by the States formally signified through a resolution of their legislatures. This would give it political legitimacy.[39] It may even be that a politically acceptable solution would lie in entrusting the Central Government with the recruitment and initial training of personnel and the State Government with complete control over them.

By the same token, the Central Government too must make provision for the managing of positions which are presently being filled with officers of the all-India services. Already, it has a number of central civil services to draw upon for managing these posts. Also, by bilateral arrangements it may obtain officers from the States, and *vice-versa*. It is true that the pay scale of the Central Government personnel would be more favourable, but an employment under the State Government will offer opportunities of working closer to the people, which itself is an exciting experience with its own rewards.

In India both the parliamentary form of government and federalism have, despite difficulties, established themselves. National unity is now no longer subject to serious challenge. These achievements have been associated with a growing politicization of the society and with a wider recognition of the need to mobilize as much political and administrative talent as possible at all levels of the system in support of the tasks of social and economic development. Yet in the evolution of a set of institutions some come to be held more sacrosanct than others and indeed acquire such primacy as virtually to determine the location of others in the system. This has been the case of the all-India services. It is the changes achieved in the political environment in which these services operate that now make it necessary to challenge their continued primacy.

NOTES

1. Members of the appropriate all-India services are also seconded to local governments by the State Governments.
2. It should be noted that the all-India services of pre-1947 origin were not abolished abruptly or altogether. A decision to abolish a particular service meant discontinuing fresh recruitment to it, thus enabling its painless extinction through the natural process of retirement, resignation and casualties of its members. Independent India deliberately retained in 1947 only two all-India services; the Indian Civil Administrative Service (which included the old Indian Civil Service) and the Indian Police Service. It inherited, however, the other all-India services as well, which were on their way out. The last member of the Indian Civil Service will retire in 1979.
3. *Report of the Royal Commission on the Superior Civil Services in India*, Simla, Government of India Press, 1924, p, 4.
4. *Ibid.*, chapter II.
5. It also recommended provincialization of the roads and buildings branch of the Public Works Department.
6. *Ibid.*, p. 8.
7. *Legislative Assembly Debates*, vol. IV, part V, 3-16 September 1924, p. 3261.
8. *Report of the Reforms Enquiry Committee*, Calcutta, Government of India Central Publication Branch, 1924, p. 163.
9. *Report of Indian Central Committee*, Calcutta, Government of India Central Publication Branch, 1929, p. 136.
10. *Report of the Committee appointed by the United Provinces Legislative Council to cooperate with the Indian Statutory* Commission, Allaha-bad, Superintendent, Government Press, 1929, pp. 104-05, Also see fn, 17.

11. Three view-points emerged in the committee. One section was in favour of retaining the status quo in this matter, holding that the Secretary of State for India should continue, as in the past, to bear responsibility for the recruitment of members of all-India services and for determination of conditions of their service. Another section recognized the desirability of retraining the Indian Civil Service and the Indian Police Service but wanted the Government of India to recruit and' control the members of these services. Yet another section insisted on the provincialization of all-India services. Hafiz Hidayat Husain argued: "The great objection, which to my mind seems to be insuperable, is that we are going to have provincial autonomy and if every subject is going to be transferred to the administration of the "legislative council, the retention of the Indian Civil Service and the Indian Police Service is, to my mind, fraught with considerable difficulties and inconvenience". Husain, however, did not press his views. (Indian Round Table Conference: *Proceedings of Sub-Committees*, vol. VIII, Calcutta, Central Publication Branch, 1931, p. 36). B. Shiva Rao said: "I think it would be satisfactory to work these services on an all-India basis, and at the same time ensure a proper relationship between the services and the Ministry". (*Ibid.*, p. 54). Bhimrao Ambedkar, who was also against all-India services, observed: "We are framing a Constitution in which we propose to give as large a degree of provincial autonomy to the provinces as possible, and it seems to me that no province can be deemed to have provincial autonomy if it has not the right to regulate the civil service that is going to work in its area". (*Ibid.*, p. 55).
12. Quoted in Report of Joint Committee on Indian Constitutional Reform, vol. I, (part I), London, HMSO, 1934, para 296.
13. *Ibid.*, para 297.
14. *Ibid.*, para 299.
15. Section 244 said: "(i) as from the commencement of Part III of this Act appointments to the Indian Civil Service, the Indian Medical Service (Civil), and the Indian Police Service (which last-mentioned service shall thereafter be known as "The Indian Police') shall until (British) Parliament otherwise determines, be made by the Secretary of State".
16. Sir Shafaat Ahmed Khan observed: "Provincial self-Government logically necessitates control by the provincial government over the appointment of its servants. A public servant cannot serve two masters. If he is appointed by the Secretary of State, it may be extremely difficult for the provincial

Government to exercise sufficient control and supervi-sion. The authority of such government may be undermined, and in some case actually flouted by a public servant who is determined to assert his legal rights". *The Indian Federation*, London, Macmillan, 1937, p. 216.

17. *Vide* his 'explanatory' note in the Report of the Committee appointed by the United Provinces Legislative Council to cooperate with the Indian Statutory Commission, *op. cit.*, pp. xxviii-xxxiv.
18. The North-West Frontier Province, ruled by the Congress, remained unrepresented on the first day of the conference.
19. The Indian National Congress has passed a resolution in 1931 at its Karachi session fixing a ceiling on the salary of civil servants at five hundred rupees per month. Hence, this payscale. It should be noted that the Karachi resolution was disowned shortly afterwards. 'There is a long distance between Karachi and Delhi today", said Vallabhbhai Patel in 1949. He taunted the members of the central legislative assembly: "You want forty-five rupees a day free of income-tax. What is the use of talking about Rs. 500 today ? It is very wrong." *Constituent Assembly Debates*, vol. X, 10 October 1949, p. 50.
20. *The Hindu*, 25 October 1946, p. 4.
21. Starred Question 11, *Legislative Assembly Debates*, 30 October 1946, p. 213.
22. *Ibid.*, p. 214.
23. The Constituent Assembly of India, *Draft Constitution of India*, New Delhi, Government of India Press, 1948, p. xi.
24. Article 312 of the Indian Constitution says;

    "(i) Notwithstanding 'anything in Part XI, if the Council of States has declared by resolution supported by not less than two-thirds of the members present and voting that it is necessary or expedient in the national interest so to do, Parliament may by law provide for the creation of one or more all-India services common to the Union and the States, and subject to the other provisions of this chapter, regulate the recruitment, and the conditions of service of persons appointed, to any such service, (ii) The services known at the commencement of this Constitution as the Indian Administrative Service and the Indian Police Service shall be deemed to be services created by Parliament under this article."
25. The article relating to the all-India services was Article 282 C when it came up for discussion in the constituent assembly. It was passed without a disapproving voice and in less than ten

minutes. Only three members—Brajeshwar Prasad, Muniswamy Pillai and P.S. Deshmukh—participated in the discussion. Brajeshwar Prasad, who held the view that 'all services in the country should be centralized' sought the power of creation of all-India services to be vested in the lower house of the central legislature. P.S. Deshmukh supported him: "Nowhere has the initiative in any important matter been left to any other house except the house of the people in the Central Parliament. But here for the first time ....we give the initiative to the Council of States. . . . Either the Central (*sic.*) services are desirable or they are undesirable. If they are desirable, then they should not be cramped with so many impediments created in the way of their being started. If they are undesirable, then there should not have been any provision whatsoever". Bhimrao Ambedkar, the President of the Constitution Drafting Committee, justified the provision. He observed that the States enjoyed the freedom to recruit personnel for their services and if this autonomy was to be invaded, the sanction of the upper chamber, which was the spokesman of the States, was to be secured. "*Ex hypothesi* the upper chamber represents the States and therefore their resolution would be tantamount to an authority given by the States. That is the reason why these words are introduced in Article 282 C" (Constituent Assembly Debates, vol. IX, 8 September 1949, pp. 116-19). It should be noted that Ambedkar had opposed the continuance of all-India services when he was a member of the Sub-Committee on Services, *Vide fn*. 11.

26. Vallabhbhai Patel wrote to the Prime Minister on 27 April 1948; "The draft Constitution does not provide for an all-India service. . .We will, therefore, have to make provision for these services . . . in the new Constitution". [Shiva Rao (ed.) *The Framing of India's Constitution*, vol. IV, Bombay, N.M. Tripathi, 1968, p. 332.] Patel realized even in 1949 that the civil service was feeling diffident in advising the Minister honestly and fearlessly. Central recruitment and control of the superior civil service was looked upon as an apt device to reinforce the independence of the civil service. He told the constituent assembly with his characteristic bluntness: "If you want an efficient all-India service, I advise you to allow the services to open their mouth freely. If you are a premier, it would be your duty to allow your Secretary, or Chief Secretary, or other services working under you, to express their opinion without fear or favour. But I see a tendency today that in several pro-vinces the services are set upon and told, 'No, you are servicemen,

you must carry out our orders'* . . . Today, my Secretary can write a note opposed to my views. I have given that freedom to all my Secretaries. I have told them: 'If you do not give your honest opinion for fear that it will displease your Minister, please then you had better go. I will bring another Secretary.' I will never be displeased over a frank expression of opinion. That is what the Britishers were doing with the Britishers." (*Constituent Assembly Debates,* vol. X, No. 3, 10 October 1949, p. 51.)

27. "The raison d'etre of creating all-India services, individually or in groups, is that officers, on whom the brunt of the responsibility for administration will inevitably fall, may develop a wide and all-India outlook." (*Report of the States Reorganization Commission,* Delhi, Manager of Publications, 1956, p. 232).

"The organization of these (all-India) services on an all-India basis to administer the diverse and growing responsibilities of a welfare State is of paramount importance. Their composition is indicative of the unity of India and encourages the development of a national point of view and more or less uniform standards of administration, It also ensures that the administration of every State has a leavening of officers from outside whose vision and outlook are not circumscribed by a parochial horizon since the administrative control over these officers is not vested solely in the State Governments to whom they are allotted, but jointly in the State and Central Governments, thus enabling the officers to discharge their responsibilities without being unduly subjected to the stresses and strains of local influence." (*Ninety-Third Report of the Estimates Committee* (Third Lok Sabha), New Delhi, Lok Sabha Secretariat, 1966, pp. 22-23).

28. N.V. Gadgil, a former Cabinet Minister in the Central Government, writes: 'Each department has a promotion committee. There too I found that cliques, caste, community and province play considerable part. In some cases, favourable or unfavourable reports arc arranged for in advance of the expected higher vacancy. . . . Appointments and promotions were largely a .matter of 'pull'. (*Government from Inside,* Meerut, Meenakshi Prakashan, 1968, p, 158).

29. The first ten or so candidates in each of the all-India services are still among the best products of Indian universities. There is, however, a steep fall after that. Of the 542 entrants to the IAS during 1960-65, 220 (41 per cent) graduated in first class, 284 (52 per cent) graduated in second class and the remaining

38 (7 per cent) in the third class. During the same period 365 persons joined the Indian Police Service; of this number 64 (17 per cent) graduated in first class, 221 (61 per cent) in second class and the remaining 80 (22 per cent) in third class. These numbers exclude the scheduled castes and scheduled tribes, (*Report of the Study Team on Recruitment, Selection, U.P.S.C. State P.S.C. and Training*, New Delhi, Administrative Reforms Commission, 1967, p. 6.)

30. The annual intake in the IAS alone, today, exceeds 125. This stands in sharp contrast to an intake of six or so in the old Indian Civil Service.

31. This, for obvious political reasons, is not much discussed publicly. H.V.R. Iengar, an ex-member of the 'steel-frame', observes: "In order to ensure that members of the backward classes shall have adequate representation in the services, special steps have been taken to give them additional leverage over members of the more advanced communities . . . I think there has been, for the time being, a weakening of administration because people who have not had the necessary training have been put into positions of responsibility for which they are not yet completely fitted." (*Administration in India: A Historical Review* Bombay, Bhartiya Vidya Bhavan, 1967, p.43.)

32. Reproduced in Shiva Rao, B. (ed.), *The Framing of India's Constitution, op cit.* 1968, pp. 332-33.'

33. This, however, does not imply that a State Government or the Central Government is completely precluded from availing itself of the services of civil servants belonging to the other. Depending on the good will and mutual confidence, there may be Centre-State or Inter-State loaning of officers.

34. A member of an all-India service starts his career in the State Government to which he has been allotted just after his selection. He also comes to the Central Government for a fixed spell of service. Such interchanges continue until he reaches a certain stage in his career. The state administrative pyramid is narrower at the top than the centre's. As there are not many senior positions in the State, after twenty years of service or so, he joins the Central Government almost permanently. The latter has a fairly large number of senior positions—and extensive patronage—under its command. Consequently, the State Government lets itself part with his services at a time when he is at his best. This to be sure, is not mandatory under the rules but happens as a result of the interplay of various considerations. As an officer's reversion to his State Government is apt to make him suffer a cut in his emoluments

he lobbies support for his continuance at the Centre.

35. *The Statesman*, 23 February 1969, p. 7.
36. Ajoy Kumar Mukherji made this observation on 13 September 1970 while inaugurating a conference on state autonomy sponsored by the Tamil Nadu Government. *The Statesman*, 14 September 1970, p. 9.
37. Ministry of Home Affairs. *Report* 1969-70, New Delhi, Government of India, 1970, p. 4.
38. The Central Government is committed to the policy of allowing the candidate, to write their answers in the competitive examination in English, Hindi and other regional languages. The Union Public Service Commission moved in this direction with effect from the competitive examination of 1969.
39. K. Santhanam made this suggestion in 1961: Vide Parliamentary Debates: *Rajya Sabha*, vol. XXXVI, No. 7, 5 December 1961, c. 1164-7. He repeated it after the fourth (1967) general election. "I think the organization of the new (all-India) services should not be proceeded with without "obtaining a fresh consent from the non-Congress governments." *Vide* his article 'Centre-State ties need to be revised' in *The Statesman*, 22 March 1967, p. 8.

13

Reform of the Civil Service

The former Prime Minister of India, Mrs. Indira Gandhi criticised the machinery of public administration for acting as 'the stumbling block' in the way of the country's social and economic progress. She preferred a civil service consisting of persons "who would think and see that certain things which are necessary for our progress are implemented properly"[1] The note on 'Basic Economic Issues,' submitted to the requisitionists' All India Congress Committee held in Delhi in November 1969 complained: "The present bureaucracy under the orthodox and conservative leadership of the Indian Civil Service with its upper-class prejudices can hardly be expected to meet the requirements of social and economic change along socialist lines. The creation of an administrative cadre committed to national objectives and responsive to our social needs is an urgent necessity."[2] More recently, Jagjivan Ram in his presidential speech to the requisitionists' Congress, (held in December 1969 at Bombay) referred to the 'neutrality' of the civil service as a 'hindrance', adding further that "the theory of neutral bureaucracy is hardly relevant to Indian conditions". We need a service committed to the ideal of democracy, socialism and secularism".[3]

A criticism of the bureaucracy by a political party which held uninterrupted sway right since Independence till 1977 is unusual When a certain political party remains in power for a long duration, the civil service is often suspected by other parties of imbibing a distinct political orientation, thus, weakening *Us* capability to serve under a different political dispensation with equal measure of zeal and devotion. In Canada, for example when the Progressive Conservative Party succeeded the Liberal

Party which had ruled Canada for an unbroken period of twenty years, it suspected the bureaucracy's political status complained about its infiltration by the ideolology of the Liberal Party. Thus, a criticism of the bureaucracy is not without precedent but in India it has emanated from a party which had been holding the, reins of the Central Government (and most States) uninterruptedly since 1947.

The Indian bureaucracy has been a subject of adverse criticism both at the hands of Englishmen and Indians from time to time. Lord Curzon, the viceroy of India (1899- 1905) once likened the Government of India to an elephant—"very stately, very dignified but very slow in its movement." He wrote in his own inimitable style: "Government here. ..has become very ponderous and slow. I am prodding up the animal with most vigorous and unexpected digs, and it gambols plaintively under the novel spur. Nothing has been done hitherto under six months. When, I suggest six weeks, the attitude is one of pained surprise; if six days, one of pathetic protest; if six hours one of stupefied resignation."[4] He was indignant at the bureaucracy's, passion for noting, and the note that he Wrote to highlight its evils and to suggest remedial measures is of freshness and validity even today. "I am grappling with this vile system in my own department, but it has seated itself like the Old Man of the Sea upon the shoulders of the Indian Government, and every man accepts, while deploring, the burden "[5] Mahatma Gandhi considered the Indian administration as "top-heavy and ruinously expensive", adding "for me, even law, order and good government would be too dearly purchased if the price to be paid for it is to be the grinding poverty of the masses."[6] Jawaharlal Nehru was always outspoken in his criticism of the Indian bureaucracy, and this trait he exhibited right through his prime ministerial days. In 1936 he wrote: "...Of one thing I am quite sure, that no new order can be built up in India so long as the spirit of the Indian Civil Service pervades our administration and our public service. That spirit of authoritarianism is the ally of imperialism, and it cannot co-exist with freedom. It will either succeed in crushing freedom or will be swept away itself. Only with one type of state it is likely to fit in, and that is the fascist type. Therefore it seems to me quite essential that the Indian Civil Service and similar services must disappear completely, as such, before we can start real work on a new order. Individual members of these services, if they are willing and competent for the new job, will be welcome, but only on new conditions. It is quite inconceivable that they will get the absurdly high salaries and allowances that are paid to them today. The new India must be served by earnest, efficient workers who have an ardent faith in the cause they serve and are bent on achievement, and who work for the joy and glory of it, and not for the attraction of high salaries. The money motive must be reduced to a minimum."[7] Soon after becoming the Prime Minister in the interim Central Government in 1946, he observed at the Meerut session of the Indian National Congress: "...The (civil) services were fossilised in their mental outlook. They were wedded to by-gone and obsolete methods and refused to move with the times It remains to be seen how long we can function in these circumstances. The experience of the past three or four months has shown us that the conduct and attitude of the officers have not changed."[8] In 1953 he characterized Delhi as a jungle of experts and felt that one was sure to get lost in its administrative mazes and labyrinths. The machinery of public administration was afflicted with a tendency to spread itself, not on all fronts but in a lop-sided way. "If only the hands and legs are to increase but not head, then there will be no real development. There will be development quantitatively but qualitatively there will be deterioration."[9] Many a time he criticised the civil servants for their 'ivory tower' living and alienation from the common man and felt unhappy that the farmer was absent from the conferences supposed to deal with his problems although everyone else was present on such occasions!

Political independence in 1947 brought with it the sovereign right to take decisions on matters and issues concerning the country. A basic decision to be taken by independent India was about the form of government itself. The nation, through a long-drawn process of Constitution-making, conferred upon itself, on 26 January 1950, a democratic, republican, parliamentary, and federal form of government based on universal franchise. The bureaucracy which was really governing India till ,1947 found itself reduced to a position of subordination to the country's Parliament and the political executive.

A study of the historical process of evolution of legislative institutions in India is necessary and relevant, for it has in part influenced the style and system of mutual relations and reciprocations between the politician and the civil service. In western democracies, the political power of the people preceded—or, at least, accompanied—the constitution of the national civil service. They had, thus, two in simultaneous existence—the civil service and the politician. Each matched the other and thus a dynamic equilibrium in the society was maintained. India, on the other hand, inherited bureaucracy first. The imperial rule had created a formidable bureaucracy but did not care, until a much later date, to provide and diversify political experience to both contain and maintain the former[10]. Organized policy was a subsequent development in this country. The Indian National Congress was the first crystalization of organized polity, and was founded in 1885 while the civil service in India had emerged in a completed form by 1854. Although our first legislative assembly was born in 1853, it could acquire a somewhat popular base only under the Montagu-Chelmsford Reform of 1919. The Government of India Act of 1919 marked an humble but distinct departure from the old system of bureaucratic rule in India and made a real beginning in introducing representative government in India. Thus, in India democracy followed, not preceded, bureaucracy. Historically speaking, bureaucracy was, thus, the supreme body exercising virtually unchecked authority in the country. It did not take kindly to the emergence, albeit gradual and halting, of representative institutions which held the prospect of keeping, ultimately, the former accountable to it. The legislature had no control over the civil service though it emerged to criticise and challenge the latter. With each wave of representative institutions there followed resignations of many of the British members of the civil service and many who chose to remain behind, sulked and balked.

Independence of the country brought with it a fundamental alteration in the mutual relations between its Parliament and the civil service. Under the Constitution, the Parliament is a sovereign body and the civil service is necessarily subordinate to it. But the attitude and outlook of the two are not yet com-pletely or substantially identical, Indeed, both are sociological strangers. The Members of Parliament (including the Ministers) and of the senior civil service do not share a common educational, cultural or social background. Parliament is composed of members whose main qualification is victory in the election held on universal franchise. They represent the common man of the land. They may not lay claim to any superior schooling and upbringing. A member of the civil service, on the other hand, is selected on the basis of merit confirmed by an open competitive examination. The interview, called personality test, places in effect premium on such not very relevant aspects as the department of the candidate, his dress, the fluency with which he speaks English, his accent etc. It certainly does not test whether the applicant could be a *good public servant*. The personality test, by introducing the class bias of the interviewers, perpetuates the oligarchic character of the Indian civil service. Since these are the qualities (plus average intelligence) which are important in gaining entry into the civil service, a candidate who expects to be successful is generally one who has been educated in an English-medium school and has perhaps inherited a distinct breeding and upbringing. Besides, a civil servant gets a salary which is out of all proportion to the per capita national income of the country. The constitutionally guaranteed security of tenure makes him secure in his post for life and keeps him beyond the reach of the elected members who are likely to be dismissed at .the next election, Clothed that he is with governmental authority, he is feared and respected in the society, and he indeed conies to believe quite early in his career that he is superior to the rest of the human beings. He lives in an exclusive locality and in a big house which, again, conveys to him, in no uncertain term, his distinctly superior position in the society. Whenever he goes he stays in circuit houses, guest houses, rest houses, etc. The consequence is .that he remains aloof, domineering and insensitive to the nations social and .economic environment and milieu. Let it be frankly and honestly stated that, in view of the forgoing, the term 'public servant' is a mere euphemism today. A governmental official has to travel a long distance to consider himself, psychologically and emotionally, a servant of the people. He is in the citizen's eye, a *sahib* or a *barra sahib*.

As stated earlier, the form of the political system adopted in India is of the nations's own choosing. But a similar claim cannot be made about the administrative system of the country.

The country did not set out to design it itself. The administrative system, which was built up by the British to subserve their own interests, was inherited by independent India.

It is axiomatic that the system of a country's public administration including the bureaucracy, must fit into and respond to its overall political system. The civil service enjoys permanence of tenure and has the attributes of political neutrality and anonymity. The Government comes and goes, depending upon the wishes of the electorate but the civil service of the country is permanent. It is enjoined to serve whatever Government is in power with equal competence. As the Council of Ministers formulates the policies of the Government and a Minister decides on policies concerning his own charge, and, further, as Parliament holds the Minister and the Council of Ministers accountable for all acts of the Government, the civil service necessarily and rightly remains anonymous, neither getting credit nor blame.

Mrs. Indira Gandhi is reported to have further added: "The country would be in a rut if it followed the British system in which civil servants were not supposed to be concerned about which political party was in power."[11] This observation is fraught with dangerous implications and consequences. A civil service which gets motivated by 'which political party was in power' would be one which knowingly practices discrimination between the various political parties of the land, This would be fatal, for a bureaucracy with such an in-built or induced capability is the accompaniment of totalitarianism. A civil service designed to serve both the levels of the union, and the Governments of all political persuasions would render itself unacceptable to the country's political system if it is made to venture on such a path of deliberate discrimination.

A 'committed' bureaucracy in this sense (regulating its tune in accordance with 'which political party was in power') is apt to be a sinister and disruptive force and in practice, completely unworkable in a coalition system of Government. India has, since 1967, entered an era of coalition Governments, of short-lived Governments, rather kaleidoscopic political changes. We are to witness strange political bed-follows with all possible combinations and permutations. Which political party (or parties) in a coalition Government the country's bureaucracy ought to serve more loyally and which one (or ones) with diminished, or even complete lack of, commitment are questions which readily expose the impracticability of the theory of commitment. In an era of political fluidity and longer legislative hibernations, the bureaucracy is sure to acquire more and more power. Indeed, the power and strength of bureaucracy will show an increase in direct proportion to the frequency of changes in Government. Just as the country's polity is firm and unanimous in discouraging the army to actively interest itself in any way in the political matters of the land, it should adopt a similar attitude with reference to the country's bureaucracy. A direct provocation to it to get committed in the above sense is a move towards the general weakening of the larger political system of the land. At any rate, what is first needed is the social commitment of the politician himself.

'Political neutrality' is the hall-mark of our civil service. A civil servant is precluded from indulging in activities of a political nature and canvassing for political support on behalf of any political party. He has, like rest of the citizens, a right to vote but he must exercise it silently. His political beliefs are his private concern, and no one else need—indeed, should—know about them. He is under an obligation to serve whichever political party is in power. This is what is meant by the term 'political neutrality'. When, historically speaking, the civil service transited from a system of spoils to permanence of tenure, it had necessarily to abandon an active political role in favour of one of strict neutrality. Neutrality is the price which the civil service paid for securing permanence of tenure.

The term 'political neutrality' is, nevertheless, not entirely without ambiguity: it degenerates into a drag and a stumbling block when given an over-stretched or broader meaning. Neutrality does not mean absence of emotional involvement, so vital for the completion of complex tasks. It does not imply indifference towards action in hand or passivity of mind. It does not suggest inertia, mechanical application to work or work to rule practices. It does not connote soul less ness in implementation of policies. It does not convey an absence of dynamism, zeal, enthusiasm, push and drive. Above all, it does not postulate a lack of commitment to the basic philosophy and injunctions of the Country's constitution. The concept of 'neutrality of the civil service' must; not be invoked to cover or justify non-performance, poor performance, or shoddy performance, of tasks.

Different political parties are operating in the country, each having its own, party programme. Nevertheless, a large area of basic agreement exists, in reality, among them all. This is not unnatural. Each political party is necessarily called upon to come to grips with the country's major problems and to formulate solutions. But the country's basic problems are evident enough and it is also evident as to what needs to be done. The point of dispute and contention generally is how soundly or poorly a particular programme is being administered. In other word is the major political, economic and social problems and issues ultimately boil down largely to the problems of efficient administration. A civil servant must ever remain 'committed' to such an area of common national agreement and to the need for providing an efficient administration. Indeed, our Constitution with its heavy socio-economic overlay .has itself forged the direction in which the Indian nation is to move, and both the country's polity and its bureaucracy cannot be allowed to shy away from it. More concretely, the national five-year plan spells out this common area of agreement, and the civil service should implement it with, 'flaming enthusiasm'. It is this quality which distinguishes some like V.P. Menon from the rest of their tribe.

A word needs especially be said about the country's diplomatic civil service. A member of the latter when posted in a foreign country, virtually performs the functions which, on the domestic front, are primarily the responsibility of a Minister—outlining, upholding and promoting the policies of the Government fie represents. He cannot expect to leave an impact on the country of his posting if he himself is not emotionally dedicated to the policies of his government and functions with missionary zeal with a 'sense' of commitment. The Committee on the Indian Foreign Service (1966) pointed to "the need for a diplomat to have faith in his government's policies and to speak in a clear and unambiguous voice presenting them". It rightly emphasized: "Whatever other forms of communication may be available and be used for inter-governmental contact, an ambassador or high commissioner remains the principal channel of communication between his government and the government to which he is accredited. On him devolves the duty of explaining, interpreting and defending the policies and views of his government, both at the official and at numerous other levels. This is a positive function, going far beyond the mechanical one of 'saying one's piece', and calls for inter-pretative skill of a high order. To succeed in persuasion, however, skill needs to be sustained by integrity of mind and purpose. Where he differs from headquarters, the representative has the freedom to seek, through the channels and subject to the limits prescribed by established procedure, a modification or reconsideration of particular policies. In no circumstances, however, should he let others outside get even the remotest hint of such differences of opinion; that would not only seriously compromise his government's position but also eventually reduce his own effectiveness".[12]

A civil servant enjoys full internal freedom to express his views while tendering service to his senior officer and to the Minister. Its importance cannot be emphasized too greatly. Vallabhbhai Patel elaborated it so bluntly: "If you want an efficient all-India service, I advise you to allow the services to open their mouth freely. If you are a Premier, it would be your duty to allow your Secretary, or Chief Secretary, or other services working under you, to express their opinion without fear or favour. But I see a tendency today that in several provinces the services are set upon and told, 'No, you are servicemen, you must carry out our orders.'. . . Today, my Secretary can write a note opposed to my views. I have given that freedom to all my Secretaries. I have told them, 'if you do not give your honest opinion for fear that it will displease your Minister, please then had better go. I will bring another Secretory'. I will never be displeased over a frank expression or opinion. That is what the Britishers were doing with the Britishers."[13] Just as a civil servant should advise his senior officer with honesty and frankness, he should encourage the officers under him to behave similarly towards him and comment fearlessly. Many an officer, today, neither gives honest advice nor is in a mental frame to tolerate it from the subordinate functionaries. A functionary has even come to expect personal commitment from his underlings. All this eats into the vitality of administration.

Once, however, a decision has been taken, it is a civil servant's bounden duty to carry it out enthusiastically, faithfully and competently. He should ever draw inspiration from Attlee's following observation: "I recall...., a time when I was working with the late Lord Addison, Minister of Agriculture in the second Labour Government, when he was framing the Agricultural Marketing Bill. Sir Arthur Street an outstanding civil servant, offered a most strenuous opposition to it, but three weeks later one could have got an affiliation order against him as its only begetter.[14]

It is of paramount importance that the policy is clearly defined, leaving no room for ambiguity and confusion. Once laid down, it must not be changed or modified too often. Frequent changes in policy are indicative of a vascillating attitude, which precludes firmness and consistency in execution. Also it should not be overlaid with riders. Such a course is sure to provide one to say: "You show me the person and I will quote the suitable rule". Riders have a tendency to obscure, obstruct and defeat the over-all policy. There must be adequate provision for follow-up and feedback. Having fixed definite responsibility, lapses on the part of any should be instantly visited by punishment. Finally, it must be clearly borne in mind that there is no substitute to a policy. As Lyndall Urwick so pointedly mentions, "administration and organisation cannot be more than means to ends. And they may be directed with great deficiency to bad ends as well as to good."[15]

But bad administration of even a good policy is apt to spell misery and hardship. The civil service, under the pretext of political neutrality, should not lose sight of the spirit pervading a policy. There are innumerable instances in India of policies being implemented in such a way that the original purpose underpinning them was completely defeated. It should remember the old adage: 'example is better than precept': it must itself practice that it has been called upon to implement and administer. It is common knowledge that the policy of prohibition has met with failure because the civil servants themselves do not practise abstinence. The national policy regarding the gradual adoption of Hindi as the official language has not made any headway because the civil servants themselves have no faith in it.

The country's bureaucracy suffers from lack of professionalism and achievement-orientation, not lack of competence. In sheer intellectual attainments, it can hardly be surpassed by any other profession in the land, but its besetting sin, today, is rampant careerism, which has enfeebled its sensitivity to public interest.

The political executive must set an example to others by its devotion to public interest, integrity, hard work, sincerity of purpose, austerity and firmness. It must itself practise what it professes; it cannot be permitted to have a duplicate character-one private and another public.[16] An effective remedy may lie in a suitable strengthening, both qualitative and quantitative, of the political wing of the Government. Each Ministry should have, in addition to the Minister, a few junior Ministers, depending upon the nature, variety and volume of work. The political wing should, with crusader's zeal, address itself to the task of laying down, in full consultation with the civil service, clearly defined policies, preparing time-bound programmes compatible with these policies, and overseeing their implementation in accordance with the time-schedule. In other words, it is absolutely necessary that a Minister has a mind and will of his own, and gives clear and definite orders on matters coming before him. 'The bulk of our ministers", complains Acharya Kriplani, "seem to have no mind of their own". He continues, "They are generally appointed on tribal, caste, communal and regional considerations."[17] It may not here be out of place to refer to the personal cabinet which a Minister in France constitutes on assumption of his office. The personal cabinet of the French Minister has a capability to offer the advantages of the prevalent American practice of choosing top departmental officers from the political supporters of the administration in power, ensuring a quicker and faithful execution of party programmes. Contrary to popular expectation, the personal cabinet does not have many politicians on it; instead, it consists of civil servants, of rather junior level, temporarily detached from their departments and a few experts. This has over a period of years become a device to gain faster promotions in the department, not to prod the bureaucracy on. Nor is it a brains' trust of the Minister, strictly speaking. Besides, it entails two other disadvantages. It sometimes secures political coordination at the expense of administrative coordination; the minister's policy is kept to the fore, but its detailed execution suffers because the members of this cabinet possess less experience in administrative work than the permanent officials of longer standing. Secondly, the existence of the personal cabinet which has some junior civil servants on it dampens the morale of the senior civil service.

The maladies afflicting the administrative machinery are too pervasive and deep to be cured by stray, isolated or half-hearted measures. The machinery of administration is groaning under its own size; it must considerably reduce its weight in order to be active and resilient. There is a lot of deadwood the administration has accumulated gradually but steadily, which must be got rid of. The functions have been allowed to grow and multiply as the Government apparently makes no discrimination between the subjects figuring under the union list and those under the state list under the Constitution;[18] indeed the Central Government is most anxious to become the State Government also. Coupled with this deep-seated reluctance to reconcile itself with the federal character of the Constitution is the centre's desire to have 'nation-wide' coverage for every scheme and plan, and its refusal to be guided by a stern sense of priority.[19]

Public administration has been over the years eating more than it can chew. Good administration lies in a realistic assessment of available resources—Manpower and others—of requisite quality and quantity, which should determine the upper limit of a scheme or plan. This thought is seldom taken into account in this country. It is naively believed that finance is the only relevant criterion to determine the acceptance of a scheme, and, if this is assured, the scheme encounters no difficulty. It is little realized that the greatest limitation in the way of implementation of a scheme is paucity of qualified personnel itself. As development of personnel is a long-drawn educational process, persons cannot be made available over-night. A consequence of such an abstract administrative thinking is a significant deterioration in the quality and quantity of work expected of a particular office, the cumulative effect being a wide gap between what was hoped and what finally ensued. A contributory factor has been the civil servant himself, who, instead of concentrating on his job, remains ever on the look out for a better one or drowned in laziness. As a result, his own output is necessarily less and his supervision over his subordinates is apt to be superficial and inadequate, leading to reduced output all along the line. This is, then, sought to be offset by a demand for more hands. Thus occurs a steady proliferation of personnel without a clearer realization that an unnecessarily large staff is itself the begetter of delays and inefficiency and grievances in addition to generating infructuous work of a housekeeping nature. A complete inventory of the functions the Central Government has been presently performing needs to be prepared and the non-essential activities should be disbanded forth with, and the non-priority ones de-emphasized by reductions in their budget and personnel. This should bring about a more than corresponding reduction in the number of governmental personnel, for the Government already has too many employees on its payroll.[20]

It has happened that while the line jobs are generally under-staffed the staff jobs, which have indiscriminately proliferated, have an excessive concentration of personnel. The staff jobs are cushy and have an especially irresistible appeal to action shy comfort-loving Indians.[21] The imbalance must be rectified by a rational deployment, after necessary training, of the surplus personnel. Officials in key posts should be kept in their jobs for at least three or four years to enable them to produce the results expected of them. Responsibilities should be clearly defined for all levels of administrative hierarchy and all functionaries. Responsibility should carry commensurate authority. A civil servant must operate at his level; he must neither seek to over-stretch and over-reach nor fall below the requirement and expectation of his post in the administrative hierarchy. Habits of devotion to one's work, good behaviour, punctuality, discipline and courtesy which are all but gone from the intermediary and lower levels of administration must be restored by effective supervision backed by advice, warning and punitive action. Resort to committees, conferences and seminars must be reduced drastically. Loquacity is our national trait; our emphasis should be on action rather than[22] on mere talk.

Administration is essentially team work involving a group of persons. Fulfilment of a task makes it essential that there should exist in the group feelings of brotherliness and camaraderie. These qualities are summed up in the word 'morale', which holds the key to successful administration. Morale in the bureaucracy is very low, which may be ascribed largely in the adoption of the present form and style of 'merit' as the basis for promotion. This certainly sounds paradoxical, yet is true.

A deliberate denigration of seniority and extolling of 'merit' has triggered off an unseemly rivalry in the civil service for getting an 'outstanding' character roll. As a consequence, colleagues who have to bend their energies together to get jobs accomplished have become concealed rivals and competitors, creating a relationship characterized by all-round suspicion, mistrust and lack of confidence. The openings at the higher levels are necessarily fewer in number. In this scramble for 'merit', therefore, only a few stand to succeed while all are apparently in the race. The result is an enormous growth in frustrations of civil servants. Assuming that the promotions are made on a 'fool-proof' system of merit, it is wise to have an army of angry, discontented persons on the payroll? Both security of tenure and inadequacy of employment opportunities outside tend to keep them to their jobs; they remain behind, nursing frustrations and chanting grievances. The term 'merit' itself is highly subjective, more so when a character roll is made the sole basis for assessment of merit. Often, it is difficult to distinguish merit-scouting from sheer arbitrariness. As this term is interpreted today in Government, it, at its worst, stands for disguised favouritism and; at its best, a measure of personal social relationship between the supervisor and the subordinate. N.V. Gadgil, recalling his experiences as a Union Minister, observed: "Each department has a promotion committee. There too I found that cliques, caste, community and province play considerable part. In some cases, favourable or unfavourable reports are arranged far in advance of the expected higher vacancy . .. appointments and promotions were largely a matter of 'pull'."[23] A large number of otherwise public-spirited, achievement-oriented, conscientious civil servants are soon over-taken by a feeling of despondency and disappointment when they see those indulging in intrigues and politicking reaping all rewards and their own hard work remaining unrecognized.

There is, today, a deliberate attempt, to inflate the ratings of governmental employees, There has occurred a steady growth in the number of officials getting the rating of 'outstanding'. This implies that the efficiency in the civil service has improved, which is doubtful. Even otherwise only a small percentage of persons, ranging between 10 to. 20 may be rated as 'outstanding' and most would be 'average', for this is the meaning of this term. In Indian bureaucracy, however, 'average' is an unacceptably negative term. A reporting officer seldom dares to record his honest opinion.[24]

'Merit' should be built into, and should emerge from, seniority. Seniority is a fact; merit a matter of mere opinion. It is not true that seniority and merit are dichotomous. As recruitment for public services is already made on the basis of merit, seniority is merit plus 'X' years of service. If the public service commission is doing its job well—and supervisors theirs— seniority is merit. If, however, seniority is considered to be such a great sinner, the cure should be sought right at the stage of recruitment (and also that of probation). The fallings and foibles of the public service commission, if any, should not be transferred to and foisted upon the principle of seniority.

To make the principle of seniority fool-proof as the basis of promotion, it must take into full account one possibility and ask for supportive action. As our civil service is recruited at an early age, it is likely to have some who turn out to be 'early deteriorates', and some who are 'late developers'. The former class must be identified and segregated from the rest. Those who are discovered deficient persistently must be made to leave Government on proportionate pension—as is already a practice in the army. As regards the 'late developers', this is more a myth than a reality. At any rate, an organization frames its rules and regulations for an average employee, not for an extra-brilliant person. One need not show unnecessary concern for him; he, being extra-brilliant, can be safely trusted to take care of himself.

The Indian civil service has a core of exceptionally hard-working, dedicated, conscientious persons but they, today, stand overwhelmingly outnumbered by those not so well endowed. Generally speaking, the bureaucracy suffers from a sense of complacency which it must be made to shake off. It allows itself to remain obsessed with factors like status, rank and emoluments, which it must overcome. It is also rather too much addicted to habits of personal luxury and indolence, which it must shed. The bureaucracy at present enjoys excessive security of tenure; it should have less of it. An increased flow of personnel at different age-groups, from as well as to the public administration is over-due. In short, the Indian bureaucracy must consciously set out to professionalise and humanize itself. At present, it is not endowed with these qualities in sufficient measure. It must spiritually align itself with the following advice given by the Father of the Nation. Mahatma Gandhi said, "I will give you a talisman. Whenever you are in doubt, or when the self becomes too much with you, try the following expedient. Recall the face of the poorest and the most helpless man whom you may have seen and ask yourself if the step you contemplate is going to be of any use to him. Will it restore him to a control over his own life and destiny? In other words, will it lead to Swaraj or self-rule for the hungry and spiritually starving millions of our countrymen? Then you will find your doubts and yourself melting away."[25]

The reform of the civil service has ultimately to take into account an external factor which, when considered in perspective, is of undoubted importance to its health and vigor. Indeed, this is valid for any social institution operating in today's society with its necessary feature of increasing inter-dependence and inter-action among institutions, groups and people. The effectiveness of an institution is sustained and conditioned by the efficiency of the infra-structure in the society. The reform of the bureaucracy also demands that the society's infra-structure—political parties, voluntary associations, interest groups, economic organizations, educational institutions, to name a few—should be strong, resilient and vigilant.

NOTES

1. Mrs. Indira Gandhi's speech at the meeting of the Congress Parliamentary Party on 16 November 1969. *The Hindustan Times,* 17 November 1969, p. 5.
2. *Ibid.,* 1 December 1969, p. 9.
3. *The Statesman,* 29 December 1969, p. 9.

4. Earl of Ronaldshay: *The Life of Lord Curzon*, vol II (London, Ernest Benn; 1928), p. 27.
5. *Ibid.*, p. 27.
6. Quoted in *Mahatma Gandhi: The Man and His Mission*, (Madras: G.A. Natesan &Co., 1930) (eighth edition), pp. 40-41.
7. Jawaharlal Nehru: *An Autobiography*, (London: The Bodley Head, 1955), p. 445.
8. *The Indian Annual Register*, July-December, 1946, vol. II, Calcutta, the Annual Register Office, (year of publication not given), pp. 289-90.
9. Jawaharlal Nehru's address at the twenty-fourth session of the Central Board of Irrigation and Power. *The Times of India* (Bombay), 27 October 1953, p. 5.
10. An absence of polity to interact with the bureaucracy, made the latter a worshipper of abstract efficiency. The following episode narrated by Edwin Montagu, the Secretary of State for India during 1917-22, is fairly representative of the bureaucracy in India. Montagu came across an Indian Civil Service officer, Marris. He writes: "He told him (Marris) I had never met a man with greater devotion to duty and greater industry; I had never met a man with a better natural style and more real command of language. But, he failed, like everybody else in India failed, from having no political instinct, of despising political science, and I told him that I did not think he was capable of making the best argument he could, or of intelligible exposition; that the Indian Civil Service had been so long accustomed to state their conclusions without reasoning them. I therefore told him that, whilst leaving him to do the drafting, I must insist that I must be the judge of whether what I wanted to say was brought out or whether what was said was intelligible." Montagu, Edwin S.: *An Indian Diary*, (London: William Heinemann, 1930), pp. 358-59.

    Ramsay Macdonald, who later (in 1924) became the Prime Minister of Great Britain, had the following to say about the Indian bureaucracy. "India is governed by bureaucracy which, though officers may come and officers may go, goes on for ever, without a break beyond the fluctuations in policy natural to its own being. No general election changes its majority, no new premier comes to alter its course, no parliamentary complication modifies its will. It runs in ruts. It has no machinery for self-criticism. *The Awakening of India*, p. 11.
11. *The Hindustan Times*, 17 November 1969, p. 5.

12. *Report of the Committee on the Indian Foreign Service* (Delhi, Manager of Publications, 1966), p. 40.

13. *Constituent Assembly Debates*, vol. X, No. 3, 10 Oct. 1949, p, 15. L. Urwick points out the danger, both material and spiritual, befalling an organisation in which internal freedom of expression is denied or remains narrowly restricted. He writes:

    "That is why the greatest crime the administrator can commit is to be too authoritative, too impatient of criticism and discussion, too quick to resent as disloyalty frank difference of opinion as to policy. Disloyalty arises when decisions have been taken, in lack of energy in implementing them, never, in the processes through which they are formulated. To treat opposition as something to be crushed or swept aside is to start the insidious process by which candid officials are turned into 'Yes-men', creatures who first enquire what will be "liked" by their superiors before formulating their own views, who have lost the taste for honesty when thinking about the affairs of the organisation, Once that process is started it will corrupt a whole undertaking like a leprosy. The direction will be robbed of the greatest contribution the personnel can make to the undertaking, unbiased and fearless statement of the best thought of which they are capable. Enthusiasm will be stifled, ability frustrated and energy turned inwards to concentrate on self-seeking. The administrator who gives way to the temptation to use his authority to suppress rather than to develop the views of his subordinates is committing the sin against the Holy Ghost".

    The Elements of Administration (London: Sir Issac" Pitman & Co., 1947), p. 89.

14. Earl, Attlee, 'Civil Servants, Ministers, Parliament and the Public', in William A. Robson, *(Ed.): The Civil Service in Britain and France* (The Hogarth Press, 1956), p. 17.

15. L. Urwick.: *The Elements of Administration*, (London: Sir Issac Pitman & Co., 1947) p. 8.

16. Mahatma Gandhi has correctly observed: "There is in modern life a tendency to ignore altogether the character of a public worker so long as he works efficiently as a unit in an administrative machinery. It is said that everybody's character is his own private concern. Though I have known this view to have been often taken, I have never been able to appreciate, much less to adopt, it. I have known the serious consequences overtaking organisations that have counted private character as a matter of no consequence."

17. Kriplani, J.B., 'Bureaucracy Lacks Courage', in *The Hindustan Times*, 26 January 1978.
18. The Economy Committee, set up by the Central Government in 1948, expressed its concern at "the increasing encroachment by the Central Government, particularly in the Ministries of Education, Agriculture, and Health, over the functions of provincial Governments. It observed: "It is appreciated that these subjects cannot be treated as matters of purely provincial concern. For India to develop on healthy lines, it is essential to ensure that the economic and social development of the various provincial and states' units is, as far as possible, uniform. The Centre has a useful function to perform in action as a coordinating and advisory body and in assisting provinces in the implementation of their development schemes. But it would be wrong for the Centre, under the guise of coordination or, on the plea that the provincial administrations are inadequately equipped, to undertake directly activities which are essentially provincial functions. It is perhaps difficult to draw a line as to where advice ends, and interference, begins, but the examination of the Ministries and their activities have convinced us that at least as far as major provinces are concerned, the Centre could with advantage restrict its 'advice'. As regards minor provinces, the primary difficulty seems to be the inability of the provincial services to cope with the tasks that fall on them. The proper solution in such cases is for the Centre to assist the provinces in developing their own services. Provincial autonomy without provincial responsibility is detrimental to the growth of a healthy governmental machinery." *General Report of the Economy Committee*, pp. 5-6.
19. "...in all sectors, in every tier and at each level, the size of government machinery has grown and appears to be growing unabated." *The Study Team Report on Personnel Administration*, (Delhi, Manager of Publications, 1967), p. 18.
20. The Central Governmental expenditure on the wages and salaries of its employees was 124 crores in 1950-51; it rose to Rs. 468 in 1964-65.
21. Because of foreign rule in the country, Indians came face to face with the administrative challenges of a modern society with a lack of many centuries of administrative experience. Coupled with it has: been our well-known speculative bent of mind. As a consequence, we are deficient in action mindedness of a scale required to telescope both, time and space.
22. In 1953 Jawaharlal Nehru expressed his concern for an unusually large number of conferences held in India. He felt

that time had come to 'draw a curtain' on these conferences and stop them. "People should instead do work silently" he observed. *The Times of India* (Bombay), 27 October 1953, p. 5.

23. Gadgil, N.V., *Government from Inside,* Meerut (Meenakshi Prakashan, 1968), p. 158.

24. Stated by B.N. Chakravarty, Governor of Haryaua, while inaugurating the seminar on civil services in a developing democracy, held at Chandigarh in 1969. Chakravarty was a member of the Indian Civil Service. He continued: "The reason is that the confidential report has to be shown to the subordinate and this almost invariably leads to unseemly controversies. It is the reporting officer who is put on the dock and has to defend his report. The junior officer has nothing to lose by making the wildest allegations of mala fides. Failure to prove such allegation does not bring him any punishment. The relations between the two get strained and thereafter the senior officer can neither enforce discipline nor get work out of his junior".

Bibliography

Adiseshiah, M.S., *Administrative Reorganization in the Madras University*. Madras, University of Madras.

Agarwal, U.C., Good governance: Cutting edge of administration. *Indian journal of Public Administration*, 44(3) July-September 1998, p. 428-38.

Aivalli, Veeranna, Single-line administration: An Administrative experiment in Jammu and Kashmir. *Indian Journal of Public Administration*, 43(3) July-September 1998, p. 604-08.

Ali, Ashraf, *Municipal Bureaucracy and Urban Development*, Patna. A.N. Sinha Institute of Social Studies.

Anter Singh, *Rajasva Prasashan: ek Sarvekshan. Rajasthan*, G.V.M.V., Banasthali Vidyapith.

Arora, Ramesh K. and Goyal, Rajani, *Indian Public Administration: Institutions and Processes*. New Delhi, Wiswa Pra., 1995, 61 p.

Bandopadhyay, A.R., Public administration in the twenty first century: Preparing for a new society. *Management in Government*, 26(1-4) April 1994-March 1995, p. 9-26.

Bandyopadhyay, D., Administration, decentralisation and good governance. *Economic and Political Weekly*, 31(48) 30 November 1996, p. 3109-14.

Basu, Prahlad K., Strategic issues in administrative reorganisation: Developing countries perspective. *Economic and Political Weekly* 27(22) 30 May 1992, p. M-46-58.

Basu, P.K., Administrative reorganisation in India: Some strategic issues. *Indian Journal of Public Administration*, 44(3) July-September 1998, p. 661-87.

Battistella, Roger, "Health services Reforms: Political and Managerial Aims - An International Perspective", *International Journal of Health Planning and Management*, 8(4), October-December 1993.

Bennett, Sara and Viroj Tangcharoensathien, "A Shrinking State? Politics, economics and Private Health Care in Thailand", *Public Administration and Development*, 14(1), February 1994.

Bhargava, Prabha, *Administration of Justice Through Lok Adalat System in Western Rajasthan*. Bikaner, Dunger College.

Bhattacharya, M., *Bureaucratic Response to Emergency: A Study of West Bengal Flood Relief*. Calcatta, University of Calcutta.

Bhattacharya, Mohit, Public Administration today and tomorrow. *Indian Journal Public Administration*, (Special Number) 43(3) July-September 1997, p. 323-30.

Bhattacharyya, Mohit, Restructuring public administration: Essays in rehabilitation. New Delhi, Jawahar Pub., 1997, 20 p.

Bhaumik, Drubojyoti and Sarka, Dilip Kumar, *The Darjeeling Gorkha Mill Council: An Alternative Politico-Administrative Arrangement at the Sub-State Level*. Darjeeling, North-Bengal Univeristy.

Bureaucratic-Administrative machine in India. *Monthly Commentary on Indian Economic Conditions*, 34(8) March 1993, p. 21-24.

Calden, Gerald E., Future of public administration. *Management in Government*, 26(1-4) April 1994-March 1995, p. 27-46.

Calden, Gerald E., What reality is public maladministration? *Indian Journal of Public Administration* 37(1) January-March 1991, p. 1-16.

Chaturvedi, H.R., *Local Bureaucracy and Development: A Comparative Study of Citizens Participation in the States*. Delhi, Centre for the

Civil service reform and world Bank. *Indian Journal of Public Administration*, 44(3) July-September 1998, p. 722-23.

Crone, Donald K., "State, Elites, and Social Welfare in Southeast Asia", *World Development*, 21(1), January 1993.

Damle, Y.B., *Citizens Participation in Rural Development and Urban Administration: A Comparative Study*. Pune, University of Poona.

Das, M.N. and Manpoong, C.M., *District Administration in Arunachal Pradesh*. Dibrugath, Dibrugarh University.

Dauda, Bola, Philosophical issues in public service reform, *Journal of Public Enterprise*, 18(3-4) July-December 1995, p. 127-43.

Dey, Bata K., Ethics in public administration: Maladies and remedies. *Indian Journal of Public Administration*, 41(3) July-September 1995, p. 451-61.

Dhamala, Ranju R., *A Study of Panchayati Raj Institutions Sikkim*. North Bengal, University of North Bengal.

Dhar, T.N. and Basthwal, C.P., Administration in mountain regions: Challenges and paradigms case of Uttaranchal. *Indian Journal of Public Administration*, 44(3) July-September 1988, p. 584-95.

Dhawan, Rajeev, (i) Research into Policy Aspects of Judicial Decision Making, (ii) Research into Socio-Political Aspects of the Concept of

Validation in Laws and Legal Theory. New Delhi, Indian Law Institute.

Dube, S.N., *Decision-Making in Zila Parishads in Maharashtra: An Exploratory Study*. Bomaby, Tata Institute of Social Sciences.

Dubhashi, P.R., Restructuring and reforming of Indian political administrative and economic system. *Indian Journal of Public Administration*, (Special Number) 43(3) July-September 1997, p. 362-68.

Duggal, Ravi, Nagaland; Issues in governance. *Economic and Political Weekly*, 34(50) 11 December 1999, p. 3498-3501.

Dunn, Delmer D., *Politics and administration at the top: Lessons from down under*. Pittsburgh, University of Pittsburg Press, 1997, 194 p.

Evans, Ivan Thomas, *Bureaucracy and Race, Native Administration in South Africa*, Berkeley, University of California Press, 1998.

Gandhi, H.S., *Dais as Partners in Maternal Health*. New Delhi, National Institute of Health Administration and Education.

Ghate, Prabhu, Reforming the civil service-meeting crucial need for exertise. *Economic and Political Weekly*, 33(7) 14 February 1998, p. 359- 65.

Goel, B.B., *Survey of Research in Cooperation Administration*. Chandigarh, Panjab University.

Goyal, S.K., *Regulatory Administration of Private Corporate Sector in India*. New Delhi, Indian Institute of Public Administration.

Guiding principles on civil service reform. *Indian journal of Public Administration*, 44(3) July-September 1998, p. 707-13.

Gupta, V.S., *A Study of Sociological and Administrative Implications of Transfer of Government pesonnel*. Gwalior, Arts and Commerce College.

Haldipur, R.N., *Legislation Relating to Town Planning and Development: Authorities and Their Implementation*. New Delhi, Indian Institute of Public Administration.

Hetcalte, Les, International policy coordination and public management reforms. *Management in Government*, 26(1-4) 1995, p. 157-80.

Ibrahim F.I, Shihata, Civil service reform in developing countries. *Indian journal of Public Administration*, 44(3) July-September 1998, p. 732-35.

Inamdar, N.R., *District Planning in Maharashtra: A Political Administrative Study*. Pune, University of Poona.

Inamdar, N.R., *Study of Education Administration in Zila Parishad in Maharashtra*. *Pune*, University of Poona.

Ishwar Dayal, *Bench Mark Studies of Field Administration in India*. New Delhi, Indian Institute of Public Administration.

Ishwar Dayal, *Study of the Process of Transformation of the Kurukshetra University*. New Delhi, Indian Institute of Public Administratin.

Jain, R.B., *Bureaucracy and Development: A Comparative Study in Orientation and Behaviour of Bureaucracy Engaged in Development and Non-Development Tasks*. Delhi, University of Delhi.

Jangam, R.T., *Recent Theories of Administration and Management*. Dharwar, Karnatak University. January-March 1999, p. 80-85.

Jha, M.L., *Functional Analysis and Administrative Practices of Uttar Pradesh Universities: A Pilot Study. Patna*, Lalit Narayan Misra Institute of Economic Development and Social Change.

Jitender Kaur, *Panchayati Raj and Political Perception of Electorate*. Delhi, Centre for the Study of Developing Societies.

Joshi, O.P., *Appropriate Technology for Tribal Development: A Study in a Tribal District of Rajasthan*. Jaipur, The HCM Rajasthan State Institute of Public Administration.

Joshi, R.P., *Panchayati Raj and Rural Development in Rajasthan*, Jaipur, University of Rajasthan.

Kapur, Vijay, Term limits for local administration. *Man and Development*, 19(1) 1997, p. 149-59.

Khanna, B.S., Study of Decentralization for Strengthening Rural Local Government in India and other South Asian Countries: Bangladesh, Pakistan, Nepal and Sri Lanka (The Study of recent politico-administrative decentralization for strengthening rural local government in selected South Asian Countries: National Perspective and Comparative Analysis-India, Bangladesh, Nepal, Sri Lanka). Chandigarh, Punjab University.

Kothari, Rajni, Public administration and the democratic upsurge. *Indian journal of Public Administation*, (Special Number) 43(3) July-September 1997, p. 289-92.

Kshire, V.K. and Nandekar, V.G., *Public administration in India*. Jaipur, Rawat, 1994, 271 p.

Kulkarni, V.M. *Preparation of a Special Volume on Social Welfare and its Administration in the Indian Setting*. New Delhi, Indian Institute of Public Administration.

Madhava Menon, N.R., Civil society and the quest for good governance: Some reflections. *ISDA journal*, 8(2-4) April 1998, p. 97-101.

Mahapatra, Jayat Kumar, *Fiscal Problems and Austerity Management Policy in Selected Orissa Municipalities*. Orissa, Berhampur University.

Maheshwari, S.R., *Administrative reform in India*. New Delhi, Jawahar, 1993, 239 p.

Maheshwari, S.R., *Indian administrative system*. New Delhi, Jawahar, 1994, 258 p.

Maiti, Ashok Kumar, *Panchayati Raj and Rural Development: A Study in West Bengal*. Kalyani, University of Kalyani.

Managing the civil service reform lessons from advanced industrialised countries. *Indian journal of Public Administration*, 44(3) July-September 1998, p. 724-26.

Mathur, Kuldeep, *The Response of the State Government. Its Administration, Organization, the Community and the Family to the Scarcity Conditions Caused by Drought in Maharasthra*. New Delhi, Indian Institute of Public Administration.

Mathur, Kuldeep, ed., *Development policy and administration*. Delhi, Sage, 1996, 306 p.

Mathur, Reeta, *Politics, policy and administrative change-Paul Appleby's perspective*. Jaipur, Arihant, 1994, 168 p.

McCarthy, Florence E. and Shelley Feldman, "Administrative Reforms in Bangladesh; Incorporation or Democratization?", *International Journal of Contemporary Sociology*, 24 (3-4), July-October, 1987.

Mehrajuddin, Mir, *Corruption in Administration of Justice: An Empirical Study*. Srinagar, University of Kashmir.

Montgomery, John D., "Bureaucrat, Heal Thyself! Lessons from Three Administrative Reforms", *World Development*, 24(5) May, 1996.

Mukherjee, Davesh Chandra, *Socio-Legal Research on Laws in Andaman and Nicobar Islands*.

Muttalib, M., *Administration of Development Programmes of the District, Block and Village Level in Andhra Pradesh*. Hyderabad, Osmania University.

Nanda, Debidas, *The Administrative Culture in Urban Government - A Case Study of the Varanasi Nagar Mahapalika*. Varanasi, Banaras Hindu University.

October-December 1995, p. 793-98.

Pai Panandikar, V.A., *Bureaucratic Skills and Capabilities in Development*. New Delhi, Centre for Policy Research.

Pandaya, H.J., *Leadership in Panchayati Pattern: Towards Technological Innovative Administration*. Pune, University of Poona.

Patil, V.T., Rural Elites and Panchayati Raj: A Case Study of Dharwad District. Dharwad, Karnataka University.

Prabhavalkar, B.H. and Kagalkar, P.C., Political environment, personnel and legal aspects of urban local administration: A study. Bombay, All India Institute of Local Self Government.

Qureshi, M.A., *The Administration and Statutory Control of Waqfs in India with Special Reference to Madhya Pradesh*. Jabalpur, University of Jabalpur.

Raghavinh, Y., *The Role of Laymen in University Administration: A pilot Study of the Role, Functions and Performance of Laymen in Osmania and Kerala Universities*. Hyderabad, University College of Arts and Commerce.

Rama Rao, C.V.S., *Organizational Structure and Behaviour in Government in the Context of Development Admimstration-A Comparative Study of Two Community Development Blocks in South Arcot District, Tamil Nadu: A Pilot Study*, Pondicherry, Pondicherry Multipurpose Social Service Society.

Ranga Rao, S.P., *Administration of Primary Health Centre*. Hyderabad, Osmania University.

Rao, Nirmala, Representing the people? Testing assumptions about local government reform. *Public Administration*, 77(2) 1999, p. 257-271.

Rao, Vasudeva D., *Health Services Management in Hyderabad Slums*. Hyderabad, Council for Social Development.

Rashid, S.K., *Socio-Legal Study of the Administration of Wakfs in Jammu and Kashmir*. Aligarh, Aligarh Muslim University.

Reddy, B. Ratan, Code of conduct and ethics for civil servants in India and United Kingdom. *Indian journal* of *Public Administration*, 45(1) January-March 1999, p. 17-33.

Rosenberg, Marie B., "Gender Images in Public Administration: Legitimacy and the Administrative State", *Women and Politics*, 17(3), 1997.

Sahay, B.B., *Implementation of the Integrated Rural Development Programme: Administrative and Organisational Issues - A Case Study of a District in Bihar*. New Delhi, C-II, 60, Shahjahan Road.

Sangitn, S.N., Reforms for effective and responsive administration in Karnataka. *IDSA journal*, 8(2-4) April 1998, p. 119-47.

Sapru, R.K., Development administration: Crises and continuities. *Indian Journal of Public Administration*, 44(4) October-December 1998, p. 768- 79.

Saxena, H.S., Administration of Scheduled and the Tribal Areas: The Constitutional Background. (Located in the North Eastern India).

Sehgal, Jiwan Lal, *Organization and Management of a University*. Jaipur, Malviya Regional Engineering College.

Seshadri, K., Study of Villages between Panchayati Raj Leadership and State and Central Leadership. Hyderabad, National Institute of Community Development.

Seth, A.N., *Reorganisation of Panchayati Raj Institution: A Survey*, Ghaziabad, Centre for Agrarian Research, Training and Education.

Sexena, R.N., *Functioning of Bureaucracy in Districts of Madhya Pradesh and Delhi*. Aligarh, Aligarh Muslim University.

Sharat Kumar, Administrative reforms in the context of political and economic restructuring. *Indian Journal of Public Administration*, 41(4)

Sharma, B.D., Study of the Administration of Tribal Development Blocks. New Delhi, Ministry of Home Affairs.

Sharma, Rajesh, Milestones of the discipline of public administration. *Indian Journal of Public Administration*, 42(2) April-June 1996,

p. 197- 201.

Sharma, Ravindra, *A Case Study of the Organization and Working of the Three Nyaya Panchayats in Rajasthan*. Jaipur, University of Rajasthan.

Sharma, Ravindra, *The Recruitment and Training of Village Extension Workers in Rajasthan*. Jaipur, University of Rajasthan.

Shivaramakrishna, K.C. and Datta, A., *Organizational Framework for Planning and Development Administration in the Metropolitans*. Cities, New Delhi, Indian Institute of Public Administration.

Shrivastava, R.C., *An Investigation into the Faculty and Pupil Particpation in the Administration of Colleges in Delhi. Delhi*, Central Institute of Education.

Simeon, James C., "Prime Minister's Office and White House Office; Political Administration in Canada and the United States", *Presidential Studies Quarterly*, 21(3), Summer 1991.

Singh, D.P., Public administration in India: The British legacy, *Administrative Change*, 23(1-2) July 1995-June 1996, p. 26-36.

Singh, Shekhar, Ethics and administration, *Indian Journal of Public Administration*, (Special Number) 43(3) July-September 1997, p. 331-44.

Singh, C.B.P., *District Administration-The Problem of Coordination. Bhagalpur (Bihar)*, Bhagalpur University.

Singh, Chandra Mauli, *Administration of Rural Primary Education in Rajasthan: A Research Project for Evaluation*, Jaipur, Indian Society for Public Affairs.

Singh, M.M., *State Administration in West Bengal*. Calcutta, University of Calcutta.

Singh, P. and Bhandarker, Asha, *IAS project: Myths and realities*. New Delhi, ICSSR.

Singh, S.N., *Caste in decision making amongst the civil servants of Uttar Pradesh*. New Delhi, ICSSR.

Singh, S.S., Liberalisation and public service: Agenda for reforms, *Indian Journal of Public Administration*, 42(3) July-September 1996, p. 383-91.

Singh, S.S., Public accountability and misfeasance in public office-Satish and Shiela Cases. *Indian Journal of Public Administration*, 45(1).

Singhwi, S.S., Working of Subordinate Judiciary and Its Effect on the Administradition of Justice in the State of Rajathan. Udaipur, University of Udaipur.

Sinha, P., Bureaucrats and Political Development in Bihar. Patna, University of Patna.

Sisodia, Y.S., *Panchayat Raj Ka Kriyanvayan evam Anusuchit Jati Mahila Varg Ka Netratva: Ujjain Sambhag Ke Vishesh Sandarbh Mem Ek Adhyayan*. Ujjain, Institute of Social Science Research.

Subramaniam, Changing administrative values in India. *Indian Journal of Public Administration*, (Special Number) 43(3) July-September 1997, p. 261-74.

Subramaniam, V., Administrative legacy ancient India in relation to modern public administration. *Indian Journal of Public Adminsitration*,

Sundaram, P.S.A., Recent initatives for administrative reform in India. *Indian Journal of Public Administration*, (Special Number) 43(3) July-September 1997, p. 553-59.

Tawale, S.N., *A Study of Inter-Relationship between Bureaucracy and Political Leadership in Development: Western Maharashtra*. Pune. University of Poona.

Thudipara, Jacob Z., *Privatization of Municipal Services: A Study on the Impact of Pay and Use Toilet Complexes on the Life of Slum Dwellers in Indore City*. Indore, Indore School of Social Work.

Tripathi, S.I., *The Role of Ethical Values in Socio-Economic Development and Its Implication for Public Administration*. New Delhi, Commissioner of Income Tax.

Trivedi, Harshad R., Public administration: Breath taking perspectival change. *Indian Journal of Public Administration*, 43(4) October-December 1997, p. 904-09.

Tummala, Krishna K., Politics and administration in changing socieites. *Administrative Change*, 23(1-2) July 1995-June 1996, p. 138-44.

Vajpayee, Atal Bihari, Indian Administration today-remedying. *Indian*

Journal of Public Administration, 45(1) Janaury-March 1999, p. 1-4.

Vasquez, Maria and Isabel Rodriguez, *Modernization and Organizational Culture: The Challenges of Public Administration in Venezuela,* International Sociological Association, 1998.

Venkatachar, C.S., Indian administration: Myths of the legacy. *Monthly Commentary on Indian Economic Conditions,* 35(1) August 1993, p. 13-14.

Venketachalapathi, B., *Rural Education in Andhra Pradesh-A Study of the Cuddapath District.* Tirupati, Sri Venkateswara University.

Watson, Robert P., "Politics and Public Administration: A Political Profile of Local Bureaucrats in Alabama", *Administration and Society,* 29(2), May 1997.

Yasin, M. and Sengupta, P.K., Constitutional dynamics and administrative development: The Indian experience. *Administrative Change,* 23(1-2), July 1995-June 1996, p. 117-30.

Index